Conduct
Sociology and Social Worlds

Edited by Liz McFall, Paul du Gay and Simon Carter

Manchester University Press
Manchester and New York
distributed exclusively in the USA by Palgrave
in association with

The Open University

This book is part of a series published by Manchester University Press in association with The Open University. The three books in the Sociology and Social Worlds series are:

Security: Sociology and Social Worlds (edited by Simon Carter, Tim Jordan and Sophie Watson)

Attachment: Sociology and Social Worlds (edited by Peter Redman)

Conduct: Sociology and Social Worlds (edited by Liz McFall, Paul du Gay and Simon Carter)

This publication forms part of the Open University course *Making social worlds* (DD308). Details of this and other Open University courses can be obtained from the Student Registration and Enquiry Service, The Open University, PO Box 197, Milton Keynes, MK7 6BJ, United Kingdom; tel. +44 (0)845 300 6090; email general-enquiries@open.ac.uk.

Alternatively, you may visit The Open University website at http://www.open.ac.uk where you can learn more about the wide range of courses and packs offered at all levels by The Open University.

To purchase a selection of Open University course materials visit http://www.ouw.co.uk, or contact Open University Worldwide Ltd, Walton Hall, Milton Keynes MK7 6AA, United Kingdom for a brochure, tel. +44 (0)1908 858785; fax +44 (0)1908 858787; email ouw-customer-services@open.ac.uk

Conduct

Sociology and Social Worlds

Manchester University Press
Oxford Road
Manchester M13 9NR, UK
and Room 400, 175 Fifth Avenue, New York, NY 10010, USA

www.manchesteruniversitypress.co.uk

First published 2008

A catalogue record of this book is available from the British Library

ISBN 978 0 7190 7813 2 *paperback*

Library of Congress Cataloguing-in-Publication Data

CIP data applied for

Edited and designed by The Open University.

Typeset in India by Alden Prepress Services, Chennai.

Printed and bound in the United Kingdon by TJ International Ltd, Padstow.

1.1

Contents

Notes on contributors

Tony Bennett is Professor of Sociology at The Open University, a Director of the ESRC Centre for Research on Socio-cultural Change (CRESC), and Visiting Professor in the Department of English and Cultural Studies at the University of Melbourne. His interests focus on the relations between culture and the social, and he has published widely in this area. His recent books include *Culture: A Reformer's Science* (Sage, 1998) and *Pasts Beyond Memory: Evolution, Museums, Colonialism* (Routledge, 2004).

Simon Carter is Lecturer in Sociology at The Open University. He has a particular interest in science and technology studies, especially as applied to issues of health and medicine. He is the author of *Rise and Shine: Sunlight, Technology and Health* (Berg, 2007) and many articles in sociological and medical journals.

Francis Dodsworth is a research fellow in the ESRC Centre for Research on Socio-cultural Change (CRESC). His interests lie in the history of freedom and its relation to government in eighteenth-century England, particularly in relation to control of conduct and administrative architecture. He has published in *Social History*, *The British Journal of Criminology*, *The Journal of Historical Sociology* and in M.L. McCormack (ed.) *Public Men: Political Masculinities in Britain, c. 1700–2000* (Palgrave, 2007).

Paul du Gay is Professor of Organisational Behaviour at Warwick Business School. His work is located on the cusp of the sociology of organisations and cultural studies. His publications include: *Consumption and Identity at Work* (Sage, 1996), *In Praise of Bureaucracy* (Sage, 2000), *Questions of Cultural Identity* (Sage, 1996, edited with S. Hall), *Cultural Economy* (Sage, 2002, edited with M. Pryke) and *Organizing Identity: Persons and Organizations 'After Theory'* (Sage, 2007).

Liz McFall is Lecturer in Sociology at The Open University. Her work is situated within the historical sociology of economic life with particular emphasis on the role of promotional practices in the 'making' of markets and consumers. She is the author of *Advertising: A Cultural Economy* (Sage, 2004) and a number of articles exploring nineteenth-century promotional culture, consumption and life assurance.

Charles Turner is Senior Lecturer in Sociology at the University of Warwick. His interests include social and political thought, the politics of commemoration and the history of sociology. He is author of *Modernity and Politics in the Work of Max Weber* (Routledge, 1992) and co-editor (with Robert Fine) of *Social Theory after the Holocaust* (Liverpool University Press, 2000) and (with Ralf Rogowski) of *The Shape of the New Europe* (Cambridge University Press, 2006).

Series preface

Sociology and Social Worlds is a series of three stand-alone books designed to explore the characteristics and benefits of sociological approaches to the social worlds in which we live. The books form the main study materials for the Open University course, *Making social worlds* (DD308), which aims to demonstrate the insights that sociology offers into everyday life, individual behaviour, the relationships between people and between people and things. The series considers how social worlds meet – and sometimes fail to meet – individual needs for security, attachment and order. Supported by examples ranging from Harry Potter to concentration camps, the books demonstrate that sociological approaches can help explain how individuals operate in the world, how social experience is shaped by nature and the material world, and how individual, social lives are made meaningful through culture and the media. The series takes account of the way in which sociology has been shaped by other disciplines and intellectual approaches, including cultural studies, media studies, history, psychology, anthropology and women's studies.

The first book in the series, *Security*, examines what security means in a variety of social and individual contexts. Authors consider issues ranging from geopolitical concerns such as global warming, terrorism and asylum seekers through to the intimate world of home and psychological development to help explain how security intersects with the making of social worlds. Through critical, sociological analyses of the character of material, natural, political and psychological 'threats' the authors show how security is constructed at different times and places.

The second book, *Attachment*, addresses attachment as a fundamental – and frequently overlooked – dimension of social life. Attachments between people, and between people and objects, make up the social worlds we inhabit. This book brings together a range of approaches (such as social constructionism, psychoanalysis and the anthropology of material culture) to investigate how the processes of attachment and detachment occur. Exploring a number of areas – including the nature of attachment to characters and plotlines in reality television shows, intimacy in parent–child relationships, and sport and the masculine body – the book offers a clear and accessible introduction to attachment as an issue of sociological concern.

Conduct, the final book in the series, offers an innovative perspective on how individual behaviour is ordered in social worlds. It aims to show that matters of conduct – habits, attributes, capacities, manners, skills and behaviours – and the norms, techniques, laws and rules which regulate them offer a crucial means through which sociologists can understand how social worlds are put together, change and break apart. Topics including self-service shopping, personal finance, violence and drunkenness are used as part of a sustained analysis of the close links between individual conduct and particular social worlds.

Open University courses are produced by course teams. These teams involve authors from The Open University as well as other institutions, course and project managers, tutors, external assessors, editors, designers, audio and video producers, administrators and secretaries. Academics on the *Making social worlds* course team were based mainly in the Sociology department within The Open University's Faculty of Social Sciences, but the course team also drew upon the expertise of colleagues in the Economic and Social Research Council (ESRC) Centre for Research on Socio-cultural Change (CRESC) and from other universities and institutions in order to construct a course with interdisciplinary foundations and appeal. While book editors have primary responsibility for the content of each book, the assignment of editors' names to books does not adequately convey the collective nature of production at The Open University. I'd like to thank all my colleagues on the course team for their intellectual energy, hard work and unfailing good humour. Particular thanks are due to Lucy Morris, who has, among many other things, been a resourceful, professional and efficient Course Manager.

Liz McFall, Course Chair

On behalf of the *Making social worlds* course team

Introduction

Paul du Gay and Liz McFall

Contents

1 Conduct and social worlds

This book is concerned with exploring the relationship between forms of human conduct and the making of social worlds. Its main line of argument is that attention to questions of conduct – to dispositions, attributes, capacities, habit, bearing, comportment, manners, gesture and so forth, and the norms, techniques and practices mediating them – offers a central means through which sociologists come to understand how distinctive social worlds are put together, change and break apart. If we turn briefly to the *Oxford English Dictionary* (*OED*) and consider some of the central meanings attributed to 'conduct', we can quickly see why it might be (indeed should be) of interest to sociologists. In the *OED*, 'conduct' is defined as:

> The action of conducting or leading; guidance ... The action or manner of conducting, directing, managing, or carrying on (any business, performance, process, course, etc.); direction, management ... Manner of conducting oneself or one's life; behaviour; usually with more or less reference to its moral quality (good or bad) ... Conveyance, carriage ... A channel, passage, means of communication.
>
> (*OED Online*)

So, 'conduct' refers to the manner in which people behave in particular circumstances, occasions or contexts – as, for example, in 'the conduct of the police during the riots'; 'the drunken fans were arrested for disorderly conduct'; 'her conduct was deemed unprofessional'; or 'members of the Board of Directors are bound by a code of conduct'. The sense here is of individuals as certain sorts of people – members of the police service, directors of companies – being expected to behave in a specified way, taking responsibility for managing their own behaviour in line with those expectations, and, in failing so to behave, potentially or actually leaving themselves open to some form of sanction – moral or legal.

However, and not unrelatedly, conduct also refers to the ways in which an organisation, activity or process is put together, carried out, managed and regulated – as, for instance, in the 'the conduct of the elections'; 'the conduct of the trial'; or 'the conduct of the meeting'. Here the focus of the term is on the form and the manner in which something is directed and performed, on the techniques, practices and materials constituting the activity in question, but also on the authorities who are involved in doing the organising, managing and directing, whether an individual musical conductor directing an orchestra, or a public body, such as a local authority charged with directing and monitoring the conduct of council elections.

Finally, conduct also refers to a process of transmission and conveyance. The original form of the word conduct was *conduit* – channel, passage, and means of communication. Thus, the term 'aqueduct' refers to an artificial channel for the conveyance of water; in physics we have the term 'conduction' to refer to the transmission of a form of energy such as electricity or heat. However, this idea of conveyance, transmission, and mediation applies equally to questions of human conduct. Here, the shaping of bodily conduct – gesture, posture, carriage, manners, etiquette, certain styles of dress – can be seen as a way of transmitting or communicating certain meanings in distinctive social worlds. One need only think of the particular comportments, styles of dress, and model gestures enjoined upon individuals in the conduct of soldiering, waiting tables, or judging, for instance, to appreciate the extent to which particular forms of embodied conduct transmit or convey distinctive meanings.

As a result of this brief definitional detour, it should be reasonably easy to see why questions of 'conduct' might be of central concern to sociological enquiry. After all, sociology, as an academic discipline, is crucially concerned with exploring the relationship between the individual and the social (conduct as the manner in which a certain sort of person behaves in a particular context), with analysing how activities, organisations and indeed categories of person are assembled and sustained (conduct as the manner in which an organisation or activity is materially put together, directed and carried out), and with examining how meaningful action and interaction is produced in particular situations (conduct as the transmission, conveyance or mediation of meaning). It is worth holding onto these three elements of conduct – the relationship between the individual and the social; the materials necessary to assemble and sustain given activities, organisations and persons; and the forms of mediation through which social meanings are transmitted or conveyed in both intangible and tangible ways – as we will be referring to them a number of times in what follows, and they act as something of a common thread linking the concerns of the individual chapters of this book.

Given the apparent centrality of questions of conduct to the concerns of sociology, it is tempting to turn immediately to a sociological dictionary or textbook to begin to see how 'conduct' has been approached by sociologists over time. This may prove a rather unproductive move, however, for a cursory inspection of the subject index of any major sociology textbook, or quick flick through the many dictionaries of sociology available, is unlikely to reveal an entry under 'conduct'. If 'conduct' is, as we have suggested, such an important sociological topic, why the omission?

One of the first things to note is that this omission is of relatively recent origin. Questions of conduct were an explicit interest of the early, so-called 'founding' figures, of sociology such as Émile Durkheim and Max Weber (see Chapters 1 and 3 in this volume for discussions of certain aspects of the work of Weber and Durkheim), and the vocabularies of conduct they deployed – including concepts such as 'habit' (generally defined as that disposition or tendency to act or behave in a certain way, normally acquired by frequent repetition) or 'habitus' (generally used to refer to the durable and generalised dispositions that suffuse a person's action throughout an entire domain of life; see Chapter 3 in this volume) – were crucial to the way their work was organised. For example, Durkheim (quoted in Camic, 1986, p. 1052) wrote that sociologists needed to pay considerable attention to 'the habits ... for these are the real forces that govern us', and 'which have the most influence on our conduct'. Similarly, Weber's work on the emergence of capitalistic forms of economic life, what he termed 'the capitalist spirit' (Weber, 1930 [1904–5]), was centrally concerned with 'the development of a particular *habitus*', and he saw forms of ascetic Protestant Christianity as producing 'a psychological vehicle that tended to create a typical conduct' (quoted in Hennis, 1988, pp. 15, 16). Weber's analysis was of the emergence of a particular type of 'conduct of life' (*Lebensführung*), and his focus was 'on the aspect most difficult to grasp and prove, relating to the inner habitus' (quoted in Hennis, 1988, p. 18).

This concern with questions of conduct among classical sociologists was only really written out of sociological theory by a later generation of sociologists, often armed with grand or totalising ambitions for the subject, frequently modelled on the natural sciences. From the heights of this more grand sociological theory, questions of conduct often appeared inherently superficial, deriving whatever significance and meaning they were deemed to possess from some other, more fundamental factor: social structure, ideology, capitalism, class, or patriarchy, for instance.

This reduction of questions of conduct to the status of explanatory 'add-ons' (what we might call 'epiphenomena') can be evidenced in many of the discussions of the relationship between individual and society within sociology. Generally speaking, sociologists agree that individuals do not exist outside of social worlds or 'societies'. However, attempts to characterise this relationship – between the individual and the social – have given rise to the division of sociological thought into what the sociologist Alan Dawe (1970) called the 'two sociologies': those concerned with the importance of structure and structural constraint, on the one hand, and those concerned with questions of action and agency, on the other (see Chapter 1 in this volume). This division has tended to result in conceptions of the relations between individual and society that treat the latter as if they were two static and isolated objects, two separate and distinct realities. Thus, certain structural theories seek to explain social order by positing the hypothesis that order emerges from the internalisation of social norms by individuals, what came to be established in sociology as the concept of 'socialisation'. Here conduct is simply the expression of the internalisation of particular social norms by individual human beings. The problem with such a hypothesis, however, is that it depends upon the assumption that social orderliness is somehow entirely external to the activity of human beings. In other words, social order is a process that somehow goes on 'behind the backs' of human beings.

Attempts to oppose the determinism of structural sociological approaches with theories of action and **agency** nonetheless reproduce the idea of individual and society as two separate entities, by proposing that social order and human conduct are the products of the interaction of fundamentally free human beings, individuals emancipated from pre-existing 'external constraint'. As the sociologist Norbert Elias (quoted in van Krieken, 1998, p. 46) put it, 'one of the strongest motive forces of people who insist on starting their theoretical reflections about societies from "individuals *per se*" or from "individual acts" seems to be the wish to assert that basically an individual is free' (see also Chapters 1 and Chapter 2 in this volume). In such accounts the autonomous individual is the basic unit of social analysis. This entity determines its own conduct; for the structuralist sociologists the very opposite is true. What unites both sociologies, though, as we suggested above, is the latent assumption that individual and society are two static, separate, isolated objects. What these two sociologies signally fail to account for is how exactly any entity – whether a human being or a formal organisation (a business corporation, a public body), say – is equipped to act as a social agent of a certain sort. In other words, neither of the two sociologies addresses as fundamental the *question of conduct*.

It is easy to see how, for both structural and action-oriented sociologies, questions of conduct would be considered as either superficial or suspicious, and thus unworthy of analysis in their own terms. For the former, the charge of superficiality is often a way of expressing doubt about whether instituting changes at the level of manners, comportment or habit, for instance, could ever contribute to significant social and political change. Because social relations are assumed to be underpinned and determined by a certain fundamental structuring device – class, patriarchy, capitalism and so on – it is therefore assumed that only by radically transforming the totality of that structure will meaningful change be instigated and sustained. In this instance, social change appears to be a case of 'all or nothing at all': if you can't change the whole, you won't really change anything substantially.

For many agency-focused sociologies, on the other hand, forms of positive conduct are to be measured against the benchmark of inner, self-directed action by an individual agent. From this perspective, all kinds of conduct that fail to meet that criterion of value are considered both superficial and/or suspicious. Because manners, for example, appear simply as social conventions or various customary courtesies and proprieties, they breach the rule that nothing whatsoever should be done by an individual agent without that agent first subjecting it to rational evaluation and free choice. This is the fantasy of subjective power which Norbert Elias suggested always seems to accompany sociologies that start from the basic premise of the free individual as the building block of society and social relations. For Elias, as for a number of other sociologists working both before and after him, to make this autonomous individual, with a unique inner self, the explanation of conduct, as opposed to something whose existence needs to be explained empirically in terms of conduct, is something of a category mistake. The philosopher Gilbert Ryle (1949) coined this phrase when discussing certain – what he considered inappropriate – approaches to the concept of mind. In an analogy with the concept of mind, Ryle gave the example of the visitor to Oxford who asks to be shown the University, not realising that the University of Oxford is nothing more than the organisation of its constituent colleges. So too, with questions of conduct and individual agency, rather than seeing the modern self as the central generating mechanism for explanations of conduct, it is upon conduct itself that we need to focus, for if we do we might begin to see that this 'integrated' self is really only the contingent and fragile outcome of a particular assemblage of conduct, and not its origin.

As we have already suggested, conduct, as a sociological topic, immediately raises questions concerning why and how individuals are enjoined to act as persons of a certain sort in particular social situations or worlds (our first meaning of conduct outlined above). The capacity to interrogate one's conducts and abilities by relating them to an inner principle of self-scrutiny and control – the basic features of the inner, self-directed individual agent – is undoubtedly a real capacity, but it is not the foundation of these abilities and it does not provide an explanation for the development of all forms of social life. Historical and anthropological research teaches us that not all human abilities undergo introspective interrogation at all times in all cultures. To think they do requires us to adopt a particular, historically rare, understanding of what it means to be a human being as if it were the universal basis for investigating the historicity of being human (Rose, 1996). The point, rather, is to explore how it is that personal capacities and deportments – conducts – are formulated and formed in particular contexts and circumstances. This is one of the key aims of this book, and in pursuing this objective it allies itself with a diverse but distinctive tradition of sociological enquiry in which 'conduct' has been a key organising motif.

As we indicated earlier, this 'tradition' was largely written out of sociological theory in the second half of the twentieth century, with only a few authors attempting to write it back in. However, in recent years conduct has once again become a central focus of sociological scholarship, due in no small part to the influence exerted on their fellow practitioners by sociologists such as Elias (see Chapters 1, 2, 4 and 5 in this volume), Pierre Bourdieu (see Chapter 3 in this volume), Bruno Latour and Michel Callon (see Chapters 1 and 2 in this volume), and from outside of sociology by the historian and philosopher, Michel Foucault (see Chapters 3 and 4 in this volume). As we also suggested earlier in this Introduction, questions of conduct have operated as a frame through which a distinctive group of sociologists have sought to explore some of the key concerns animating sociological enquiry – the question of how we can best understand the relationship between individual human beings and the social worlds they inhabit; the character and status of matter and the material world, vis-à-vis the social world; and the role of mediation in transmitting and conveying meanings within and between social worlds. We can begin to see how 'conduct' lends itself to such an endeavour by turning briefly to the work of three theorists whose work has addressed one or more of these sociological concerns through an explicit engagement with 'questions of conduct'. The three theorists in question are: Weber, one of the earliest sociologists of conduct; Foucault, whose work on the 'arts of government' – where government is understood as an activity fundamentally concerned with 'the conduct of conduct' – has had a major influence across the social sciences and the humanities; and, finally, Elias, a historical sociologist who, perhaps more then anyone in recent times, has reoriented the discipline towards 'questions of conduct'. We begin with one of the earliest exponents of a sociology of conduct: Weber.

In recent years, a somewhat stereotypical image of the sociologist Weber as a 'grand' theorist of the 'instrumental rationalisation' of modern life has been challenged by a range of work emerging from the social sciences and the humanities (Hennis, 1988, 2000; Mommsen, 1987; Turner, 1992). In the 'traditional image' – influenced in particular by the reading of Weber's *oeuvre* associated with the work of the sociologist Talcott Parsons – Western history is represented as a process involving the rationalisation of all social relations and of increasing disenchantment, in which all world views become progressively devalued. Although diverse, these recent interpretations have sought to undo this image of Weber as a sociologist of 'rationalisation' and have instead begun to paint a picture of a historical anthropologist whose concerns centred on the problem of *Kulturmensch*, on 'man' as a cultural being.

For this Weber we are cultural beings because 'we are not natural, living, social, religious or political beings' (Turner, 1992, p.44). We have no 'essence' waiting to unfold itself but are instead remarkably malleable creatures whose capacities and dispositions are formed and reformed in the various spheres of life in which we are placed and place ourselves. In other words, because we are not 'natural' but 'cultural' beings, our becoming a certain sort of person – a politician, a bureaucrat, a priest – is dependent upon historically contingent sociocultural conditions of training and practice. Thus, as we saw earlier, in his famous essay on the relationship between Puritan ethics and the development of a capitalistic way of life, *The Protestant Ethic and the Spirit of Capitalism* (1930 [1904–5]), Weber stresses the sets of ethical techniques and practices through which members of the Protestant sects learned to conduct their lives in the absence of collective guarantees of religious salvation. The Puritan ethics that Weber describes can be viewed as a set of practices and techniques in which the status and attributes of a particular form of Christian personhood are attached to an inner – conscious and conscientious – principle of monitoring and self-control. Weber's Puritan internalises in the form of an ever watchful inner conscience the public norm embodied in the predestinarian doctrine or code, rather than externalising that norm in religious ceremonies and images or, for that matter, in a legal system. The manner of bearing one's person, he argues, depends on a diversity of factors, and has no general or necessary form.

For Weber, the question is not how well a particular persona equates with the truth of human experience or subjectivity in general, but how one gets individuals to bear that form of personhood which fits the circumstances of a given sphere of life (Saunders, 1997). Weber is therefore concerned with offering an account of the ways in which individuals learn to conduct themselves as certain sorts of person, an account which shows the actual 'conducts of life' involved and the technical conditions for producing and deploying them.

According to one of the most acute contemporary analysts of Weber's work, Wilhelm Hennis (1988, 2000), the most important parts of Weber's vast work take the 'conduct of life' (*Lebensführung*) as their explicit topic. Among the writings Hennis points to is the famous essay *The Protestant Ethic and the Spirit of Capitalism*, with, as we just indicated, its treatment of 'the methodical conduct of life' instilled by the Puritan sects. Along with the Puritan, Weber explored the 'conducts of life' of persons in what he called other 'departments of existence' or, what we might term, social worlds; for example: the bureaucrat in the administrative office of government and business; the politician in parliament; the university scholar in defeated post-First World War Germany; and the peasant in the agrarian life order of eastern Germany. For Hennis, Weber's great lesson concerns the extraordinary amount of work and materials that go into fashioning, assembling and sustaining a particular sort of person in a given 'department of existence'.

Accordingly, it is not so much the complexity but the relative simplicity of Weber's theme that has proved, for Hennis, to be such an obstacle to its comprehension within sociology. For what Hennis (1988, p. 104) considers to be a social science often obsessed with high theory and the desire, as Weber himself put it, 'to shift its location and change its conceptual apparatus so that it might regard the stream of events from the heights of reflective thought', the relationship between 'persons and life orders' could 'have little interest' (as cited in Hennis, 1988, p. 104). If one can come down from those heights, Hennis (1988, p. 104) argues, once again paying sufficient attention to actual conducts of life, then the relations of 'persons and life-orders' might become rather more important. Weber's central sociological focus can therefore be seen to be upon the relationship between forms of human personhood and the conducts of life in particular settings that animate them. Weber's 'special sociologies' of conduct therefore suggest a particular understanding of the relationship between the individual and the social. As Weber (1994 [1919], pp. 362–3) put it, 'we are placed in different orders of life, each of which is governed by different laws'. The result is that different social worlds give rise to plural forms of human personhood, such that persons and the conducts that support them are diverse and variable across time and circumstance. For Weber, attempts to hold onto the idea of the individual with a distinctive inner self as the common thread uniting and underpinning all 'departments of existence' is precisely a category mistake. He put this question to those who continued to believe that an ethic of unified or integrated 'selfhood' functions as just such a common thread: 'But is it true that any ethic of the world could establish substantively identical commandments applicable to all relationships, whether erotic, business, family, or official, to one's relations with one's wife, greengrocer, son, competitor, with a friend, or an accused man?' (Weber, 1994 [1919], p. 357).

Weber was clear that the answer was 'No'. For him, the error of a unified conception of the person lay precisely in its failure to recognise that different forms of conduct in different departments of existence gave rise to their own particular and specific forms of personhood – the priest, the bureaucrat, the lawyer, the journalist and so on. Sociologically speaking, nothing was to be gained from trying to make these different persons add up to a coherent whole person located in the inner 'self'. Weber's sociology of conduct is therefore fundamentally concerned with exploring the relationship between the individual and the social, through an examination of the extraordinary work that goes into fashioning novel forms of personhood suited to the exigencies of particular social settings. So, Weber's work equates with our first meaning of 'conduct': conduct as the manner in which people behave in particular circumstances, occasions or contexts. In particular, Weber is concerned with individuals as certain sorts of people being expected to conduct themselves in specified ways.

In the final decades of his life, Foucault's work moved in directions remarkably consistent with those of Weber, in particular in the latter's focus on 'the conduct of life'. Indeed, it is probably not coincidental that Foucault spoke, at this point, of Weber's growing contemporary importance (Gordon, 1987, p. 296). The connection between Weber and Foucault's interest in questions of conduct is perhaps most clearly articulated in the latter's preoccupation in his final lecture courses with a field of research he termed 'governmental rationality', or, in his own neologism, **governmentality** (see Gordon, 1987, 1991; also Chapters 3 and 4 in this volume).

So what exactly is this topic of 'governmental rationality'? Foucault proposed a very wide definition of 'government'. Rather than referring exclusively to the personnel and organisations with responsibility for directing and running the affairs of a state, Foucault defined the term in general as meaning 'the conduct of conduct': that is to say, a form of activity aiming to shape, guide or affect the conduct of some person or persons (Gordon, 1991, p. 2). Thus, one could talk of the government of a nation or a state, but equally of the governing body of a school, or of a captain governing the crew of a ship, or of the need for an individual to govern their own habits or demeanour, their tongue, their temper. Foucault was therefore interested in government as an activity or practice, and not simply as a structure or institutional complex. The government is only one of many possible governments, each of which, as Nikolas Rose (2005, p. 151) has indicated has 'its own jurisdiction, powers, ambitions and techniques'. These are linked by the fact that they all involve authorities who seek to govern: to educate, to control, to influence, to guide, to regulate, to administer, to reform, to manage. Government, in this sense, has a very clear connection with our second meaning of 'conduct': the form and the manner in which something is directed and performed, the techniques, practices and materials constituting the activity in question, and also the authorities who are involved in doing the organising, managing and directing.

For Foucault, practices of government are deliberate attempts – deploying more or less rationalised schemes, techniques and devices – to shape conduct in particular ways in relation to certain desired objectives (see Chapters 3 and 4 in this volume). As Rose has argued, in relation to Foucault's schema:

> Attempts at governing may be formally rationalized in programmatic statements, policy documents, pamphlets and speeches – for example, Keynesian economic management, Beveridge's strategies of social insurance, the new forms of risk management coming to shape the provision of mental health services across the English-speaking world … But others are less formally articulated, and exist in the form of a variety of practical rationalities within particular types of practice – for example, much social work or police work is of this type.
>
> (Rose, 1999, pp. 3–4)

As Rose's comments make clear, one of the crucial features of Foucault's work on government as 'the conduct of conduct' is its focus on the practical means, devices or *materials* that have been invented to govern the conduct of human beings, to shape or fashion their conduct in certain specified directions. This is why throughout Foucault's work on government we find a liberal scattering of the term 'technology'. At first sight, 'technology' seems somewhat out of place in discussions of human conduct; perhaps because the technological and the human are so regularly counterposed to one another. Yet if we consider almost any modern information technology, we can soon see that its introduction has implications for human conduct in all sorts of ways – in terms of reshaping roles for humans vis-à-vis machines, in requiring modifications in body techniques so as to use the device effectively, and in mental techniques required to think in terms of new forms of communication, for example. Even in its conventional sense, then, technologies require for their effectivity a certain shaping of conduct (see, for instance, the discussion of Bruno Latour in **Carter and Davey Smith, 2008,** and of Michel Callon and Latour in Chapter 1 of this volume).

Technologies of government are technical means explicitly imbued with aspirations for the shaping of conduct in the hope of producing desired effects. In this instance it is human capacities, in particular, that are to be understood and acted upon by technical means. The capacity to exercise freedom of choice within a supermarket, for example – to conduct oneself as a particular sort of person, a self-servicer – requires all sorts of technical devices, props or tools to be in place: packaging, so that goods can be divided up and displayed in a way that enables an individual to 'help themselves' to them rather than waiting to be served by someone; the provision of shopping baskets or trollies into which an individual can place their goods and transport them around the store in an orderly fashion; labels with information about pricing, and about content, so that an individual can decide for themselves which, among a range of tinned soups, frozen pizzas or instant coffees, they wish to purchase, and so on (see Chapter 1 in this volume). Here, attempts by retailers to transform the conduct of shopping in order to optimise the economy and efficiency of operations work through the capacities of the individual shopper for their own self-government. The experience of ourselves as creatures with the freedom to choose in the domain of shopping and consumption therefore depends upon, rather than being antithetical to, a range of technologies, devices and materials – from open shelving and end-of-aisle gondolas, to cooler and freezer cabinets, and trollies and baskets. Without such technologies, self-servicing conduct would not be possible, and the person associated with them – the self-servicing consumer – would not exist.

This focus on 'technologies' in Foucault's work on the arts of government therefore alerts us to the importance of material equipment in shaping human conduct, and, in the process, bringing certain sorts of person into being. Here, in Foucault's governmental 'technologies', our second meaning of conduct – the form and the manner in which an activity is directed and performed; the techniques, practices and materials constituting the activity in question; and the authorities who are involved in doing the organising, managing and directing – is clear and evident.

This focus upon the materials – technologies, props, devices, mechanisms – necessary for the production of certain forms of conduct is closely bound up with the question of mediation, transmission or conveyance: our third meaning of conduct. The concern with mediation or conveyance refers to the various ways in which human beings are enjoined to acquire the norms, habits and comportments that comprise different forms of socially sanctioned conduct.

In his classic work, *The Civilizing Process* (1994 [1939]), Elias sketched an explanation of the links between the pacification of manners in social encounters and the internal pacification of territory in the formation of the modern state. Looking at over 500 years of Western European history, Elias argued that as greater numbers of people became enmeshed in ever more extensive **webs of interdependence**, as they were forced increasingly to live at peace with one another, their 'habitus' gradually changed: from generation to generation they slowly developed more intricate mechanisms of habitual self-restraint. In arguing his case, Elias provides many concrete examples of the ways in which explicit codes of bodily conduct – manners, etiquette and the self-monitoring of bodily functions and actions – were enjoined upon different categories of person (most notably the nobility at the royal court).

The History of Manners, the first volume of *The Civilizing Process*, identifies gradual changes in how people approached their own bodily functions and emotions and in expectations of how people *should* conduct themselves throughout European countries. In tracing changes in manners from the Middle Ages, Elias draws on evidence from many sources, including literature, painting and various historical documents depicting how people were said to have behaved. His main sources, however, were 'manners books' and 'conduct books', important literary genres throughout Europe, which, from the thirteenth to the nineteenth century, set out to articulate the standards of acceptable behaviour, particularly for those in the highest echelons of a given social order (most notably those at court in an age of absolutist monarchies).

These texts took many forms, including court dialogue, parental advice and treatises on civility and commerce. The premise of such books was that manners could be learned – through imitation and practice – and that deportment was an 'art form'. In this way, manners books acted as crucial mediators of conduct which taught particular categories of person to learn and acquire habits and dispositions in relation to certain specified activities or domains. Conduct books were, in other words, devices of mediation which acted to transmit meanings in particular social worlds.

The books that preoccupied Elias, particularly those of the earliest periods he investigated, dealt with questions of 'outward bodily propriety'. They tell their intended recipients how to handle food and conduct themselves at table; how, when and where not to fart, burp or spit; how to blow their noses; and how to behave when in the proximity of someone urinating or defecating, etc. Elias focused on these 'basic instincts', as it were, because they are things that humans cannot biologically avoid doing, no matter what cultural milieu or age they live in. Therefore, if changes occur in the manner in which these activities are conducted, they can be seen quite clearly (see Chapter 4 in this volume).

Through an engagement with these manners books, Elias suggests that typical medieval conducts in relation to these functions were characterised by their relative simplicity and naivety, emotions were 'expressed more violently and directly' and there were fewer psychological nuances and complexities in 'the general stock of ideas' (1994 [1939], p. 38). Elias discovered that, as time passed, standards applied to violence, sexual behaviour, bodily functions, table manners and so on all became more sophisticated, with an increased threshold of shame and repugnance. In medieval society:

> Compared to later eras, social control is mild. Manners, measured against later ones, are relaxed in all senses of the word. One ought not to snort or smack one's lips while eating. One ought not to spit across the table or blow one's nose on the tablecloth (for this is used for

wiping greasy fingers) or into the fingers (with which one holds the common dish). Eating from the same dish or plate as others is taken for granted. One must refrain from falling on the dish like a pig, and from dipping bitten food into the communal sauce.

(Elias, 1994 [1939], p. 87)

In regard to blowing one's nose, for instance, medieval people used their fingers. By the sixteenth century, people are being instructed that any mucus that falls to the ground is to be trodden immediately under foot. Handkerchiefs were known only as a luxury good at this time and were not in common usage. To blow one's nose on one's clothes was already being seen as 'rustic', but it was still quite common. By the later seventeenth century, upper-class folk had large quantities of handkerchiefs and their use had become obligatory. Eighteenth-century books indicated polite ways of using them and for a person to look at the product of their nasal exertions was deemed disgusting (Elias, 1994 [1939], pp. 120–1).

Gradually, Elias argues, more and more aspects of earlier forms of human behaviour become regarded as distasteful, and the distasteful was removed behind the scenes of social life. This is most obvious in the case of urination and defecation being rigorously confined to places set apart for this purpose, and in the increasing privacy of the bedroom. But it is also seen, as we indicated above, in the greater attention to care and discretion when blowing one's nose. This hiding behind the scenes of what has become distasteful is, for Elias, one of the defining features of what he calls 'the civilizing process' in Europe. From the Renaissance, increasingly refined standards of civility required people to consider others more carefully, to 'look about them' and 'check their behaviour' (Elias, 1994 [1939], p. 101). For Elias, the civilising process is characterised by the progressive refinement of outward manners, the advancing threshold of embarrassment and repugnance, and the hiding of what is deemed to be distasteful behind the scenes of social life. And 'conduct books' provide one of the key means – mediators – through which these new standards of behaviour are enjoined upon individuals, and through which they learn to conduct themselves according to these new norms of civility (see Chapters 2 and 4 in this volume).

Another crucial, and crucially related, form of mediation promoting orderly habits and civilised manners is the subject of *State Formation and Civilization*, the second volume of Elias's *The Civilizing Process*, as well as of his *The Court Society* (1983 [1969]): namely, the 'courtly' forms of institutional organisation associated with the functioning of absolutist monarchies. New forms of 'civilised' conduct were shaped by what Elias terms a process of 'courtisation'. Here, the 'warrior nobility' and the difficult bishops were drawn away from their regional power bases into the royal court, and, in becoming dependent upon the patronage of the monarch, they were gradually transformed into pliant courtiers.

The emerging 'absolute' sway of royal rule flows from the fact that all the groups that huddle together at court need the recognition of the monarch for their relative and absolute standing. It was in this context that French court society became such a notorious forcing-house for the cultivation of manners. A royal decision, for example, as to who would hold the King's right sleeve during the morning dressing ritual served as a 'literal documentation of social existence' (Elias, 1983 ([1969], p. 94). The meticulous daily round of royal rituals and entertainments were as essential as they were inescapable. For it was by these means that the shifting distributions of power, rank, favours and prestige were symbolised and so determined.

'Court rationality', wrote Elias (1983 [1969], p. 93), 'derived its specific character ... from the calculated planning of strategy in the face of the possible gain or loss of status'. In this continual competition for status, where reputations could rise and fall almost by the minute, to successfully enact one's prestige, to create and maintain the appropriate distance between oneself and every other courtier required powers of circumspection and observation: the cultivation of a keen sensitivity to one's own and other's appearance and conduct: the nuances of posture, gesture and speech; 'the moulding of facial muscles ... and facial expression' (Elias, 1982, p. 276); the capacity to read other's behaviour and discern their probable motives. All this demanded the continual reading of the social scene and the ability to control emotions in the face of what one saw or felt. These arts of existence were, of course, the subject of those 'conduct books' mentioned earlier. They supplied the means by which the courtier might learn to rein in their aggressive urges, sublimate them into courtliness and polish away coarse behaviours. Good courtly manners emphasised mode of satisfaction over instinctual source, aim and object. In this way, the early modern conduct book helped make the absolutist court 'the cocoon in which ravening ... baronial caterpillars were transformed into the beautiful noble court butterflies of the old regime' (Murphy, 1996).

As well as providing an exemplary lesson in the mediation of conduct, Elias's books give the lie to the idea that instituting changes at the level of manners and conduct could ever contribute to significant cultural and social changes. The policing of courtly manners, he argues, provided as important a prototype for the conversion of 'external into internal compulsion' (1983 [1969], p. 221) as Weber's study of the Protestant Ethic. Questions of conduct, he argues, are not second-order or superficial objects of sociological concern. Rather, they form an essential part of any understanding of how social worlds are put together, change and disintegrate.

2   Structure of the book

The primacy of questions of conduct to an understanding of how social worlds work and how individuals fit within them is dealt with in all five main chapters of this book. The book begins with an analysis of conduct in relatively orderly, routine and everyday situations and moves steadily towards a discussion of conduct in increasingly disorderly, violent and, finally, extreme situations. This ordering is designed in an explicit attempt to open up questions about the conditions through which social worlds work, change and sometimes seem to fail.

Chapter 1 addresses the fundamental question of precisely *how* people are equipped to act in particular situations. This question, Paul du Gay explains, has particular resonance because the ability to act – to have agency – has often been seen in sociological theory as a prerequisite of being 'a person'. Using the development of self-service shopping as a case study, du Gay appraises the character of the relationship between the individual and the social via a close interrogation of the concept of 'agency'. As du Gay demonstrates, even the simplest choice in the supermarket is underpinned by a welter of techniques, practices, props, devices and prostheses. To be a self-service consumer involves the acquisition of specific attributes and modes of comportment, it requires the consumer's involvement in the production of a certain assembly, what Callon (2005) calls an **agencement**, of trolleys, aisles, shelves and packaging. What this points to, du Gay concludes, is the need for sociologists to investigate how different sorts of person arise as the outcome of socially organised forms of training and practice.

Chapter 2 continues the investigation into how particular forms of conduct have emerged historically through a discussion of the role of prudence as an ideal in the realm of personal finance. Prudence offers a useful perspective on the nature of the relationship between the social and the individual, in part, because it has such a long and diverse history. In the context of personal finance, prudence is an ideal, at times a virtue to be cultivated, a habit to be acquired or a skill to be learned. What it is not, on the whole, is an attribute which individuals are thought to already possess. Making people prudent is therefore a task, one that has been undertaken in different social worlds in a variety of ways with distinct purposes in mind. In financial conduct, prudence requires extensive advice and specialist equipment, tools and techniques to help individuals learn how to set aside short-term passions in favour of appropriate long-term goals. Even equipped with the right training and the right material, acquiring prudent financial habits, Liz McFall argues, remains a distant ideal for many as immediate demands prevail over future contingencies.

Questions about the role of habit in governing social conduct come under closer scrutiny in Chapter 3. Following the *OED* definition of 'habit' as 'a settled disposition to act a certain way, esp. one acquired by frequent repetition of the same act', Tony Bennett explores the links between 'habit', the nature of social change and the governance of conduct. Habit can be used in two main ways to focus analyses of how conduct is organised socially. First, a discussion of habit and the related concept of habitus flags the role of repetition and routine in durably shaping, shifting and sustaining social conduct over time. Second, habit opens up questions of conduct by representing forms of behaviour which, from a variety of perspectives, have been seen as requiring change, management or regulation. Using examples including attempts in the late nineteenth century to curb public drunkenness through liberal arts policies, Bennett exposes the range of ways in which the mechanisms of discipline and those of liberal government have been brought to bear on the management of conduct. His analysis points to the different ways these mechanisms have worked on individuals, either to make them docile and useful, or by enjoining them to manage themselves through their own autonomy and freedom. These different strategies for managing conduct, Bennett explains, have been, and continue to be, connected to ways of dividing societies into different categories of persons accorded different positions, different responsibilities and different kinds of freedom, autonomy and individuality.

The need to govern or direct conduct also forms the backdrop of the discussion of violence and social ordering in Chapter 4. Here Francis Dodsworth explores how closely bound up the governing of conduct is with the creation of the modern categories of 'society' and 'the social'. One of the things which marks out 'modern' Western society as 'civilised' is that violence is, normatively, the preserve of specific state institutions and even then only when sanctioned by the law. This, Dodsworth explains, is a very different situation from the early modern period in which violence was not so much something that needed *to be regulated* but something that could be used *to regulate*. During this period, violence in, for example, the ritualised form of 'rough music' was used by male heads of households and communities as well as by the state to enforce particular modes of conduct. By the turn of the nineteenth century, violence was seen less as a mechanism of ordering as a form of disorder. Dodsworth reviews a series of explanations for this transformation of violence, concluding that the key shift overall lies in the increasing significance of mediating institutions responsible not only for administering normative social values but also for providing the conditions under which it becomes possible for people to mould their own conduct in accordance with such values.

The final chapter completes the shift away from human conduct in 'normal circumstances' through a study of the questions provoked by examining conduct in circumstances in which the seemingly normal rules of behaviour are suspended. Charles Turner poses the question of how we are to make sense of human conduct in the kind of 'extreme situations' exemplified by wars and the Nazi and Soviet camps. Extreme situations have exerted an enduring fascination on philosophers, historians and psychologists – if not sociologists – in part because as Todorov (2000) remarked they seem to offer the promise of acting as a sort of magnifying glass that might bring into focus things which, although present, are blurry in the normal course of human affairs. While extreme situations may not offer the insight into the nature of morality and human evil Todorov hoped for, Turner concludes, they do offer something of a technical lesson for sociologists on the nature of the relation between the self and the social world.

This is a lesson which is rehearsed throughout the book – that the relation between individuals and social worlds requires constant and considerable work. In other words, both the individual as a particular sort of socially instituted person, and the social world as a certain sort of material, technical and cultural ensemble or association have to be accomplished in practice and do not come ready made, or 'guaranteed'. The various chapters of the book use the minutiae of human conduct to investigate precisely how these remarkable achievements take place and how easily they can be made to fall apart or dissolve.

References

Callon, M. (2005) 'Why virtualism paves the way to political impotence: a reply to Daniel Miller's critique of *The Laws of the Markets*', *Economic Sociology: European Electronic Newsletter*, vol. 6, no. 2 (February): pp. 3–20. Available online at http://econsoc.mpifg.de/archive/esfeb05.pdf (Accessed 24 July 2007).

Camic, C. (1986) 'The matter of habit', *American Journal of Sociology*, vol. 91, no. 5, pp. 1039–87.

Carter, S. and Davey Smith, G. (2008) 'Health and security' in Carter, S., Jordan, T. and Watson, S. (eds) *Security: Sociology and Social Worlds*, Manchester, Manchester University Press/Milton Keynes, The Open University (Book 1 in this series).

Dawe, A. (1970) 'The two sociologies', *British Journal of Sociology*, vol. 21, pp. 207–18.

Elias, N. (1982) *The Civilizing Process*, Vol. 2, *Power and Civility*, Oxford, Blackwell.

Elias, N. (1983 [1969]) *The Court Society*, Oxford, Blackwell.

Elias, N. (1994 [1939]) *The Civilizing Process*, Oxford, Blackwell.

Gordon, C. (1987) 'The soul of the citizen: Max Weber and Michel Foucault on rationality and government' in Lash and Whimster (eds) (1987).

Gordon, C. (1991) 'Governmental rationality: an introduction' in Burchell, G., Gordon, C. and Miller, P. (eds) *The Foucault Effect: Studies in Governmental Rationality*, Hemel Hempstead, Harvester.

Hennis, W. (1988) *Max Weber: Essays in Reconstruction*, London, Allen & Unwin.

Hennis, W. (2000) *Max Weber's Science of Man*, Newbury, Threshold Press.

Lash, S. and Whimster, S. (eds) (1987) *Max Weber, Rationality and Modernity*, London, Allen & Unwin.

Mommsen, W. (1987) 'Personal conduct and societal change' in Lash and Whimster (eds) (1987).

Murphy, T.R. (1996) 'Conduct Books' in Hillerbrand, H.J. (ed.) *The Oxford Encyclopedia of the Reformation*, Oxford, Oxford University Press.

Rose, N. (1996) 'Identity, genealogy, history' in Hall, S. and du Gay, P. (eds) *Questions of Cultural Identity*, London, Sage.

Rose, N. (1999) *Powers of Freedom*, Cambridge, Cambridge University Press.

Rose, N. (2005) 'Government' in Bennett, T., Grossberg, L. and Morris, M. (eds) *New Keywords*, Oxford, Blackwell.

Ryle, G. (1949) *The Concept of Mind*, London, Hutchinson.

Saunders, D. (1997) *The Anti-Lawyers: Critics of State as Heirs of Religion*, London, Routledge.

Todorov, T. (2000 [1986]) *Facing the Extreme: Moral Life in the Concentration Camps*, London, Phoenix.

Turner, C. (1992) *Modernity and Politics in the Work of Max Weber*, London, Routledge.

van Krieken, R. (1998) *Nobert Elias*, London, Routledge.

Weber, M. (1930 [1904–5]) *The Protestant Ethic and the Spirit of Capitalism*, Oxford, Blackwell.

Weber, M. (1994 [1919]) 'The profession and vocation of politics' in Lassman, P. and Speirs, R. (eds) *Weber: Political Writings*, Cambridge, Cambridge University Press.

Chapter 1
Organising conduct, making up people

Paul du Gay

Contents

1   Introduction

> BP Marketing Men saw one customer read the instructions several times, scratch his head, push a pound note up the nozzle and shout at the pump through cupped hands 'Four gallons of commercial please'.
>
> (*The Times*, 17 August 1972, p. 23)

I came across this passage when I was undertaking some historical research into the emergence of self-service shopping practices in Britain after the Second World War. It is taken from an article in *The Times* newspaper concerning the human and technical problems encountered by the oil company BP when it began to introduce self-service techniques into its petrol stations in the 1970s. The executives at BP were faced with some difficult issues to resolve. For instance: How do you get people to adopt a certain technology – in this instance using a petrol pump for themselves – when those people have little to no previous experience of that technology and when its use goes against their understandings of the proper way to conduct a given activity? How do you get them to see something that they have conceived of as work, undertaken for them by other people for a wage, as something they should do themselves, for free? And how do you get them to see themselves as enhancing their own liberty or freedom in so doing?

Seen from the vantage point of the present the picture painted in the opening quotation may seem both humorous and quaint. After all, those of us who drive rarely encounter any other mode of refuelling. Indeed, I would say that I only experience the levels of anxiety and bewilderment described above if I have to use a petrol station where there is still personal as opposed to self-service, so inured to self-service techniques am I! But that, as it were, is the point. Changes in the accepted way of undertaking a given activity, in this instance, something as mundane as filling a car with petrol, have implications for human conduct. They require both a change in the habitual ways we think about the activity – someone should come over and fill my car with petrol, I shouldn't have to do this myself – and physically do it – how do I operate this pump correctly? How do I know when the tank is full? The lack of practical – physical and mental – know-how can certainly lead to fear, anxiety, anger or bewilderment. Such feelings are only likely to be assuaged once one has become familiar with and learned the relevant bodily and mental capacities necessary for the conduct of the activity in question.

Now read the following short passage from an essay entitled 'Techniques of the body' by the anthropologist and sociologist Marcel Mauss (1973 [1935]). (It's worth noting, as you do so, that Mauss was writing some time ago so some of his language, and the examples he uses, may seem strange to you.) When you have finished, jot down some examples that spring to your mind of bodily and mental attributes or forms of conduct that are acquired through imitation of what Mauss refers to as 'body techniques'.

Reading 1.1 Marcel Mauss, 'Techniques of the body'

A kind of revelation came to me in hospital. I was ill in New York. I wondered where previously I had seen girls walking as my nurses walked. I had the time to think about it. At last I realised that it was at the cinema. Returning to France, I noticed how common this gait was, especially in Paris; the girls were French and they too were walking in this way. In fact, American walking fashions had begun to arrive over here, thanks to the cinema. This was an idea I could generalise. The positions of the arms and hands while walking form a social idiosyncrasy, they are not simply a product of purely individual, almost completely psychical arrangements and mechanisms. For example: I think I can also recognise a girl who has been raised in a convent. In general, she will walk with her fists closed. And I can still remember my third-form teacher shouting at me: 'Idiot! Why do you walk around the whole time with your hands flapping wide open?' Thus there exists an education in walking, too.

...

Finally, in *running*, too. I have seen, you have all seen, the change in technique. Imagine, my gymnastics teacher, one of the top graduates of Joinville around 1860, taught me to run with my fists close to my chest: a movement completely contradictory to all running movements; I had to see the professional runners of 1890 before I realised the necessity of running in a different fashion.

Hence, I have had this notion of the social nature of the '*habitus*' for many years. Please note that I use the Latin word – it should be understood in France – *habitus*. The word translates infinitely better than '*habitude*' (habit or custom), the '*exis*', the 'acquired ability' and 'faculty' of Aristotle (who was a psychologist). It does not designate those metaphysical *habitudes*, that mysterious 'memory', the subjects of volumes or short and famous theses. These 'habits' do not vary just with individuals and their imitations; they vary especially between societies, educations, proprieties and fashions, prestiges. In them we should see the techniques and work of collective and individual practical reason rather than, in the ordinary way, merely the soul and its repetitive faculties.

Reading source

Mauss, 1973 [1935], pp. 70–88

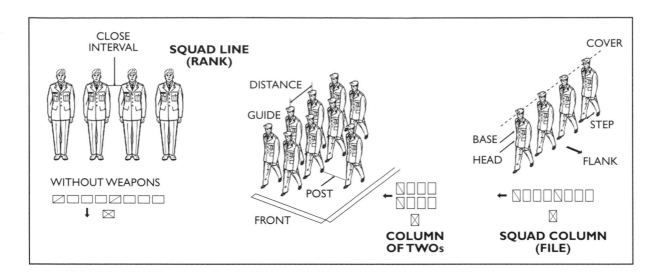

Figure 1.1

Learning how to do military drill

As seemingly banal as all this may seem, I feel it hints at something of considerable sociological significance, namely that humans' bodily and mental capacities are not 'naturally' given, that they depend in great measure on, and vary with, social beliefs, practices and techniques. In other words, rather than being the self-evident concomitants of human experience, human capacities – whether for language use, mathematics, spitting, swimming or, yes, filling up a car with petrol – can all be seen as the products of certain forms of training and practice.

This is an important point, not least because it tends to go against the grain of a considerable body of sociological theory that approaches the question of the formation and regulation of personal conducts and capacities by focusing upon the subject of 'human agency'. For sociological work in this vein, the capacity for willed voluntary action – what is often termed 'agency' – is viewed as the sine qua non of what it means to be a person. In other words, for many sociological theories 'agency' is something that is uniquely contained within, or is the essential property of, a human being. Individuals are assumed to 'have' agency by dint of being human. They are 'preformatted', as it were, with some uniform muscle of the spirit that enables them to exercise a capacity for voluntary willed action in any situation they happen to find themselves in. Following on from this, the most important sociological questions are seen to refer to whether that capacity is facilitated or constrained by existing social arrangements, and thus how those social arrangements might be altered to best allow the full flourishing of the human capacity for voluntary willed action.

While there is no doubt much to be learned from general sociological discussions of the relations between social structure and human agency,

against agency

such discussions tend to overlook – not least because of the general and abstract ways in which they are often conceived – the sorts of questions about human capacities raised by Mauss, and which I briefly discussed in relation to the use of the petrol pump. These are such questions as: 'How exactly are individuals equipped to act in particular situations?' and 'If the capacity to act freely or voluntarily defines what it means to be a person, to what extent are all individuals persons in all situations they find themselves in?'

This chapter seeks to offer some sociological guidance in approaching these complex questions, and to do so through examples derived predominantly from the world of organisations and economic life. The chapter is divided into three main sections, each of which engages, more or less directly, with one or more of the three core sociological concerns of the course. Thus, Section 2 will outline some of the key assumptions framing what is often referred to in sociological discourse as the 'agency and structure' debate. For a number of years, this debate has been one of the most prominent bones of contention in sociological theory. As I suggested above, this debate revolves around the question of how social arrangements determine what individuals can do for themselves; how these arrangements, commonly referred to as 'social structures' to indicate their relatively enduring characteristics, can constrain or facilitate individuals' capacities to act independently and exert 'their agency'. The debate thus impinges upon the question of how we understand the relationship between individual human beings and the social worlds they inhabit: the sociological question of *individual and society*. In exploring this debate I shall have cause to question many of its core assumptions and terms of reference, indicating in particular the limits they impose on a sociological understanding of the ways in which individuals are equipped – practically and technically – with the capacities to act or conduct themselves as certain sorts of social person.

In Section 3, I return briefly to the topic of 'self-service' and discuss the ways in which forms of agency can be seen as multiple and diverse rather than singular, homogeneous and human-centred. In exploring changes in retail practices in the period after the Second World War I seek to show how the introduction and development of self-service techniques altered the conduct of shopping and helped put together or assemble a certain sort of person – the self-servicing consumer. Here our main sociological concerns are with the *material culture* of the retail domain and the *mediating* role of socio-technical devices in equipping human beings with certain capacities to act in the field of shopping and consumption.

Alongside this emphasis on the distributed nature of agency comes recognition of the social variability, contingency and plurality of 'personhood', another topic dealt with some time ago by Mauss, as well as by one of the founding figures of modern sociology, Max Weber. In Section 4, through a brief engagement with the work of these two authors, we return once again to the question of the relationship of individual and society. I explore the ways in which forms of social personhood are not necessarily, or even frequently, congruent with the idea of the individual human agent as a unique entity with a distinct consciousness and will. Not only have conceptions and practices of personhood varied considerably both culturally and historically, but even today not all persons are individuals for all purposes, and not all individuals are persons in every situation they encounter. In the legal domain, for instance, personhood 'refers to the particular devices by which the law creates or recognises units to which it ascribes certain powers and capacities' (*Black's Law Dictionary*, 1999, p. 1162). Thus we find non-humans defined as legal persons.

In the final section, I sum up the main arguments of the chapter and indicate their sociological implications for understanding the questions of conduct and, more broadly, the 'making up of social worlds'.

1.1 Teaching aims

The aims of this chapter are to:

■ explore how individuals are equipped to act as certain sorts of person in particular social worlds

■ review sociological discussions of 'agency', and to assess the extent to which forms of agency can be seen as multiple and diverse, rather than singular, homogeneous and human-centred

■ examine the variability, contingency and plurality of forms of 'personhood' over time and between different cultural milieux

■ highlight the ways in which personal capacities and deportments are formulated and organised in the context of particular normative and technical regimes of conduct.

2   Action, structure and the problem of 'agency'

Can 'agency', as a capacity to act and give meaning to action, be contained in a human being? The answer to this question within sociological discourse is often a resounding 'Yes'. Agency as a property of human beings is assumed by many sociological theories, even those which highlight the constraining role of 'society' or 'social structure' on the capacity of individuals to exert voluntary willed action. Indeed, it would be no exaggeration to say that the history of sociology has in many respects been a history of 'two sociologies' (Dawe, 1979) – a sociology of action on the one hand, and a sociology of structure or system on the other – which never quite manage to meet and settle their respective 'takes' on the relative weight to be allotted to 'human agency' in the formation and reproduction of social worlds. The former, for instance, tends to emphasise the knowledgeability of human actors and highlight their active role in creating social worlds. The latter pays considerably more attention to the role of social structures in constraining or determining human action, in some cases to the point where human agents are conceived primarily as the 'bearers' of these structures. Frequently, arguments between adherents of these two sociologies become somewhat circular: they have the same endless possibilities as debates over which came first, the chicken or the egg (try replacing the word 'agency' with the word 'chicken, and the word 'structure' with the word 'egg', and you can quickly get the drift!).

This is a point made very forcefully by the sociologist Norbert Elias in a classic piece of historical sociology entitled *The Civilizing Process* (2000 [1939]). Looking at over 500 years of Western European history, Elias sketched a sociological explanation of the links between the pacification of manners in social encounters and the internal pacification of territory in the formation of the modern state. Elias argued that as more and more people became enmeshed in ever more extensive **webs of interdependence**, as they were forced increasingly to live at peace with one another, their **habitus** (remember the use of this term by Mauss in Reading 1.1) gradually changed: from generation to generation they slowly developed more intricate mechanisms of habitual self-restraint (see also the discussion of the term 'habitus' in relation to the work of both Mauss and Pierre Bourdieu in Chapter 3 in this volume). In arguing his case, Elias provides many concrete examples of the ways in which explicit codes of bodily conduct – manners, etiquette and the self-monitoring of bodily functions and actions – were enjoined upon different categories of person (most notably the nobility at the royal court).

You should now read the following extract from Elias's *The Civilizing Process*. As you do so, focus in particular upon what Elias says about the notion of the *homo clausus*, and how it sets up a particular way of thinking about the relationship between 'individual and society'.

Reading 1.2 Norbert Elias, '*Homo clausus* and the civilizing process'

People to whom it seems self-evident that their own self (or their ego, or whatever else it may be called) exists, as it were, 'inside' them, isolated from all the other people and things 'outside', have difficulty assigning significance to all those facts which indicate that individuals live from the first in interdependence with others. ... This kind of self-perception appears as obvious, a symptom of an eternal human state, simply the normal, natural and universal self-perception of all human beings. The conception of the individual as *homo clausus*, a little world in himself who ultimately exists quite independently of the great world outside, determines the image of man in general. Every other human being is likewise seen as a *homo clausus*; his core, his being, his true self appears likewise as something divided within him by an invisible wall from everything outside, including every other human being.

But the nature of this wall itself is hardly ever considered and never properly explained. ... and although this omission to investigate one's own presuppositions is hardly appropriate to scientific procedure, this preconceived image of *homo clausus* commands the stage not only in society at large but also in the human sciences. ... As philosophers did before them, many sociological theorists today accept this self-perception, and the image of the individual corresponding to it, as the untested basis of their theories. They do not detach themselves from it in order to confront it and call its aptness into question. ... As a result, the ideas of social theorists constantly find themselves in blind alleys from which there seems no way out. The individual – or, more precisely, what the present concept of the individual refers to – appears again and again as something existing 'outside' society. What the concept of society refers to appears again and again as something existing outside and beyond individuals. ... In order to pass beyond this dead end of sociology and the social sciences in general, it is necessary to make clear the inadequacy of both conceptions, that of the individual outside society and, equally, that of a society outside individuals. This is difficult as long as the sense of the encapsulation of the self within itself serves as the untested basis of the image of the individual, and as long as, in conjunction with this, the concepts 'individual' and 'society' are understood as if they related to unchanging states.

The conceptual trap in which one is continually being caught by these static notions of 'individual' and 'society' can only be prized open if, as is done here, these notions are developed further, in conjunction with empirical investigations, in such a way that the two concepts are made to refer to processes. ...

...

... The network of interdependencies among human beings is what binds them together. Such interdependencies are the nexus of what is here called the figuration, a structure of mutually oriented and dependent people. ... The concept of the figuration has been introduced precisely because it expresses what we call 'society' more clearly and unambiguously than the existing conceptual tools of sociology, as neither an abstraction of attributes of individuals existing without a society, nor a 'system' or 'totality' beyond individuals, but the network of interdependencies formed by individuals. It is certainly quite possible to speak of a social system formed of individuals. But the undertones associated with the concept of the social system in contemporary sociology make such an expression seem forced. Furthermore, the concept of the system is prejudiced by the associated notion of immutability.

Reading source

Elias, 2000 [1939], pp. 471–482

For Elias, the question of how human beings are equipped to conduct themselves as certain sorts of person cannot be answered in terms of the action–structure debate, precisely because its adherents are hostage to a particular view of 'the' idea of the person which they then deploy as the basic, universal datum of experience and existence. Elias describes this conception as the *homo clausus* – the individual in a box, a little world unto himself or herself. According to Elias, this image of the person (in the singular) as an entirely free, independent being, a 'closed personality', inwardly quite self-sufficient and separate from all other people, appears in many different guises in the humanities and social sciences – *homo economicus*, *homo philosophicus* and, not least, *homo sociologicus*. All these expressions of the *homo clausus* presuppose the existence of individual agents with perfectly stabilised competencies. In other words, the *homo clausus* is always already competent to act; there is little sense of the training and practice through which this category of person is actually equipped with the capacity to act as a certain sort of person.

Time and time again, Elias argues, the dependence on *homo clausus* leads social scientists to engage in futile debates about the relationship between individual and society as if they were two static and isolated objects, two separate and distinct realities. And this misconception is reinforced by a widespread tendency to speak not of persons but of 'the person' or 'the individual' in the singular as if all forms of socially instituted personhood were effectively identical.

This 'conceptual trap' can only be prized open, Elias suggests, if these static notions are made to refer to ongoing processes. In saying this, Elias (2000 [1939], p. 474) is keen to indicate that he does not view the 'self-perception that finds expression in the image of man as *homo clausus* and its many variations' as an outright illusion. It exists but it does so in specific ways in relation to specific purposes and activities. It is not a universal mode of being human, and thus it cannot act as 'a self-evident assumption incapable of further explanation' (2000 [1939], p. 474). It has in fact developed over time. In order to show how this has happened Elias introduces the notion of **figuration**.

Elias uses the term 'figuration' in Reading 1.2 to refer to 'the network of interdependencies among human beings'. It is deployed as a more dynamic term in contrast to expressions like 'social structure' and 'social system' which he regards as somewhat static, and as referring to something separate from, beyond and outside the activity of human beings. As the sociologist Robert van Krieken (1998, p. 55) puts it, 'For Elias, the structure and dynamics of social life could only be understood if human beings were conceptualised as *interdependent* rather than autonomous, comprising what he called *figurations* rather than social systems of structures, and as characterised by socially and historically specific forms of *habitus*'. The 'figuration' or network in this sense does not link human beings with already-established identities (that is to say, individuals endowed with a set of fixed attributes and stabilised competencies) to form what would be a static social structure constituting the framework within which individual actions are situated. In the 'figuration', individuals' identities, interests and objectives – everything that might stabilise their description and their being – are variable, contingent outcomes which fluctuate with the form and dynamics of the relationship between those individuals. Both figuration and person are therefore, in a sense, two sides of the same coin. One can enter the figuration through the persons it constitutes, whereby one is immediately tempted to characterise them by the shape of their relationships. Alternatively, one can focus on the figuration itself, in which case one uses the associations of the persons it constitutes to describe it. The figuration, in other words, does not connect persons with already-established identities but rather it provides those persons with their very dimensions or characteristics. The persons, their characteristics, what they are and what they can do are all dependent upon the relations in which they are involved.

What Elias enables us to see is that social relations and human attributes are necessarily interdependent. Nothing is to be gained analytically from viewing them as separate and distinct realities.

Now, Elias was certainly not alone among sociologists in seeking to overcome the stasis of the individual–society dualism as a general philosophical problem. There have been many attempts to overcome the static and circular nature of the 'action–structure' debate. Quite a few of these have also insisted upon the importance of conceiving of action and structure as mutually constitutive, and thus of understanding their relationship as a matter of process in time. Here the action–structure dichotomy is reconceived in terms of a problematic of 'structuring'. By 'problematic' I mean a field of phenomena which yields problems for investigation. This occurs on the basis of an application of theoretical assumptions and principles to phenomena in order to constitute a range of enquiry. Perhaps the most famous attempt in contemporary sociology to overcome the action–structure impasse through the problematic of 'structuring' is the structuration theory associated with the British sociologist Anthony Giddens. Giddens introduced this notion in his book *Central Problems in Social Theory* (1979). Here he attempted to overcome the division between action and structure by means of a notion of the 'duality of structure', in which structures are seen as both the medium and outcome of human action. This focus was designed to indicate the mutual dependence of structure and agency. And of crucial importance was the idea of 'structuration' or 'structuring' as a process happening in time.

This idea that time is the common medium in which social relations and human agents generate one another is a core assumption informing the work of many different forms of sociology, from the social-interactionist studies of sociologists such as Anselm Strauss (1977), to the studies of social reproduction undertaken by Bourdieu (1977). Strauss, for example, argued that individual 'identities imply not only personal histories but social histories ... individuals hold memberships in groups that are themselves products of the past. If you wish to understand persons – their development and their relations with significant others – you must be prepared to view them as embedded in historical context' (1977, p. 164). This is not simply a matter of recognising the historical background to the present. Rather, as the historical sociologist Philip Abrams (1982, p. 16) put it, 'it is an attempt to understand the relationship of personal activity and experience on the one hand and social organization on the other as something that is continuously constructed in time'. It makes the continuous process of construction the focal point of social analysis. At one level, this all makes good sense. After all, it does provide a way of understanding what Giddens called one of the central problems of sociological analysis: how the actions of human agents constitute a social world that in turn constitutes the conditions of possibility of the actions of those agents.

And yet, the overcoming of a simple dichotomy between action and structure, or individual and society, by seeing these two entities as somehow made in process by their mutual interaction and interdependence, does not really overcome, but perhaps merely relocates, the central problem: the problem of the *homo clausus* outlined by Elias. One of the crucial problems is the conception of social agency that these approaches deploy. Here, social agency is identified with the capacities and attributes of the human being. Other forms of social agency, including various forms of institutional or corporate agency, are either relegated to a minor role, written out of the account or, more often than not, represented as ultimately composed of and hence reducible to human agents. And, as we saw in the Introduction to this chapter, another substantial act of conflation is made between human agents and the actions of persons as individuals. However, since Mauss's highly influential work, which I will discuss further later in this chapter, sociologists have been aware that categories of person, self and individual are themselves dependent upon, and the products of, certain historically distinctive practices and techniques. These categories cannot be used as if they were universal data of human experience and existence as they are in attempts to found a general sociological theory upon them. As the sociologist Mitchell Dean puts it:

> Attempts to grasp the properties of social relations ... from such categories of agency [human-centred] cannot be sustained. When such categories are combined in basic sociological concepts themselves, such as in the famous 'duality of structure', they form an unstable amalgam sliding between a structure whose effectivity knows no limits and a form of agency that knows no determination.
>
> (Dean, 1994, p. 9)

For Dean, theories of 'structuration' or 'structuring' never quite manage to get around to describing how human beings are actually equipped to act in particular situations. This is not a problem shared by every sort of sociology, however. An opposed idea that views forms of agency as multiple and diverse finds its classic expression not only in the work of authors like Mauss and Elias – but also in the work of Weber and that associated with sociologists such as Bruno Latour and Michel Callon, which we will encounter in Section 3 – and has continuities, *inter alia*, in the research programmes of Michel Foucault and Bourdieu, whose work you will engage with later in this book (see Chapter 3). For all of these authors, in their own particular ways, agencies are made up of human bodies but also of various prostheses, tools, technical devices and other equipment. These socio-technical arrangements serve not only to organise conduct, they also make up certain sorts of personhood. We can see this more clearly by turning our attention to the world of economic organisations and, once again, to the example of 'self-service'.

3 The conduct of shopping: self-service as *agencement*

Leave us to do the thinking, sweetheart, it takes equipment.
(Chandler, 2001 [1955], p. 431)

As we saw in Reading 1.2 by Elias in Section 2, many branches of social science operate with a version of the *homo clausus*, and economics is no different in this respect. Classical economics explicitly or implicitly theorises actors as equivalent to individual human beings (*homo economicus*).

Economic sociology has regularly contested this idea of the actor as an atomistic individual. From the work of Karl Marx and Émile Durkheim up to and including a large body of literature in what has come to be known as the 'new' economic sociology, sociologists have been keen to demonstrate the social character of economic activity and to highlight, for example, the 'embedding' of economic action in networks of interpersonal relations and in cultural and political circumstances (Granovetter, 1985). In recent years, however, a rather different approach has developed from the work of the French sociologist Callon (1998).

Callon's approach to economic life is part and parcel of the 'actor-network theory' that he developed with Latour (see **Carter and Davey Smith, 2008**). One of the most distinctive – and controversial – features of actor-network theory is its openness as to the nature of actors, which for its adherents can potentially include non-human entities as well as human beings. Callon's approach to studying markets and economic behaviour thus differs from much traditional economic sociology (even 'new' economic sociology) in its conceptualisation of the actor (Hardie and MacKenzie, 2006). 'Action', writes Callon (2005, p. 4), 'including its reflexive dimension that produces meaning, takes place in hybrid collectives', collectives that incorporate 'material and technical devices, texts, etc.' as well as human beings.

In Callon's analysis an economic actor is not conceived of as an individual human being, or even a human being 'embedded in institutions, conventions, personal relationships or groups' (Callon, 2005, p. 4). Rather, for Callon, an actor is 'made up of human bodies but also of prostheses, tools, equipment, technical devices, algorithms, etc.' –

in other words, an actor is made up of what he terms an *agencement* (Callon, 2005, p. 4). In French, as Hardie and Mackenzie (2006, p. 3) point out, the notion of *agencement* involves a deliberate wordplay. The verb *agencer* means to arrange or to fit together: in one sense, then, *un agencement* is an assemblage, arrangement, configuration or format. The referent in everyday speech is quite banal: in French parlance, *les agencements* are fixtures and fittings, and to be *bien agencé* is to be well-equipped. But *agence* also refers to agency. For Callon (2005), as for Mauss, actors do not have inherent properties or a fixed essence. Their characteristics are constituted by the *agencements* – those fixtures and fittings, arrangements and devices – which furnish them with particular characteristics and thus make them up as certain sorts of person:

> Depending on the nature of the arrangements, of the framing and attribution devices, we can consider agencies reduced to adaptive behaviours, reflexive agencies, calculative or non-calculative agencies, or disinterested or selfish ones, that may be either collective or individual ... (Re)configuring an agency means (re)configuring the socio-technical *agencements* constituting it, which requires material, textual and other investments.
>
> (Callon and Caliskan, 2005, pp. 24–5)

Thus, for Callon, different forms of agency depend upon the nature of the *agencements* – technical, material and indeed normative arrangements – that constitute them. Callon's view of the economic actor implies that different *agencements* will create different forms of economic action. We can observe this if we return to the example of self-service.

As I indicated in the Introduction to this chapter, it is sometimes difficult to believe that self-service techniques – whether for choosing goods in a shop, refuelling a car or for getting money from a cashpoint – have any sociological significance for understanding human conduct or the making of social worlds. Yet, as we saw earlier, people don't intuitively know how to 'do self-service'. They have to learn, to be taught, to become habituated to conducting themselves as self-servicers. Not only this, their capacity to act as self-servicers – in shops, petrol stations, banks and elsewhere – requires a lot of equipment to be in place. Becoming capable of acting as a self-service consumer requires a lot of devices, each having the capacity to provide you – the consumer – with the possibility of choosing goods for yourself. After all, even such a mundane decision as to which yoghurt or pack of sliced meat to purchase in your local supermarket involves there being in place lots of instruments and devices that equip you – the shopper – with the very capacity to make such choices, from labels, trademarks, bar codes, lists of ingredients, and so on. The crucial point here is that you – the shopper – are sustaining this mental and cognitive competence – this capacity to act as a consumer – 'as long as you subscribe to this equipment. You don't carry it with you; it is not your own property' (Latour, 2005, p. 210). In other words, your ability to act as a certain sort of shopper – someone who services themselves – does not reside in you as a unique individual agent but is distributed throughout the formatted setting of the supermarket or self-service store. All of what we might term, following Latour (2005, p. 210), as 'the competence building technologies' that enable you – the shopper – to act as such – shopping trollies, marketing information, checkouts – need to be put together in such a way as to make 'self-service' practicable. The self-service store and the sort of shopper or consumer that is related to it are both the product of a certain *agencement* – a particular configuration of devices and instruments.

For instance, can you really imagine acting as a self-servicer without these and many other devices being in place: refrigeration units, pre-packaging materials, checkouts – and so forth? 'If there is one thing that is not "in" the agent, it is those many layers of competence builders that we have to ceaselessly rely upon and deploy in order to gain some ability for a while' (Latour, 2005, p. 211). Try living without them and see how quickly your self-servicing 'agency' in the shop setting begins to wither away.

You should now read the extract from 'Publicizing Goldilocks' choice at the supermarket' by Franck Cochoy and Catherine Grandclément-Chaffy. As you read, jot down what you consider to be the main themes and issues the authors are raising. In particular, think about the importance the authors allot to product packaging and branding in mediating the relationship between retailers and consumers, and to equipping shoppers with the capacity to act as 'self-servicers'.

Reading 1.3   Franck Cochoy and Catherine Grandclément-Chaffy, 'Publicizing Goldilocks' choice at the supermarket'

The material artifacts that are part and parcel of the choices we make at the supermarket – product packaging, shopping carts, labels – may seem trivial, insignificant, paltry things. ... however, ... these fragile metal, paper or plastic interfaces between producer and consumer have completely transformed the identity and competence of the modern subject.

...

Before the invention of packaging, many food products were presented and sold in ... bulk. ... Bulk selling meant products of different grades could be sold under a single product name, a situation that greatly facilitated fraud and unfair competition. In 1882, an American producer named Crowell (using new, costly machines that enabled him to make quality cereals) had the idea of packaging his products and putting a brand name on them: Quaker Oats. Constructing a market for high-quality oatmeal meant signalling the difference to consumers so there could be no unfair competition from lower-quality products that looked exactly like the superior product; it meant helping consumers find that product in local markets so that traditional retailers could no longer substitute one product for another. Packaging thus developed as both a condition and consequence of brand strategy. ...

... Packaging made it possible to name, invent and underscore product differences. What's more, tasting the product immediately before purchase was now impossible, so the consumer had to turn to indirect, written product-assessments. With time and practice, consumers learned the new methods and criteria for examining and assessing products, and physical sensations were supplemented or replaced by consideration of products' chemical, scientific or even cultural dimensions.

Moreover, packaging made consumers aware of product features that until then had been completely inaccessible. ... How could we evaluate product weight, for example, if '500g' were not written on the box? ... How could we complain and demand reparation for purchase of a defective product if there were no writing on the package informing us that 'Leader Price' is accountable for it? Here we have come upon the fundamental paradox of packaging: The wrapping is a screen that simultaneously conceals what it shows and shows what it conceals but shows it differently, ultimately teaching us more about the product than we could learn by ourselves, without packaging. ...

Some question the value of such wrapping, conceding the 'necessity' of indicating legal and nutritional information but decrying as useless and indeed harmful the presence of other types of information, such as symbols and logos. ... These authors more or less explicitly suggest that it would be a progressive move to amputate these features, but they don't for a second imagine what our commercial world would be like if we took their injunctions seriously. ...

...

The reason people simply go about their business at the supermarket is that the supermarket round has become natural to us. People pretty well know why they're going there and what they want to take home;

carts and cart-pushers have become an ordinary, familiar, universal and universally accepted sight. ... Still, it is only recently that we have come to take all this for granted. The hybrid cluster composed of a cart and its 'members' is so ordinary that it has become virtually invisible, and very few shoppers or researchers pause to contemplate it. But this was not always so. Sylvan Goldman, the Oklahoma grocer who invented the shopping cart, learned this the hard way: His customers at first refused to use the thing and only acquiesced after he had hired extras to 'demonstrate' it, and dispel the customers' fear of looking ridiculous.

...

If we think about it, the Three Bears' house was history's first 'self-service, no obligation to buy' shop – but a poorly stocked, unwitting shop it was. Today the bowls, chairs and beds have been replaced by cornflakes boxes, shopping carts and family deliberations. The Three Bears – manufacturers, distributors, advertisers? – now fling open their doors to bring in and keep visitors, rather than trying to scare them away. And with this series of transformations, Goldilocks herself has changed. She didn't perform very well in the fairy tale. Though she chose the most fitting product each time, she learned the hard way – that object size is hardly a sufficient selection criterion. What appears to be the best product may be disappointing or ill-made or dangerous (especially if one gives oneself over to it entirely, by falling asleep in it, for example). Today's Goldilocks chooses differently. First, she deals not with naked products but with well-wrapped ones. Thanks to packaging, she no longer has to test three bowls, three chairs, or three beds to find the one that suits her, but is directly informed of product properties and can thus circumscribe her choice by means of her own preferences and those the manufacturer suggests. Second, as we have said, she is no longer alone. The shopping cart, which brings people together (Goldilocks and those who accompany her), has transformed the figure of the solitary consumer into a plural entity.

Reading source

Cochoy and Grandclément-Chaffy, 2006, pp. 646–57

As Cochoy and Grandclément-Chaffy argue, self-service shopping has its own techniques, devices, instruments – *agencement* – just as much as any other organised environment, whether a financial trading room, a government bureau or a hotel. They are keen to stress the ways in which contemporary shoppers no longer possess – if they ever did – an unmediated relationship to products. Product packaging and the shopping trolley not only mediate the shopper's relationship to

Figure 1.2
Branding/de-branding

Figure 1.3
Little boy pointing the way *(left)*; Getting last orders for the shopping *(right)*

products, they also help equip them with the capacity to make choices and serve themselves within the supermarket.

Their main point is that without that particular *agencement* much of what we take for granted as contemporary consumers would not exist. There are many people who would welcome the dissolution of this *agencement,* or at least its replacement with something different. Naomi Klein's popular attack on corporate branding and the seemingly ceaseless commodification of all aspects of human existence – *No Logo* (2000) – is a clear case in point. What Cochoy and Grandclément-Chaffy suggest, though, is that it is always important to explore the details of particular market *agencements* so that we are better able to judge what sorts of impacts are likely to arise from attempts to alter them and thus are better able to see what the costs of these proposed interventions might be. By stressing the details of particular *agencements,* those details that grander social theories often pay no attention to (such as those preoccupied with the action–structure debate), Cochoy and Grandclément-Chaffy show that 'equipping' individuals to conduct themselves as certain sorts of person isn't easy; the techniques employed in such an endeavour do not come ready made. They have to be invented, refined, disseminated, implanted and stabilised. This all takes a lot of hard work, work that sometimes fails.

Again, while it may seem strange from the perspective of the present, self-service itself almost failed in Britain. A brief historical examination of the introduction of self-service shopping techniques into British retailing after the Second World War shows that retailers were very aware of the difficulties of equipping people with the capacity to shop for themselves, not least because self-service posed serious challenges to predominant assumptions about the conduct of shopping and its relationship to work. Taking a brief look in Section 3.1 at the problems of learning to shop in post-war Britain that arose from the introduction of self-service will alert us both to the serious work that accompanies changes in conduct and to the importance of the milieu-specificity of those changes.

3.1 The material culture of self-servicing: learning to shop for oneself in post-war British retailing

At its most basic, the term 'self-service' is used in the retail environment to describe any method of displaying goods in a manner that enables customers to help themselves. There are, then, many degrees of 'self-service' – as the trade terms 'partial self-service' and 'assisted self-service' testify. One of the earliest British retail trade journals devoted to self-service *Shop Review* (1955, pp. 35–42) gives a broad definition. A self-service system is one in which:

1   Every item of stock must be pre-packaged and clearly price-marked and displayed within reach of the customer in an easily-seen, suitably-classified, quickly identified section of open shelving, bins, trays or gondolas.

2   Each customer must be handed or pick up a basket (or light trolley) as they enter, into which all their purchases must be placed.

3   Customers must leave the self-service store, shop or department via a check-out counter, where the borrowed basket is emptied, the cost of the goods added up, payment made and the goods placed in the customer's own basket or a free bag provided for this purposes by the store.

4   There must be an adequate and efficient system of quick and constant replenishment of stock from an immediately adjacent store-room.

5   The lay-out must be such that freedom of movement is assured and that executives and staff have an uninterrupted view of the whole self-service area.

(Shop Review, 1955, p. 40)

Now, this definition would not hold for every instance of self-service shopping one might have come across in 1955, nor would it correspond to every instance one might encounter today. Nonetheless, the basics are pretty recognisable. So are the benefits assumed to flow to the retailer from its operation. These were described in the same article as:

1   Increased sales turnover due to increased custom and additional spend per customer.

2   Reduction in overheads through reduced staff costs.

3   Greater efficiencies due to more rational management of the store; for instance more statistical information available through the cash register thus enabling better comparison of profitability of different departments and thus ability to mix product selection.

(Shop Review, 1955, p. 42)

One of the things that these retail trade reports continually stress is the superiority of self-service to all other forms of organising the conduct of shopping. Self-service, we are told, will be economic, efficient and effective for the retailer and, a clear and immediate hit with the shopping public. However, things were not quite so simple. For instance, the high street multiple retailer Tesco converted one of their stores to self-service in 1947, only to have to return it to counter service when customers complained of the inconvenience (Humphrey, 1998, p. 73). Similarly, opening day at the first Sainsbury's self-service store in Croydon found a queue consisting of only one person – the branch manager's wife! The idea that, once unveiled and put to work, self-service just took over the retail environment cannot be taken at face value. Despite much rewriting of the historical record for promotional purposes, many of the established household names in contemporary

British retail did not enthusiastically adopt self-service. Instead, they were very concerned about the impact on their customers of going self-service, and took a distinctly cautious and experimental approach to the technology.

In order to understand the reasons for this caution, it is first necessary to consider the situation in which retailers found themselves immediately after the Second World War. For one thing, rationing continued to be the norm for many goods. At the same time, the British Government continued to exercise very detailed controls on prices to help ensure relatively fair distribution to all sections of the population (Towsey, 1964; Seth and Randall, 1999). Competition on price was therefore restricted and this had a negative pull on the willingness of many retailers to invest in new methods. Given this, it is hardly surprising that many were extremely cautious about adopting self-service.

Second, early failures of self-service were frequently represented in the national press as the result of a consumer distaste for serving oneself (*The Times*, 21 January 1957, p. XVI). Established, often class-based, cultural norms about 'service' and the relative responsibilities of shopper and worker did not always tally with the more individualised and impersonal ethos of self-service and, in particular, the redistribution of responsibilities for serving from workers to consumers that it instigated (Bowlby, 2000; Humphrey, 1998). Lord Sainsbury's experience at the opening of the Purley self-service branch might serve as a paradigm of what retailers to the middle classes most feared from the self-service experiment. Lord Alan Sainsbury, the managing director of the company carrying his name, stood at the entrance to this store on opening day shaking hands with customers as they entered and passing them a shopping basket. The company history reports the wife of a local judge screaming abuse at Lord Alan and throwing the basket back with contempt when she discovered that she was required to do the work of a shop assistant and then to carry home her own purchases (Bowlby, 2000). This perhaps is the crux of the problem facing the would-be self-service retailer. How do you get people who are used to being served over the counter, or even to not having to go to the shops at all, to agree both to do the work previously done by assistants on their behalf, and to see this as enhancing their economic and personal freedom?

The effort to persuade sceptical or uninitiated shoppers to see 'self-service' in a positive light began with the development of a large network of competence builders – not simply retailers, but manufacturers, packagers, marketers, advertisers, fixture makers and fitters, and psychologists – all of whom had a specific part to play in the job of getting the housewife – for the object of their attentions was nearly always this category of person – to see the activity of shopping in a different light (Bowlby, 2000; Cochoy, 1998, 2003; Humphrey, 1998).

Extensive advice on this very subject was available from a range of sources including the numerous trade journals of the period – such as *Shop Review, Self-Service and Supermarket, Shop Equipment News* – devoted to spreading the word about 'self-service'. These focused on everything from store design, shop layout and promotional techniques to technological developments in the area of cash registers, refrigeration, and packaging materials. At the same time, the spatial management of the store and the temporal habits of the shopper were also considered to be of considerable significance. All the main trade journals stressed the need for careful attention to be paid to the layout of the shelves and the product selection displayed therein. Goods were to be grouped together in meaningful clusters, where their relation to one another could spark off associations in the minds of consumers thus leading to more 'impulse buys', a favourite catch phrase of the time (Galvani and Arnell, 1952, pp. 20–83).

Some of the most common advice concerned the importance of placing high volume goods at strategic points throughout the store, thus enticing customers into the shop and ensuring they circulate, and of situating goods most likely to be bought on impulse – chocolates, sweets, razor blades, cigarettes and so forth – at the end of gondolas and at the checkouts, thus taking some more money from the customer – typically, the housewife – prior to her leaving the store (Zimmerman, 1955). Clearly, we are not talking about complete consumer autonomy here, but regulated freedom. The consumer is encircled within the mechanics of the shop, its intrinsic ordering directing her around its perimeters and through its aisles in a particular manner.

The biggest problem facing retailers at first, though, was getting shoppers into the stores in the first place. Promotional campaigns run through the local media, accompanied by the leafleting of adjacent residential areas, were frequently conducted prior to the opening of a self-service store. Attempts would be made to build up a sense of anticipation among the local populace, trading, in particular, on the sense of being part of something new and 'modern' (Humphrey, 1998). Once the store was open and shoppers were enticed to its doors, the promotional and the educational would be fused.

The need to preserve the element of human contact – what was described as 'the social side of shopping' – was emphasised by Mr R.G. Magnus-Hannaford, Principal of the College for the Distributive Trades, at the first national conference on self-service shopping held at the college in London in 1955. He warned delegates that too keen a focus on the economic rationality of self-service could undermine what he

considered to be the social side of the retail experience for customers. This could easily switch them off from engaging in this form of shopping. He stressed that although shoppers would in reality have no one to blame but themselves if they bought too much or bought the wrong things, they would invariably end up blaming the retailers rather than themselves (*The Gazette of The John Lewis Partnership*, 21 May 1955, p. 387). Such was the fear among retailers that shoppers would feel alienated by their new surroundings (so unused to exercising their individual freedom within the stores were they assumed to be) that they regularly deployed staff to assist shoppers around the store, gradually introducing them 'by example' to the arts of shopping for oneself. While some stores (Sainsbury's, for instance) used retired branch managers to assist the newly individualised shopper to become acquainted with her surroundings, others deployed what was known in the trade press as 'the hostess'. This category of person would stand either at the front of store greeting customers and offering assistance or would stroll around the store offering her services as and when she spotted a customer in distress. The aim, again, was to alleviate the anxiety and alienation of 'being alone' and being responsible for one's conduct inside the store and to show, through example, the proper exercise of individual shopping liberty (Towsey, 1964; Zimmerman, 1955).

This brief sketch of the efforts undertaken by British retailers and their associates to put self-service techniques to work contains some

Figure 1.4
Explanatory publicity leaflet for Waitrose customers in Wimbledon on the introduction of self-service in 1953

Figure 1.5
Self-service publicity
leaflet for Sainsbury's
customers, 1955

At Sainsbury's Self-service shopping is EASY and QUICK

1 – As you go in you are given a special wire basket for your purchases.

2 – The prices and weight of all goods are clearly marked. You just take what you want.

3 – Are you a fast shopper or a slow? You can be either when you shop at Sainsbury's!

4 – Dairy produce, cooked meats, pies, sausages, bacon, poultry, rabbits and cheese – all hygienically packed.

5 – Meat is served from Sainsbury's special refrigerated counters. Or you can serve yourself from the cabinets.

6 – Pay as you go out. The assistant puts what you have bought into your own basket and gives you a receipt.

important lessons for exploring questions of conduct and, more generally, the ways in which social worlds are made up. The example of self-service indicates that human beings are not naturally equipped with the capacity to act in any social world they happen to find themselves in. People didn't intuitively know how to do self-service. They had to learn how to conduct themselves as self-servicers. Crucially, their capacity to so act was not the outcome of their own voluntary willed action or meaning making but rather was dependent upon the provision of certain sorts of equipment. This equipment did not reside in the individual as shopper per se but was distributed throughout the formatted setting of the supermarket or store. The ability to act as a self-servicing shopper was dependent on the presence of 'competence building technologies' or material prosthetics such as shopping trollies, product packaging, and so on. These and other forms of relevant 'shopping' equipment needed to be in place to make self-service and the self-servicing shopper practicable realities. Seen in this way, the self-servicing consumer or shopper appears as the product of a certain *agencement* – a particular configuration or network of devices and instruments. Changing the *agencement* changes the character of the agent because they are two sides of the same coin. Agency – in this instance a particular economically relevant agency – is distributed and thus plural, variable, and contingent on circumstances.

4 Making up people

Throughout this chapter I have argued that agency, the ability to act and give meaning to action in different social worlds, does not possess a unitary form. Rather, as we saw in section 3, different forms of *agencement* create different forms of social agency or, as the sociologists Paul Hirst and Penny Woolley (1982, p. 120) put it, 'social agents are the differentiated terminals of the varied capacities and practices they engage in'. Social agents are not therefore reducible to the person, seen as a unique entity coincident with a distinct consciousness and will, revealed to us in speech, gesture and conduct. If we assumed, as many sociologists have done, that the person as a unique self is the foundation of social life and the ultimate maker of social worlds, then we would be in for a bit of a surprise if, for instance, we entered a law court armed with such an assumption. As I suggested in the Introduction to this chapter, in many modern societies legal conceptions of 'person' are not reducible to the idea of an individual human being with a distinctive consciousness or conscience. Rather, a legal person:

> is such, not because he [sic] is human but because rights and duties are ascribed to him. The person is the legal subject or substance of which the rights and duties are attributes ... not every human being is necessarily a person, for a person is capable of rights and duties, and there may well be human beings having no legal rights, as was the case with slaves in English Law.
>
> (*Black's Law Dictionary*, 1999, p. 1162)

Viewed historically and anthropologically, concepts of personhood have varied enormously, and not simply concepts but practices, institutions and techniques which help 'make up' or 'assemble' different persons (Hirst and Woolley, 1982, p. 118).

Mauss, whose work on 'body techniques' we briefly examined in the Introduction to this chapter, focused on this very issue in a famous essay 'A category of the human mind: the notion of person; the notion of self' (1985 [1938]). In this piece Mauss built upon his earlier analysis of a diverse range of human attributes as the contingent outcomes of an array of 'body techniques'. As we saw in the Introduction, Mauss argued that individuals and groups acquire various attributes – dancing, swimming, riding a bike, reading – as a basic outcome of a practical involvement in a given activity or way of life.

Having established this possibility, Mauss extends its remit in his essay on the notion of 'person'. There Mauss attempts two tasks. The first is to challenge the idea that the conception of person or self as a unique entity coincident with a distinct consciousness and will is a foundational human category, an essential element of what it means to be human. The second is to explore whether the capacity to conduct oneself as a 'subject' or 'self', as an entity with a distinct consciousness and will, is directly comparable with these other techniques (for swimming, spitting, dancing etc.). In other words, he asks whether the capacity to interrogate one's actions and abilities by relating them to an inner principle of self-scrutiny and control might itself be the product of special techniques and practices and not, as was often argued in his time and is argued still in our own, the foundation of all human abilities and modes of existence.

Mauss begins by indicating that forms of specification of individuals exist in all societies but that they are not necessarily specified therein as individual subjects, as unique entities with inherent capacities for self-representation and self-reflection. He points to predominantly clan-based societies where persons are special configurations of rights, statuses, capacities and traits which are invested, not in individuals, but in trans-individual forms or institutions. In the words of Ian Hunter and David Saunders (1995):

> These entities and institutions – totems, naming systems, masks, ritual genealogies – are responsible for a distribution of personhood to individuals that need not be universal and may not be permanent. For example, certain individuals acquire their persons through the forms of cultural organization in which they re-incarnate the person of an ancestor or spirit. And they do so not, as we would have it, as an expression of their inner selves but through public institutions such as ritual combat or ecstatic dance. Under these circumstances it is

possible, though no doubt difficult for us to understand, for individuals to lose their persons and for others to acquire them ... We on the contrary have come to think of our persons – our rights, duties, capacities, virtues and traits – as inalienable, as rooted in the conscience and consciousness of each individual. But the leading tendency of Mauss's essay is to relativize this conception of the 'person as self'. This conception is treated as a special case, peculiar to the modern West, of the cultural forms in which personhood is elaborated and ascribed to individuals.

(Hunter and Saunders, 1995, p. 72)

Mauss takes this modern conception of the person as a unique 'self' to be the product of a particular cultural elaboration of personhood. In particular, Mauss's analysis of the development of the modern conception of 'person as self' focuses upon two important moments of transformation, taking place in the institutions of law and (Christian) morality.

According to Mauss, the development of the modern Western conception of the person as 'self' really begins with 'the Romans, or perhaps rather the Latins' (1985 [1938], p.14). The first relatively even distribution of persons to individuals, he argues, comes about with the establishment of rights ascribed to all those individuals who were citizens under the laws of Rome (Hirst and Woolley, 1982, p. 119). While the Romans developed the concept of persona from that of a particular legally based status or role, to which were attached certain obligations, into that of a person as an independent moral entity, a being whose conduct is self-governed, it was Christianity which invested this legal and moral persona with additional attributes. The second transformation therefore occurs in the institutions of morality, most especially in the milieux of particular Christian ethical speculation and practice. Here the person became both an individual agent and an immortal soul, the well-being of the soul being dependent in part upon the conduct of the individual (Hirst and Woolley, 1982, p.119). According to Mauss (1985 [1938], pp. 19–20), Christianity produces a conception of the individual as a unity in its conduct, as a unique entity independent of particular social statuses, 'and of a transcendental value irreducible to considerations of social utility' (Hirst and Woolley, p.119). It is not until after the Reformation that identity and consciousness are linked in the individual self, with self-consciousness emerging as the ground of individual moral existence (Hirst and Woolley, 1985, p. 119). For Mauss (1985 [1938], p.21) this development is premised upon specific forms of Christian belief and practice, in particular an unmediated relationship between the individual Christian and God, a relationship based on prayer as a dialogue, on introspection and an inner regulation based upon the continual examination of 'conscience' (Hirst and Woolley, 1985, p. 119). Here, Mauss singles out the Christian sects in early modern Europe as playing a crucial role in the formation of this particular conception of the person:

> We cannot exaggerate the importance of sectarian movements throughout the seventeenth and eighteenth centuries ... here it was that were posed the questions regarding individual liberty, regarding the individual conscience and the right to communicate directly with God, to be one's own priest, to have an inner God. The ideas of the Moravian Brothers, the Puritans, the Wesleyans and the Pietists are those which form the basis on which is established the notion: the 'person' (*personne*) equals the 'self' (*moi*); the 'self' (*moi*) equals consciousness, and is its primordial category.
>
> (Mauss, 1985 [1938], p. 21)

It is here, too, that Mauss's account connects most clearly with that offered by one of the founding figures of sociology, Weber (1930), in his famous essay *The Protestant Ethic and the Spirit of Capitalism*. In this essay, Weber explores the ways in which modern forms of economic conduct – the rigorous organisation of work, a distinctively methodical approach to labour, a systematic pursuit of profit – developed out of the religious practices of the sixteenth- and seventeenth-century Puritan sects: Calvinists, Methodists, Congregationalists, Baptists, Quakers, Independents and Mennonites. Puritanism gave birth, Weber argued, to a 'Protestant ethic' characterised by the strict organisation by believers of their conduct, with the result that they came to lead highly self-controlled, methodically rational lives, and directed these systematically organised lives towards work, wealth and profit as part of a vocational calling.

In *The Protestant Ethic and the Spirit of Capitalism* Weber (1930) is primarily concerned with exploring 'the characterological effects of specific forms of piety' (Hennis, 1988, p. 129). Weber describes the development of a 'Protestant ethic' in terms of the partial dissolution of a system in which individuals acquired their religious persona through the distributive rituals of the Church and the gradual emergence of a system in which 'the status and attributes of Christian personhood become attached to an inner principle of monitoring and control: conscience and consciousness' (Hunter and Saunders, 1995, p. 73). Of crucial import to members of the Puritan sects, Weber argued, was the ethical dilemmas attendant upon a belief in 'predestination' – the idea that certain individuals were preordained to go to heaven because they had been elected by God to do so. For Weber (1930, p. 111), 'the decisive problem is: How was this doctrine borne ...?'. He argued that 'two principal, mutually connected, types of pastoral advice appear' for those seeking a sign that they are after all members of the elect. On the one hand, 'it is held to be an absolute duty to consider oneself chosen, and to combat all doubts as temptations of the devil' (1930, p. 11). And on the other hand, 'in order to sustain that self-confidence intense worldly activity is recommended as the most suitable means. It and it alone disperses religious doubts and gives the certainty of grace' (Weber, 1930, p. 112).Thus, individuals are instructed to use their lives as calculated means of at once fulfilling God's plan, and assuaging their own inner need for certainty. A conscientious and conscious, self-driven and driving existence is proposed:

> In practice this means that God helps those who help themselves. Thus the Calvinist, as it is sometimes put, himself creates his own salvation, or, as would be more correct, the conviction of it. But this creation cannot, as in Catholicism, consist in a gradual accumulation of good works to one's credit, but rather in a systematic self-control which at every moment stands before the inexorable alternative, chosen or damned.
>
> (Weber, 1930, p. 115)

For Weber it is not the doctrine of predestination alone that matters. The 'Protestant ethic' is more than this: it is a set of techniques and practices – methodical daily bible reading, constant monitoring of one's spiritual progress and so forth – through which individuals learned to conduct their lives in the absence of collective guarantees of salvation. That individuals came to see themselves as the objects of their own unique ethical attention, that they came to modify their conduct on the basis of the ethical being they aspired to be – this was the result of a particular distribution and dissemination of techniques developed in the Puritan sects. In this way, individuals came to acquire personhood in a particular internalised, individual manner. Personhood here becomes identified with an inner entity – conscience, consciousness, the self – rather than with a public institution.

The fact that a large number of individuals come to acquire the ability to locate a moral personality within their 'self' is, for Mauss and for Weber, a matter of historical contingency. The modern concept of the person as self is no less a construction placed upon certain specific human capacities and attributes than any of the other conceptions of personhood that Mauss discusses in his essay and Weber explores in his studies of the formation of distinctive 'personalities' – the bureaucrat, the politician, the journalist – in various spheres of modern life. The modern conception of person as self 'tends to obliterate this in its claims, making the person an inherent unitary, given and constitutive reality' (Hirst and Woolley, 1982, p. 121). For Mauss and Weber, this 'internalisation' of personhood does not represent the 'true' or essential form of human subjectivity; rather it is simply one among many potential ways of being a 'person'. As Mauss famously argued, 'Who knows even whether this "category", which all of us here believe to be well founded will always be recognised as such? It is formulated only for us, among us' (1985 [1938], p. 22).

5 Conclusion

In this chapter I have sought to establish the centrality of questions of conduct to understanding how social worlds are constructed and made to work, and how individuals are equipped to act as agents in those diverse worlds. A crucial purpose of the chapter has been to illustrate that human beings' mental and physical capacities and conducts are not 'naturally' given but depend in great measure upon, and vary considerably with, social beliefs, practices and techniques. Mauss's essay on 'body techniques', a brief section of which you read in Reading 1.1, is basically a catalogue of the ways in which bodily dispositions, actions and attributes – walking, running, swimming, spitting, marching, eating, squatting and so on – are acquired through various forms of training and practice that vary across time and between cultures. Mauss's work and the example of the self-service petrol pump illustrate that there are many different ways of organising the conduct of a given activity, and that social beliefs, practices and techniques affect both bodily capacities and mental functioning.

Having established that human attributes and conducts are the diverse and variable products of socially instituted forms of training and practice, I went on to consider certain sociological approaches to questions of conduct that highlighted the importance of one particular category and capacity – that of 'agency'. For some forms of sociological theory – as in the example of the 'action–structure' debate in Section 2 – a capacity for willed, voluntary action is taken as a basic human constant, and, following on from this, sociological questions about conduct are framed in terms of whether the human capacity for agency and willed voluntary action is facilitated or constrained by existing social arrangements. In contrast to this view, and taking self-service shopping as our example, we saw in Section 3 that agency is, in fact, both diverse and distributed. It is diverse in the sense that a particular agent – a shopper, a nurse, a secretary – is only intelligible in relation to 'a definite substratum of categories, practices and activities that give the agent its – complex and differentiated – form' (Hirst and Woolley, 1982, p. 120). It is distributed in the sense that the capacity to exert agency resides not simply in human beings but in the *agencement* – those fixtures and fittings, material arrangements and devices which help furnish them with certain characteristics and enable them to act in particular environments. Different *agencements* produce different forms of action. Agency, rather than being a singular, universal and human-centred capacity, is distributed, plural and contingent upon particular socio-technical arrangements. Social agency does not have a unitary form. It varies with the forms of discourse, techniques and practices defining a given activity.

Having argued that many taken-for-granted physical and mental capacities and conducts, including the capacities for willed action, are the product of socially organised forms of training and practice, I went on to explore the possibility that the modern notion of 'person' as 'self' is more historically and culturally contingent than many sociological accounts would allow. In Section 4, through a brief engagement with the work of Mauss and Weber, I examined how and why views which hold that personal existence and the experience of 'self' are a human constant are more problematic than they might first appear. I located the historical development of the notion and practice of 'the person as self' in transformations taking place in the institutions of law and Christian morality. As a result of this brief analysis, I concluded that 'persons', and the conducts that support them, are diverse and variable across time and circumstance. That many of us in the West today see personhood in terms of the possession of a unique self does not mean that such a sense of self is a universal part of being human; rather, as Mauss argued, it is in many ways a historical accident, formed only 'for us, among us', and it is fragile. It may one day disappear. Indeed, we might even say that no one conception of personhood is ever likely to be the 'true' one. This is not simply because historically there have been dramatically discontinuous changes in the characterisation of persons, though this appeared to be the case. Nor is it because anthropological and cultural research indicates that moral and legal practices, that are often treated as analogous across contexts, differ so dramatically in practice that they cannot really be held to have captured 'the' concept of a person, though this too is true. Rather, looking at persons and conducts sociologically has enabled us to see that what it means to be a person is not all of a piece, as the idea of the human agent implies, but is variable and dependent upon circumstances. Personal capacities and deportments, it might be said, are formulated and formed in the context of normative and technical regimes of conduct, such as those provided by educational, aesthetic, legal, familial, political and economic institutions. What sociologists need to do, perhaps, is to describe these different persons each in their own terms, rather than assuming they are simply variations of the one true person, the human agent or individual 'self'.

References

Abrams, P. (1982) *Historical Sociology*, Shepton Mallett, Open Books.

Black's Law Dictionary (1999, 7th edn), St Paul, MN, West Group.

Bourdieu, P. (1977) *Outline of a Theory of Practice* (trans. R. Nice), Cambridge, Cambridge University Press.

Bowlby, R. (2000) *Carried Away: The Invention of Modern Shopping*, London, Faber and Faber.

Callon, M. (1998) 'Introduction: the embeddedness of economic markets in economics' in Callon, M. (ed.) *The Laws of the Markets*, Oxford, Blackwell.

Callon, M. (2005) 'Why virtualism paves the way to political impotence: a reply to Daniel Miller's critique of *The Laws of the Markets*, *Economic Sociology: European Electronic Newsletter*, vol. 6, no. 2 (February), pp. 3–20. [Online] http://econsoc. mpifg.de/archive/esfeb05.pdf (Accessed 24 July 2007).

Callon, M. and Caliskan, K. (2005) 'New and old directions in the anthropology of markets', Paper presented to Wenner-Gren Foundation for Anthropological Research, New York, NY, 9 April.

Carter, S. and Davey Smith, G. (2008) 'Health and security' in Carter, S., Jordan, T. and Watson, S. (eds) *Security: Sociology and Social Worlds*, Manchester, Manchester University Press/Milton Keynes, The Open University (Book 1 in this series).

Chandler, R. (2001 [1955]) 'The Little Sister' in *The Lady in the Lake and Other Novels*, Harmondsworth, Penguin.

Cochoy, F. (1998) 'Another discipline for the market economy: marketing as a performative knowledge and know-how for capitalism' in Callon, M. (ed.) *The Laws of the Markets*, Oxford, Blackwell.

Cochoy, F. (2003) 'On the "Captation" of publics: understanding the market thanks to Little Red Riding Hood', Workshop on Market(-ing) Practice in Shaping Markets, Stockholm, 14–16 June.

Cochoy, F. and Grandclément-Chaffy, C. (2006) 'Publicizing Goldilocks' choice at the supermarket: the political work of shopping packs, carts and talk' in Latour, B. and Weibel, P. (eds) *Making Things Public: Atmospheres of Democracy*, Cambridge, MA, MIT Press.

Dawe, A. (1979) 'Theories of social action' in Bottomore, T. and Nisbet, R. (eds) *A History of Sociological Analysis*, London, Heinemann.

Dean, M. (1994) *Critical and Effective Histories*, London, Routledge.

Elias, N. (2000) [1939] *The Civilizing Process: Sociogenetic and Psychogenetic Investigations* (trans. E. Jephcott, revised edn), Oxford, Blackwell.

Galvani, P. and Arnell, A. (1952) *Going Self-Service? A Practical Guide to Self-Service Grocery Retailing*, London, Sidgwick and Jackson Ltd.

Giddens, A. (1979) *Central Problems in Social Theory*, Basingstoke, Macmillan.

Granovetter, M. (1985) 'Economic action and social structure: the problem of embeddedness', *American Journal of Sociology*, vol. 91, no. 3, pp. 481–50.

Hardie, I. and MacKenzie, D. (2006) 'Assembling an economic actor: the *agencement* of a hedge fund', Paper presented at the workshop 'New Actors in a Financialised Economy and Implications for Varieties of Capitalism', Institute of Commonwealth Studies, London, 11–12 May.

Hennis, W. (1988) *Max Weber: Essays in Reconstruction*, London, Allen & Unwin.

Hirst, P. and Woolley, P. (1982) *Social Relations and Human Attributes*, London, Tavistock.

Humphrey, K. (1998) *Shelf Life: Supermarkets and the Changing Cultures of Consumption*, Cambridge, Cambridge University Press.

Hunter, I. and Saunders, D. (1995) 'Walks of life: Mauss and the human gymnasium', *Body & Society*, vol. 1, no. 2, pp. 65–81.

Klein, N. (2000) *No Logo*, London, Flamingo.

Latour, B. (2005) *Reassembling the Social: An Introduction to Actor-Network Theory*, Oxford, Oxford University Press.

Mauss, M. (1973 [1935]) 'Techniques of the body', *Economy and Society*, vol. 2, no. 1, pp. 70–88.

Mauss, M. (1985 [1938]) 'A category of the human mind: the notion of person; the notion of self' in Carrithers, M., Collins, S. and Lukes, S. (eds) *The Category of the Person*, Cambridge, Cambridge University Press.

Seth, A. and Randall, G. (1999) *The Grocers*, London, Kogan Page.

Shop Review (1955) vol. 1–4, London.

Strauss, A. (1977) *Mirrors and Masks: The Search for Identity*, London, Martin Robertson.

The Gazette of the John Lewis Partnership (1955) 21 May.

The Times (1957) 21 January.

The Times (1972) 'Self-service petrol', 17 August, p. 23.

Towsey, R. (1964) *Self-Service Retailing: Its Profitable Application to All Trades*, London, Iliffe Books Ltd.

van Krieken, R. (1998) *Norbert Elias*, London, Routledge.

Weber, M. (1930) *The Protestant Ethic and the Spirit of Capitalism*, London, HarperCollins.

Zimmerman, M. (1955) *The Super Market: A Revolution in Distribution*, New York, NY, McGraw-Hill.

Chapter 2
Your money or your life: making people prudent

Liz McFall

Contents

1   Introduction

Prudence is a virtue most necessary for human life. For a good life consists in good deeds. Now in order to do good deeds, it matters not only what a man does but also how he does it; to wit that he do it from right choice and not merely from impulse or passion. And, since choice is about things in reference to the end, rectitude of choice requires two things; namely, the due end, and something suitably ordained to that due end. Now man is suitably directed to his due end by a virtue which perfects the soul in the appetitive part, the object of which is the good and the end. And to that which is suitably ordained to the due end [i.e. the means] man needs to be rightly disposed by a habit in his reason, because counsel and choice, which are about things ordained to the end, are acts of the reason. Consequently an intellectual virtue is needed in the reason, to perfect the reason, and make it suitably affected towards things ordained to the end; and this virtue is prudence. Consequently prudence is a virtue necessary to lead a good life.

(Aquinas, 1947 [1265–1275], Parts I–II, Question 57, Article 5)

[A]ppetite seizeth upon a present good without foreseeing the greater evils that necessarily attach to it. Therefore appetite perturbs and impedes the operation of reason.

(Hobbes, 1991 [1657], p. 55)

What springs to mind when you think of **prudence**? My guess is that safety, caution, judgement, thrift and self-restraint would figure somewhere, but there is a wealth of other equally likely possibilities. Check in a thesaurus and you will see that among other things prudence is associated with economy, calculation, foresight, expediency, common sense and care. This range of associations is not surprising when you consider that prudence was considered one of the ancient virtues. Its history stretches back to the fourth-century BC writings of Aristotle, and through the fourth-century theology of Augustine and the thirteenth-century theology of Thomas Aquinas. Ideas about prudence feature in the early modern political philosophies of Niccolo Machiavelli, John Locke and Thomas Hobbes and in the eighteenth-century work of philosophers like Adam Smith, which fuelled the traditions of liberal (and, according to some commentators, neo-liberal) thought. What these different traditions have in common is a sense of prudence as a desirable form of conduct, an ideal to which individuals should aspire for their own good, but more particularly for the collective, social good. Prudence is offered as a way of keeping the unruly, internal economy of passions in check to enable the achievement of external goals, including, at different times, religious virtue or goodness, effective rule, civil peace, and long-term order, safety and stability.

This chapter will focus mainly on the role of prudence in one of the domains in which it is most often marshalled as an ideal – personal finance. There are good reasons for exploring personal finance sociologically; the way we live now would be quite inconceivable without money and credit. Yet finance, including personal finance, has, since the early twentieth century, largely been seen as an 'economic' rather than a 'sociological' problem. Sociologists have an enduring fascination with material acts of consumption, with the way that objects 'talk' about class, age, gender, lifestyle, personality or subculture and what this might reveal about underlying social relations. This fascination wanes a little when it comes to the consumption of services and almost halts completely at the consumption of financial services. This is regrettable as it doesn't take a financial wizard to work out that the two – consumption of goods and of financial services – are intricately related. These links between the desire for goods, attitudes towards debt and borrowing practices are manifest in the following extract from the *Guardian* newspaper:

> The price of an average dwelling is now skimming 300 grand. Nobody has that kind of money; few people earn enough to get a mortgage on that amount. How many people on a regular, let's call it middle-class, salary could scrape together the 10% deposit that was not long ago considered requisite? People buy houses with brio rather than cash – they self-certify, they borrow from Personal Loan Peter to pay All-My-Own-Savings-Honest-Guv Paul; they make it work because the alternative is to rent, which is just as expensive, with none of the boons.
>
> ...
>
> Paradoxically, the very people who would never dream of shackling themselves with the cost of a flat are in extraordinary debt for things like, well, I don't think I am underestimating their seriousness when I call them sparkly tops. According to a survey by *More* magazine, over half the women polled owed nearly four grand on credit cards, and 80% habitually spent more than they earned. This is far more burdensome than a mortgage, since you have all the grind of repayments with none of the bonuses.
>
> (Williams, *Guardian*, 2006)

Underlying Zoe Williams's tongue-in-cheek tirade is the gap between ideals of prudent financial management and consumption practices. This gap is a tricky one to negotiate in the absence of an absolute definition of financial prudence along the lines of the Shakespearian injunction to 'neither a borrower nor a lender be'. Conforming to such a standard would make social participation almost impossible for many. Indeed, at a certain income level, increasing debt, and expenditure which exceeds income may well be deemed prudent if offset by property or other appreciating capital assets (Erturk et al., 2005). Property, even in a fluctuating market, is an appreciating asset over the longer term; the things purchased with credit cards seldom are. It is this view of prudence that Williams is getting at in championing over-extended mortgage borrowing against credit-card debt.

These are matters about which sociologists have, thus far, had little to say. Yet at a time when personal debt has reached unprecedented levels in the west, with substantial borrowing on credit cards, increasing numbers of bankruptcies, soaring house prices, and a 'looming' pensions crisis (Callaghan et al., 2007), it is clear that financial conduct should be a pressing sociological concern. Financial crises like these have been read as evidence of the failures of successive governmental initiatives since the 1980s to induce individuals to take upon themselves the responsibility for their own welfare by making informed choices in a competitive marketplace, whether by choosing their own healthcare provider, paying for their own education, or making their own pension arrangements. Such initiatives are often referred to collectively as part of a sweeping neo-liberal **marketisation** project whereby the welfare-state 'safety net' is to be minimised to foster increased individual responsibility. According to Pat O'Malley, these initiatives are part of a variant of neo-liberalism which implies that individuals

> should be prudent instead of relying upon socialized securities. They should cover themselves against the vicissitudes of sickness, unemployment, old age, accidental loss or injury by making such privatised insurances as they see fit – including taking out the private insurances they can afford. ... Better understood as prudentialism, it is a technology of governance that removes the key conception of regulating individuals by collectivist risk management, and throws back upon the individual the responsibility for managing risk.
> (O'Malley, 1996, pp. 196–7)

What O'Malley means by 'prudentialism' is a form of government designed to promote the play of market forces across a range of different domains from crime control to health and financial planning. Prudentialism employs a conception of the individual as responsible, moral, rational and calculating. Armed with the right information about the everyday risks posed by crime, illness, unemployment, debt, old age and death, and the products available on the market to help offset such risks, the individual is best placed to make such choices as necessary to conduct their lives prudently.

A very particular idea of the individual is clearly in play here. This is an individual with not only the capacity for voluntary, willed action (see Chapter 1 in this volume) but also the ability to exercise such actions informed by a high level of knowledge and reason. Equally, neo-liberal, prudentialist government is underpinned by a particular conception of the social world. This is a world in need of 'unburdening' of the weight of social insurances like unemployment and sickness benefits which constitute the welfare safety net. Through popular ideas like 'dependency culture', the welfare safety net is characterised as sapping national efficiency and productivity. The social world imagined in political projects like neo-liberalism or prudentialism involves a simultaneous image of individuals equipped with specific sets of capacities and attributes. It is the nature of this link between the social and individual capacities, attributes and practices that will occupy much of our attention in this chapter.

Whatever is to be said of the failures of neo-liberal marketisation policies to create a population of well-informed, enterprising and discriminating consumers, they are only the most recent of many attempts to engineer prudence as a social virtue. Prudence, as we shall see, has occupied a privileged place throughout history as a way of articulating ideals of proper conduct. Thanks in part to this long history, prudence, in the context of personal financial conduct, offers a revealing insight into the nature of the relationship between the social and the individual. In financial matters, prudence is an ideal – at times a virtue to be cultivated, a habit to be acquired, or a skill to be learned. It is not, on the whole, an attribute with which individuals are thought to arrive already endowed. Making people prudent is therefore a task, and not a straightforward one. Prudent financial conduct involves a battle between long-term goals and short-term passions. Winning, or even participating in, this battle requires specialist equipment, tools and techniques, whether in the form of sixteenth-century treatises on household governance, eighteenth- and nineteenth-century domestic account books, or more recently computer spreadsheets or price-comparison websites. Even equipped with such material devices and proper training in their use, financial conduct conforming to shifting standards of prudence can remain a distant ideal as immediate demands prevail over future contingencies.

This chapter will explore these issues, beginning, in the next section, with a closer look at the history of prudence. This is a history in which the meaning of prudence emerges as a matter of ongoing refashioning and reinvention. Ideas about prudence are interwoven with shifting ideas about social worlds and about what it means to be an individual. Section 2 aims to expose both the closeness and the dynamic character of the connection between the social and the individual. Section 3 will follow this up with a more practical focus on the everyday mechanics of prudence. Precisely how have individuals been enjoined to conform to ideals of prudence in the management of their personal financial affairs at different moments in time? This section will focus primarily on examples, including the role of credit and advice manuals in early modern Britain, the promotion of life insurance in nineteenth-century Britain, and the phenomenon of self-help manuals and reality-television advice shows. The chapter will close with a brief conclusion reviewing some of the tensions and failures endemic within projects aimed at engineering prudent conduct.

1.1 Teaching aims

The aims of this chapter are to:

- explore the character and history of prudence as an individual and social virtue

- review the range of different institutions, practices and technologies brought to bear on the inculcation of prudent habits among individuals

- consider the relationship between individual financial practices and the making of social worlds

- highlight some of the conflicts, tensions and failures encountered by such projects, in particular as they relate to the gap between ideals of prudent conduct and individual experience.

2   The ideal of prudence

In tracing the history of prudence as a virtue in the conduct of personal financial affairs it quickly becomes clear that prudence has always been about more than thrift and tidy bookkeeping. Shifting ideas about prudence also open to scrutiny the relationship between the individual and the social more generally. The sociologist Norbert Elias (1994 [1939]) maintained that the best insight into how the dynamic relationship between individuals and society operates was to be gained through concentrating on specific empirical examples. This logic informs the approach taken in this chapter. Through the example of prudence and personal finance, we shall also be thinking about changing ideas about the nature of human individuals and the social worlds they inhabit. The changing arrangement of personal finance offers one way of exposing the interdependencies between the individual and the social.

As you saw in Chapter 1, the notion of *homo clausus*, the individual as a closed entity or 'black box' has, according to Elias, locked social science into a long and largely fruitless debate over the nature of the relationship between the individual and society. The debate has been fruitless because of its tendency to treat the individual and the social as if they were separate and static realities. As an alternative, Elias offered the term 'figuration' to invoke a sense of the social world as comprised of a dynamic network of interdependent beings; beings whose capacities and attributes were constructed by the nature of the interdependent relations between them.

To help you understand in greater depth the significance of this notion in the context of prudent conduct, read the following short but rather dense extract from Elias's classic text *The Civilizing Process*. As you do so, try to pay particular attention to what Elias is arguing about the relationship between civilisation and the 'autonomous dynamics of a web of relationships'.

Reading 2.1   Norbert Elias, 'Chains of interdependency'

The immanent regularities of social figurations are identical neither with regularities of the 'mind', of individual reasoning, nor with regularities of what we call 'nature' ... On its own, however, this general statement about the relative autonomy of social figurations is of little help in their understanding; it remains empty and ambiguous, unless the actual dynamics of social interweaving are directly illustrated by reference to specific and empirically demonstrable changes. Precisely this was one of the tasks to which Part One of *State Formation and Civilization* was devoted. It was attempted there to show what kind of interweaving, of mutual dependence between people, sets in motion, for example, processes of feudalization. It was shown how the compulsion of competitive situations drove a number of feudal lords into conflict, how the circle of competitors was slowly narrowed, and how this led to a monopoly of one and finally – in conjunction with other mechanisms of integration such as processes of increasing capital formation and functional differentiation – to the formation of an absolutist state. This whole reorganization of human relationships went hand in hand with corresponding changes in men's manners, in their personality structure, the provisional result of which is our form of 'civilized' conduct and sentiment. The connection between these specific changes in the structure of human relations and the corresponding changes in the structure of the personality will be discussed again shortly. But consideration of these mechanisms of integration is also relevant in a more general way to an understanding of the civilizing process. Only if we see the compelling force with which a particular social structure, a particular form of social intertwining, veers through its tensions to a specific change and so to other forms of intertwining, can we understand how these changes arise in human mentality, in the patterning of the malleable psychological apparatus, which can be observed over and again in human history from earliest times to the present. And only then, therefore, can we understand that the psychological change involved by civilization is subject to a quite specific order and direction, although it was not planned by individual people or produced by 'reasonable', purposive measures. Civilization is not 'reasonable'; not 'rational', any more than it is 'irrational'. It is set in motion blindly, and kept in motion by the autonomous dynamics of a web of relationships, by specific changes in the way people are bound to live together. [...]

But which specific changes in the way people are bonded together mould their personality in a 'civilizing' manner? The most general answer to this question ... is very simple. From the earliest period of the history of the Occident to the present, social functions have become more and more differentiated under the pressure of competition. The more differentiated they become, the larger grows the number of functions and thus of people on whom the individual constantly depends in all his actions, from the simplest and most commonplace to the more complex and uncommon. As more and more people must attune their conduct to that of others, the web of actions must be organized more and more strictly and accurately, if each individual action is to fulfil its social function. The individual is compelled to regulate his conduct in an increasingly differentiated, more even and more stable manner. ... this is characteristic of the psychological changes in the course of civilization: the more complex and stable control of conduct is increasingly instilled in the individual from his earliest years as an automatism, a self-compulsion that he cannot resist even if he consciously wishes to. The web of actions grows so complex and extensive, the effort required to behave 'correctly' within it becomes so great, that beside the individual's conscious self-control an automatic, blindly functioning apparatus of self-control is firmly established. This seeks to prevent offences to socially acceptable behaviour by a wall of deep-rooted fears, but, just because it operates blindly and by habit, it frequently indirectly produces such collisions with social reality. But whether consciously or unconsciously, the direction of this transformation of conduct in the form of an increasingly differentiated regulation of impulses is determined by the direction of the process of social differentiation, by the progressive division of functions and the growth of the interdependency chains into which, directly or indirectly, every impulse, every move of an individual becomes integrated.

Reading source

Elias, 1994 [1939], pp. 444–6

You may have found this hard going. It is a tightly argued piece in which Elias teases out some of the general implications of his detailed history of the civilising process. One of these implications concerns the changing nature of the web of dependent relations between individuals, what Elias calls 'interdependency chains', in complex 'civilised' societies. The civilising process, Elias maintains, is one in which, under competitive pressures, the division of functions makes large numbers of people dependent upon one another, producing lengthening interdependency chains which lead inevitably towards increasing social discipline and greater self-restraint. This process is not uniform, and 'decivilising' moves, in which failures of discipline and restraint prevail, can also take place, but the general direction is always towards greater discipline and a 'more or less automatic self-control' (1994 [1939], p. 458).

Personal finance offers a useful place to start thinking about this perspective on the relationship between individual conduct and the social world. For one thing, money and credit relations can be seen to have played a central role in the civilising process, shoring up the monopolies of force and taxation that have lent 'the West its special and unique character' as an interdependent and competitive society on a scale 'unequalled in world history' (Elias, 1994 [1939], p. 457). With networks of interdependence stretching spatially across the globe, human conduct has to be attuned, controlled and regulated over wide areas and long chains of action have to be overseen. The difficulties and potential misunderstandings that can arise over such long chains are the subject of a long-running HSBC bank advertising campaign, using the slogan, 'At HSBC, we never underestimate the importance of local knowledge' (See Figure 2.1). Stretched interdependencies, according to Elias, make foresight, self-control – especially in regard to the emotions – and social discipline increasingly indispensable. For another thing, money and credit relations offer a robust empirical example through which we can explore in greater detail Elias's account of the relationship between individual conduct and social figurations. In particular, the connection between ideals of prudence and personal financial habits and practices forms an excellent backdrop against which to think about the nature of interdependency relations at different places and times.

What Elias concludes about the demands placed on the individual for regulated, stable, predictable and habitually restrained conduct in the differentiated, interdependent social figurations typical of contemporary Western societies strikes a chord with much early discourse on prudence. One of the virtues referred to in ancient Greek philosophy, prudence was for Aristotle a sort of practical reason that could guide decision making along ethical lines The word prudence derives from the Latin

Figure 2.1
HSBC press advertisement: 'Never underestimate the importance of local knowledge'

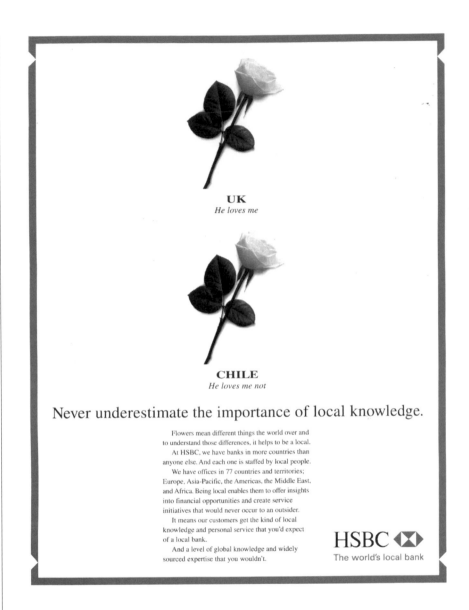

providere, meaning to foresee, to take precaution, to provide for; and it is this sense that informs the early Christian understanding of prudence as one of the four cardinal virtues alongside justice, fortitude and temperance. Prudence, in Christian thought, is about the capacity to discriminate between good and evil courses of action and to choose the good. For Aquinas, a properly developed capacity for prudence will decisively hold passions and appetites in check enabling 'man' to do good deeds 'from right choice and not merely from impulse or passion' (1947, Parts I–II, Question 57, Article 5). Prudence is thus championed as a form of reason that can be developed specifically to help attain the kind of control over the impulses, appetites, passions and emotions that Elias describes as a necessary element of the civilising process.

These notions of prudence may sound quite familiar. They also connect quite easily to the more narrow, contemporary sense of financial prudence. Think, for instance, of the balancing that is involved in trying to ensure that passionate or impulsive desires do not preside over more reasoned, rational decision making in shopping practices. The term 'impulse buy' or the excellent advice to never enter a supermarket on an empty stomach arises from the everyday operation of this balancing. The concept of prudence, however, has a more nuanced and variegated history than this might suggest. By the early sixteenth century, prudence had acquired a quite different set of connotations. Prudence in this emerging sense had more to do with expediency than with ethics. For Italian political philosopher Machiavelli, a wise, prudent ruler:

> cannot, nor should he, keep his word when doing so would be to his disadvantage and when the reasons that led him to make promises no longer exist ... But one must know how to disguise this nature well, and how to be a fine liar and hypocrite; and men are so simple-minded and so dominated by their present needs that one who deceives will always find one who will allow himself to be deceived.
>
> (Machiavelli, 1964, pp. 144–7)

This version of prudence as strategic, studied dissimulation was widespread in the sixteenth century. During this period, a 'prudential rhetoric' which emphasised the need to cultivate a certain ambiguity about one's beliefs became increasingly important in daily interactions. For English political philosopher Hobbes, writing in the seventeenth century, the key to prudent conduct lies in experience which, properly applied, can aid discrimination and foresight. This foresight can only ever be partial as providence alone can 'see' with any certainty the things that are to come:

> And though it be called prudence, when the event answereth our expectation; yet in its nature it is but presumption. For the foresight of things to come, which is providence, belongs only to him by whose will they are to come.
>
> (Hobbes, 1839 [1651], Chapter 3, p. 15)

Hobbes's account of prudence also places particular emphasis on the capacity to put off short-term satisfaction for the longer term good. This capacity did not in Hobbes's view arise naturally, as 'men cannot put off this same irrational appetite whereby they generally prefer the present good (to which by strict consequence, many unforeseen evils do adhere) before the future' (Hobbes; quoted in Vanden Houten, 2002, p. 270). While individuals may not 'naturally' possess the capacity for prudence, it is nevertheless the case that, for Hobbes, prudence was a capacity that *should* be cultivated as a tame, methodical route to the optimum gratification over the longest term. Prudence here is the proper pursuit of our own final interests and happiness. This studied pursuit of self-interested prudence was championed by Hobbes over the alternative he perceived (with good reason, given the context of the seventeenth-century religious civil wars in which he was writing) of passion-fuelled, protracted and bloody civil wars.

A not dissimilar sense of prudence can be traced in the eighteenth-century writings of Scottish moral philosopher Smith:

> The care of the health, of the fortune, of the rank and reputation of the individual, the objects upon which his comfort and happiness in this life are supposed principally to depend, is considered as the proper business of that virtue which is commonly called Prudence.
>
> (Smith, 1976 [1759], p. 213)

This version of prudence, as can be judged from the references to rank, reputation and health, is not quite so narrowly related to the pursuit of self-interest, particularly in the economic sense. Nevertheless, considerable stress is placed upon frugality, industry and steadiness and, most importantly, the ability to sacrifice 'the ease and enjoyment of the present moment for the probable expectation of the still greater ease and enjoyment of a more distant but more lasting period of time' (Smith, 1976 [1759], p. 215).

The crucial point, as far as we are concerned here, is that this idea of prudence has a long history as a standard against which individual conduct and social expectations can be gauged. The ideal of prudence went on to inform the key systems of economic and political thought which underpinned the emergence of new styles of government in the early nineteenth century, and, as we have seen, ideas about prudent behaviour were central to the neo-liberal marketisation policies pursued in the closing decades of the twentieth century. These neo-liberal policies have their roots in theories of liberal government which drew directly upon the work of political philosophers like Smith. Liberal government is a term used to refer broadly to those forms of government which rely upon individual self-rule rather than rule through coercion, and in which the 'free' market plays a central role. Liberal government employs a market-based system of organisation which aims to prompt individuals to act prudently in accordance with their own self-interests. One of the examples of *how* prudent conduct was promoted which we shall consider in the next section – that of nineteenth-century life insurance – follows very closely the emerging principles of liberal government. For now, it is worth thinking briefly about some of the difficulties and challenges that these notions of prudence as a virtue, ideal or habit might raise for the management of personal finances.

To help start this off, read the following short extract from French sociologist Pierre Bourdieu's *Distinction: A Social Critique of the Judgement of Taste*. Bourdieu is discussing the nature of the relationship between different social groups or classes within a social order and how this affects participation in a range of activities. As you read, pay particular attention to Bourdieu's comments about the role of credit in allowing members of what he terms the 'dominated classes' access to luxury goods.

Reading 2.2 Pierre Bourdieu, 'Downclassing, upclassing and the importance of credit'

The dialectic of downclassing and upclassing which underlies a whole set of social processes presupposes and entails that all groups concerned run in the same direction, towards the same objectives, the same properties, those which are designated by the leading group and which, by definition, are unavailable to the groups following, since, whatever these properties may be intrinsically, they are modified and qualified by their intrinsic rarity and will no longer be what they are once they are multiplied and made available to groups lower down. Thus, by an apparent paradox, the maintenance of order, that is, of the whole set of gaps, differences, 'differentials', ranks, precedences, priorities, exclusions, distinctions, ordinal properties, and thus of the relations of order which give a social formation its structure, is provided by an unceasing change in substantial (i.e. non-relational) properties. ...

It is no accident that *credit* is so important in this system. The imposition of legitimacy which occurs through the competitive struggle and is enhanced by the gentle violence of cultural missionary work tends to produce pretension, in the sense of a need which pre-exists the means of adequately satisfying. And in a social order which acknowledges that even the most deprived have the right to every satisfaction, but only in the long run, the only alternatives are credit, which allows immediate enjoyment of the promised goods but implies acceptance of a future which is merely the continuance of the past, or the 'imitation' – mock luxury cars, mock luxury holidays and so on.

But the dialectic of downclassing and upclassing is predisposed to function also as an ideological mechanism ... . Especially when they compare their present conditions with their past, the dominated groups are exposed to the illusion that they have only to wait in order to receive advantages which, in reality, they will obtain only by struggle. By situating the difference between the classes in the order of successions, the competitive struggle establishes a difference which, like that which separates predecessor from successor in a social order governed by well-defined rules of succession, is not only the most absolute and unabridgeable (since there is nothing to do but wait, sometimes a whole lifetime, like the petit bourgeois who acquire their own houses at the moment of retirement, sometimes several generations, like the petit bourgeois who extend their own foreshortened trajectories through their children) but also the most unreal and evanescent (since a person knows that if he can wait, he will in any case get what he is promised by the ineluctable laws of evolution). In short, what the competitive struggle makes everlasting is not different conditions but the differences between conditions.

Reading source

Bourdieu, 1990 [1984], pp. 163–4, emphasis in original

Again, you may have found this challenging reading. Bourdieu's object is to describe the dynamic tensions between classes within the social context in which he was writing – that of late twentieth-century France – and how these were manifested in the consumption practices of both material and cultural 'goods' like education, avant-garde concerts and art museums. The nature of these tensions and the processes of social mobility that Bourdieu characterises as 'downclassing and upclassing' are of less immediate concern here than the underlying implications of his argument in regard to the capacity of different groups to act 'prudently'. All groups, in Bourdieu's schema, ultimately want the same things, 'run in the same direction', but for some groups such things will always remain tantalisingly out of reach. For 'dominated', or lower socio-economic groups, access to both material and cultural goods is denied, restricted or delayed. In a social order in which 'even the most deprived have the right to every satisfaction' and in which the 'gentle violence of cultural missionary work' insistently promotes consumption through advertising, branding and marketing, members of these groups must rely upon credit.

Consumption enabled through credit is, almost by definition, imprudent; the more so, paradoxically, the poorer the borrower, as credit costs vary according to credit history and socio-economic status. The euphemistically labelled 'sub-prime' credit market, prevalent in car finance and debt-consolidation loans, targets, at premium interest rates, those borrowers deemed high risk. Underlying this argument is a view, prevalent in twentieth-century sociologies, that the prudent capacity to defer immediate gratification to enable more lasting future satisfaction is a capacity unevenly distributed according to class and/or socio-economic status. According to this view, the poor, unsurprisingly, face serious obstacles in striving to conform to standards of prudent financial conduct. These issues will be explored further in the following section as part of a discussion of some of the materials, techniques and tools that have been deployed, at different moments in history, to help engineer prudent conduct.

3   How to be prudent

The dutie of the Husband is to get goods; and of the Wife to gather them together, and saue them. The dutie of the Husband is to travell abroad, to seeke [a] living: and the Wives dutie is to keep the house. The dutie of the Husband is to get money and provision: and of the Wives, not vainely to spend it. The dutie of the Husband is to deal with many men: and of the Wives to talke with few. The dutie of the Husband is, to be entermedling: and of the wife, to be solitary and withdrawne. The dutie of the man is, to be skilful in talke: and of the wife, to boast of silence ... It is to be noted, and noted againe, that as the provision of [the] houshould dependeth only on the Husband: even so the honour of all dependeth only on the woman: in such sort, that there is no honour within the house longer than a man's wife is honourable.

(Dod and Cleaver, 1612; quoted in Shepard, 2000, p. 75)

Perhaps the most tragic thing about bad money management is this: it takes away your choices in life. Here is a sad – and all too typical – example. I recently interviewed a young woman who had just given birth to a beautiful baby daughter. Understandably, she wanted to stay home with her child. But before the baby was born, straight through the pregnancy, she and her husband had continued to manage their finances as if they were two single people with no responsibilities. They enjoyed deluxe holidays, lived very nicely (although not quite as nicely as they wished), racked up a growing pile of credit card debts, and saved not a penny.

Even after the baby was born, this young mother did not want to reduce her spending. 'I don't think it's right for me to have to do that' she told me defiantly. The result? Mother had no choice but to keep on working. By spending to the maximum of family income (and beyond), she had destroyed the possibility that she could stay at home and raise her own daughter. She was miserable, but of course it was all her own doing.

(Hall, 2002, p. 6)

You could be forgiven for wondering what these two extracts have to do with one another. The short answer is that they are both drawn from manuals designed to teach the skills of good domestic management, particularly in relation to financial management. Dod and Cleaver's *A Godlie Form of Householde Government* was one of a number of guides and treatises in wide circulation in the seventeenth century and intended to advise middle-ranking householders how to keep their houses in an orderly and godly fashion. It is clear in both these extracts that expectations of prudent conduct differ markedly according to gender. A prudent wife in the seventeenth century was expected to keep to the home, to be 'solitary, silent and withdrawn' while her husband should be locked into 'a web of commercial concerns and familiar with other men's business' (Shepard, 2000, p. 75). Alvin Hall's (2002) advice is clearly couched in very different terms and stresses questions of choice and lifestyle, but there is nevertheless an underpinning expectation that the wife should properly be able to stay at home. Both these manuals are concerned to define and convey normative standards of prudent conduct. In the contemporary context, actual practice clearly deviates substantially from such norms. Despite the exhortations of personal finance gurus like Hall, the rate of savings has seen a long, steady decline while borrowing continues to increase. Equally, in the early modern period – that is, from roughly the late fifteenth century to the middle of the eighteenth century – everyday practice was probably far more varied than Dod and Cleaver's standards imply. Historians of the period have argued that, in regard to social practice, the principles outlined by authors like Dod and Cleaver were so severely overdrawn that they verged upon fantasy (Shepard, 2000). In practice, women's lives departed from such ideals in terms of their roles and authority within and beyond the confines of the household. This is well supported by their involvement in the numerous debt litigation cases documented in court records. In this regard and in others, as we shall see in this section, the relationship between normative standards of prudent conduct, their technical articulation in advice books and manuals, and everyday practice is far from straightforward.

In sharp contrast to the Shakespearian dictate against all borrowing and lending, historians have demonstrated the absolute centrality of credit relations, in which almost all people were involved, to everyday commerce in the early modern period. As Thomas Tusser remarked in his 1573 husbandry manual, one of the most popular books of the late sixteenth century, 'Who Living but lends? And be lent to they must; else buieng and selling might lie in the dust' (quoted in Muldrew, 1993, p. 171). The nature of these credit relations helps illuminate the intricate connections between individual conduct – the practices, routines and habits of borrowing and lending – and the broader arrangements which made up the ordered social world.

Craig Muldrew (1993) has argued that the network of credit relations was so extensive and intertwined that it produced strong, moral reasons for cooperating within the social and commercial structures of the period. The pursuit of individual profit, he argues, mattered, but it could not be achieved without the direct cooperation of neighbours within the community, and this entailed trust. The extract in Reading 2.3 illustrates something of the extent and nature of the credit network.

Reading 2.3   Craig Muldrew, 'Interpreting the market: the ethics of credit and community relations in early modern England'

[B]uying and selling at this time, far from breaking up communities, actually created numerous bonds which held them together. As markets expanded, following the population growth of the sixteenth century, increasingly complex networks of credit transactions were created within this moral context. This expansion of market transactions certainly put strains on trust, but the result of such strains was that the need to maintain trust was emphasized even more strongly.

...

Probate inventories demonstrate the extent of credit, and also show that the credit market was very diffuse and certainly not dominated by usurious money lenders. One merchant from King's Lynn, for instance, was owed £1465 when he died, and another was owed debts by over 330 people on his death. In addition, contemporary diarists such as Ralph Josselin often mentioned debts. But the strongest evidence for the importance of credit is the huge number of court cases concerning failed credit relations. By 1640 there were over 28,000 cases in advanced stages of litigation in the central courts of King's Bench and Common Pleas, and in medium sized towns of about 7–10,000 people, such as King's Lynn, Yarmouth, Newcastle and Shrewsbury, it was not uncommon for over 1000 suits to be initiated in a single year! The vast majority (over 90 per cent) of this litigation concerned credit, and although sealed bonds were most commonly litigated over in the central courts of King's Bench and Common Pleas, most litigation (83 per cent) in King's Lynn, for example, concerned sales credit, and credit extended for services rendered or for work done.

Cases brought to local borough courts like King's Lynn concerned transactions which had taken place in the town, and most suits were generated by local marketing, such as the sale of beer, meat, livestock, wax, fish, bread and even hats or conny wool. Local sales could be quite large, such as one which involved over eighty barrels of beer, but there were many very small sales such as that of just 10s worth of beef. A smaller number of suits concerned goods imported and exported by sea such as coal and tobacco. Suits could also be for services rendered, such as cutting wood or cartage, and for labourer's wages owed on credit. Although the court records do not note whether transactions were made privately or in the market place, the nature of sixteenth- and seventeenth-century contract law meant that whatever the nature of the exchange, a private bargain had to be agreed upon for the transaction to be actionable.

Such bargains were a normal feature of life for most families. In a town such as King's Lynn, since it is likely that only a small portion of all transactions made on credit would have ended up in the town court, the volume of litigation gives a graphic illustration of the vast number of individual credit transactions which supported the town's economy. ... all members in urban communities, including the poor, were heavily involved in these tangled credit relationships as both creditors and debtors. Merchants traded on credit; tradesman sold or worked on credit; and many of these people were in debt to the poor for wages owed, for small sales or for work done.

Credit was so common that most people eventually accumulated numerous reciprocal debts over time. Credit was also generally fairly long term, and debts were remembered, or recorded in account books, and then mutually cancelled at convenient intervals. The standard means of payment was to 'reckon' or compare accounts, cross out equivalent debts, and then settle only the difference in cash. ... Because lending was so reciprocal, interest was not charged on sales credit to account for any risk, as opposed to money lending, or lending on bond where interest was standard by the seventeenth century.

Reading source

Muldrew, 1993, pp. 169–73

The extensiveness of credit relations meant that people were irredeemably tangled in webs of social and economic dependence based almost entirely on trust and reputation. In such a context, it was both an individual and a social imperative to prevent people from spending or lending too extravagantly. Instructional manuals, like Tusser's, accordingly aimed to set normative standards of prudence and thrift and fed into a social order which exacted severe penalties on those who lost their credit. This was a period in which the linguistic distinction between economic and social credit had not yet arisen; credit was largely synonymous with character and thus to lose credit was simultaneously to lose social standing. Tusser's manual characterised profit as the reward of good 'husbandry', or household financial management, but such profit had to be earned in keeping with certain standards. The church had long condemned profit earned through 'usury' (usury involves the charging of interest on monies lent, sometimes at any rate but more often at rates which substantially exceed the risk to the lender), and similar opprobrium was applied to the covetous hoarding of funds. It was, however, in accord with standards of prudence and good management to earn profit by sale or labour. To engage in transactions of sale and labour meant participating in credit relations and, in turn, this meant participating in a reciprocal network of trust. Getting credit in a community meant that your character was respected, while extending credit was a marker of trust that you would in turn be repaid. The centrality of trust in early modern markets, for Muldrew, reveals their operation as 'moral economies' (1993, p. 169) which required strong normative regulation to function. Part of this involved conforming to the standards and habits of mannerly and polite commercial conduct.

Individual and social interdependence here has something of the character of a property chain, in that the collapse of one link in the chain has consequences for all the other members. Tim Newton (2003) has argued that these credit relations can be seen as interdependency networks of the type outlined by Elias and described in the preceding section. Credit relations, in this perspective, position individuals in lengthy interdependency chains and thus produce a need for foresighted, controlled and disciplined conduct. Prudent individual habits of thrift, accuracy and caution in expenditure, lending and record-keeping practices may therefore be understood as contingent outcomes of a social figuration distinguished by lengthening and complex interdependencies which necessitate greater social discipline and self-restraint. Elias's account perhaps overstates the linear - inexorability, in more simple terms the inevitability, of the long historical drive towards greater social discipline and self-restraint. Instead, the early modern credit economy unravelled by historians may point to something rather more subtle and particular than Elias's account suggests. The *moral* discipline of credit relations, with their emphasis on trust, candour and sincerity, Newton (2003) argues, is quite different from prudence in the sense of dissimulation. Credit networks suggest 'that early modernity comprised *various* codes of social discipline interwoven within *particular* figurational contexts' (Newton, 2003, p. 359; emphases in original). Elias's perspective nonetheless points to the way in which codes of social discipline and self-mastery are interwoven to *make up* a figuration.

This interwoven nature of codes of discipline and self-management should become clearer by considering another example. The project of life insurance in the nineteenth century illustrates a quite different version of prudent conduct from that prevalent in the early modern credit economy. Prudent conduct in this context is exhibited not so much in conforming to standards of trust, moderation, politeness and candour, but in displaying capacities for thrift, organisation, forward planning and the deferral of gratification. Life insurance was a tricky product to establish. Across many of the countries of mainland Europe and in the USA it was at best perceived as somewhat disreputable and at worst prohibited by law as not only a usurious contract but a blasphemous idea. Britain was one of the few exceptions to this trend, with a fairly lively trade in life insurance contracts dating back to the early part of the eighteenth century. Even in Britain, however, life insurance took a long time to establish itself as a mainstream financial product. There was a sense in insurance companies, but also in governmental and charitable institutions, that, as a technique of financial planning which could claim social, moral and political benefits, life insurance was a product that should be more widely taken up. As a result, the nineteenth century bore witness to a concerted effort by insurance companies to both dispel any lingering concerns people might have about the moral propriety and financial safety of insuring and to teach people the habit of insuring.

Life insurance companies put a huge amount of energy into translating the complicated business of insurance into a form that would fit existing ideals and norms of conduct. In response to concerns that life insurance tampered with the affairs of providence, companies produced a deluge of promotional material stressing its virtuous and pious design. Figure 2.2 is typical of the imagery used in promotional matter. Here, life insurance is carefully associated with the selfless, almost sacred, business of protecting helpless widows and orphans. Public concerns about the piety and propriety of insuring were exacerbated by concerns about its financial safety, fuelled by well-publicised reports of the collapse of fraudulent and poorly managed companies. Companies responded to this by trumpeting the mathematical laws and certainties underlying insurance practice in respectable, established companies.

Insurance companies were also in competition with other, better understood, methods of financial planning, like saving. To differentiate themselves from the competition, insurance companies, interestingly, stressed not only the practical, financial benefits of their product but also its moral benefits. The great unique selling point of life insurance was that the total monetary amount of the policy, the 'sum assured', became realisable as capital in the event of death from the moment the policy was taken. Thus, where it might take many years to set aside a

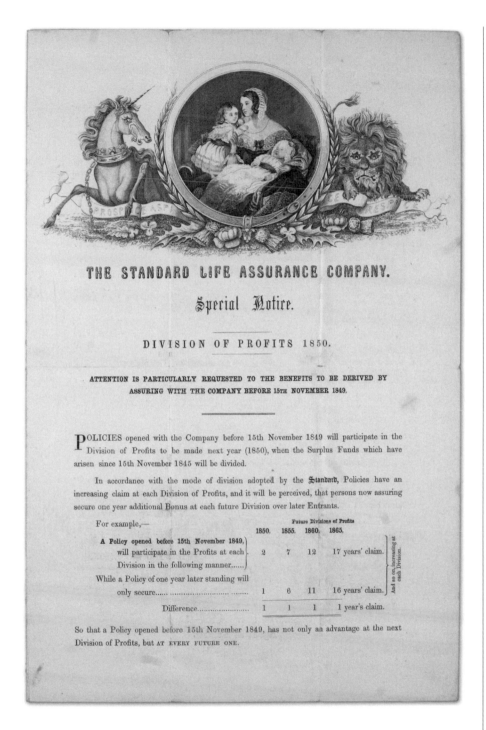

Figure 2.2
Standard Life Assurance Company promotional announcement, 1850

given sum by saving, the sum assured would be realisable even if only one premium had been paid. Life insurance companies of course made much of the financial advantages of this feature, but they were equally loquacious about its moral advantages. Individuals who set aside funds for the future well-being of their dependants via insurance were strictly separated from those funds. Then, as now, the early surrender of insurance polices would result in punitive financial penalties. In this way, the Scottish Widows Fund claimed, life insurance, 'completely obviates all those baneful evils into which a habit of saving is apt to degenerate, for such a habit although originally springing from most proper and legitimate motives, not infrequently ends in debasing the mind to a disposition of avaricious hoarding' (Scottish Widows Fund, 1837).

Avaricious hoarding, then, was to be avoided, but securing adequate means for the future well-being of dependents through a little self-denial was definitely not. Life insurance companies devoted their sizeable energies to ensuring that their agents knew just how to explain to potential customers the means by which the price of a premium might be secured, even by those with limited resources. The following extract from an agent's instruction manual offers particularly explicit advice on how to acquire the habits of prudent economy:

> To the perfectly callous you may propose the question, – 'what man possessed of a feeling heart and a well regulated mind, and who wishes to be considered a man of sense and judgement, would hesitate to secure to a beloved wife and an affectionate offspring a maintenance, when he can no longer provide for them, and that too at a trifling outlay, obtainable by a little self-denial, or wise and prudent economy?' To the industrial classes, the mechanic, the artisan, and the labourer, agricultural or otherwise – show that by the saving of a few pence weekly or by abstinence from the alehouse, and the gin-shop, or even the mere abridgment of half-a pint of his daily modicum of beer, he may secure a provision for his wife and family when he is in the grave ... To the middle classes of society, show by what small increments the means of saving may be obtained by self-denial. As it has been said a few tavern visits less, an occasional mislaying of the key of the wine cellar, a tight stopper in the spirit bottle, a few less cigars smoked, a waterside visit put off till next year, a party omitted to be given, a slight forgetfulness of the length of time a coat or a silk gown has been worn, a few less fly or cab fares to parties or scenes of amusement, Sunday trips in steamboats or on railroads, omnibus fares, and a thousand other matters of the kind, present an ample variety of sources for furnishing the small annual sum requisite to insure an ample provision for a family, when its natural protector can no longer provide a maintenance for them but is numbered with the dead ...

To all classes show that he who neglects to make a provision for his
family when he can no longer provide for them, is equally as
unnatural and as equally guilty of gross and culpable selfishness as he
who neglects to provide food and instruction for his children while he
is in health and strength; or in other words tell them that he who
leaves his children destitute and penniless at his death is no less a
detestable monster than he who will not work for their daily bread.

(NAS, *c*.1850, pp. 15–16)

Life insurance companies used a wide range of materials to get messages
like these across to customers. Advertisements, prospectuses, publicity
in newspapers and journals, essays by 'unbiased' experts, agents'
instruction manuals, tracts and pamphlets all offered detailed
information and advice to people on how insurance operated, how it
could meet the needs of every class and situation in life, and how it
might be afforded. Through such media, companies sought to define
insuring as a peculiarly prudent form of financial conduct. Purchasing
life assurance was repeatedly defined as 'not spending, but saving', 'not a
private but a public benefit', and as 'a moral, social and religious duty'.
Prudent conduct here centrally concerns thrift, foresight and familial
duty. He (it was invariably he) who would not acquire habits of thrift
sufficient to set aside the sum required to pay an annual premium was
characterised repeatedly as a wretch, a monster, an infidel. A prudent
man was one who had the self-restraint to restrict his own, and his
family's, pleasures and indulgences in the interests of preparing for an
uncertain future. The promotional address was made, in the main, to
the male householder. Companies made separate, specific addresses to
women exhorting them to help persuade their husbands to insure, or
even to refuse to marry any man who would not first insure his life.
A prudent woman, in this context, was one who ensured she had a
prudent husband. For the majority of women, this was probably the
most effective form of prudent behaviour, given that prior to the
Married Women's Property Act of 1882 the wife's property, whether
earned or inherited, automatically passed to her husband on her
marriage.

That the social arrangements underpinning prudent financial conduct
have altered substantially over the last century or so, not least in terms
of gender expectations, may not be a surprise. Yet despite the huge
upheavals in work and production, leisure and consumption that have
taken place, the idea of prudence remains a central preoccupation in the
arena of personal finance. The language used to promote the prudent
ideal has changed markedly. Advice about financial prudence now is
couched in terms of choice, enterprise and psychologically informed
self-reflection.

In the final example, we are going to turn to the contemporary context and the mediation of financial advice through self-help programmes. The primary medium of such programmes is television where they fit broadly within the spectacularly successful genre of reality self-improvement shows, which include in the UK, at the time of writing, programmes like *How to Look Good Naked, Ground Force* and *What Not To Wear.* These programmes tend to 'cross' media and are usually accompanied by paperbacks and websites offering re-versioned advice targeted at the broader population rather than the participants who form the 'case studies' of the television shows. The format for programmes like *Your Money or Your Life* (screened on BBC Two between 2000 and 2003) and *Spendaholics* (BBC Three from 2005) centres upon telling the story of an individual whose spending has so far outstripped their income that they face unmanageable debt levels. The television 'experts' investigate the true extent of the problem and then start to explore the reasons behind the imprudent spending.

Turn now to the extract from the 'Top Tips' section of the *Spendaholics* website featured below. As you read it, think about the sort of account of how to spend prudently that is being offered by the presenters of the programme, Jay Hunt and Benjamin Fry.

Reading 2.4 'Spendaholics: Top Tips'

Want to avoid becoming a Spendaholic? Get top tips from our experts Jay Hunt and Benjamin Fry.

Jay's tried and trusted shopping tips

- Always work out the CPU (cost per use against projected life span).

- Avoid shopping on a Saturday, it's too stressful for clear-headed thinking.

- Never buy anything the same day you test it to avoid 'gap' shopping – spending to fill a void in your life.

- Ask yourself will this item work for summer, winter, day and night; anything less than three out of four should be left alone.

- Use your common sense – if it seems too good to be true it probably is.

- Saving money takes time and effort. Be prepared to commit yourself. More time spent researching is less time spent spending.

- The internet is your best money-saving friend – use it to source the product you want at the best price. Be sure to check hidden costs, delivery charges and VAT before heading to the checkout.

- Ditch toxic friends who encourage you to spend.

- Suggest free or cheap activities like a trip to a gallery or a fun dance class.

- Never scrimp on a good haircut. It rarely pays.

- Write shopping lists – have a clear idea about what you need before you go shopping to avoid expensive mistakes or spontaneous splurges.

- Trade skills and items with your friends – they are a goldmine.

- Be knowledge rich not cash poor. Sometimes you just need to know what you can have to feel empowered.

- Know what you want; get what you want. Keep internet wish lists for your family and friends to access for gift ideas.

- Get off the high street, the buzz of owning a one-off is far greater than a high street transaction.

- If it doesn't fit don't buy it however much you like it - you won't wear it.

Benjamin's five most common emotional spending triggers

- Dads: If you've got unresolved issues with your dad, watch out that you're not punishing him by getting into debt.

- Low self worth: If you believe that you are worthless, you will probably feel most comfortable with nothing.

- The wounded body: Many women grow up deeply traumatised by other people's reactions and comments about their bodies. They long for their inner-swan and shop to compensate, but getting the right 'look' never heals the scars of those insults.

- Expensive tastes: If you're addicted to debt, it could be simply because you have expensive addictions; travel, eating out, drink and drugs. So, get into your issues to get out of debt.

- Loss: If you've suffered blows to your emotional security, you may be unable to bear financial security.

Reading source

BBC Three, 2007

Alongside the practical tips to develop material strategies for money management, like using the internet, shopping lists and formulae such as cost per use which relates the overall cost of an item to frequency of use, shows like *Spendaholics* offer a particular contemporary account of prudent behaviour. Here, prudence is best achieved by exploring and reflecting upon the psychological reasons behind spending. Within the context of societies like the UK, which define poverty in relative rather than absolute terms and in which as Bourdieu (1990 [1984], p. 163) put it, 'even the most deprived have the right to every satisfaction', prudence becomes an ideal in which the responsible individual makes the right choices for the right reasons.

These choices about how, what, where, when and why to spend may seem trivial, but they are fundamentally about 'how to operate in this world' (see Chapter 5 in this volume). They are about selecting the props we need in order to function as the selves we see ourselves as (think, for instance, about the language used in picking clothes: 'It's not me'; 'It's very becoming'). This involves choosing from a bewildering array of alternatives. The prudent individual in the contemporary context makes decisions not only about what to wear, eat, drive, live in, but also about what to listen to, read and see and, increasingly, as we saw in the Introduction to this chapter, about education, healthcare and retirement. The overwhelming complexity of these choices and the level of skill and foresight required to make informed choices between, say, different investment or pension plans, have caused some sociologists to conclude that neo-liberal marketisation policies have simply led individuals to be complicit in their own exploitation as they are 'mis-sold' financial products from pension plans to endowment mortgages (Aldridge, 1998). Whether or not this version of events is accepted, what is undoubtedly the case is that without the *material* tools, devices and equipment that comprise financial practice – the cheque books, ATMs, price-comparison websites, bank statements – and the *mediation* of information through advice manuals, handbooks, advertising, promotion, self-help literature, and television, it would simply be impossible to work out the difference between the information a prudent person has to attend to and what can, with impunity, be ignored.

According to sociologists like Michel Callon, such **socio-technical devices** and equipment have proliferated over the last fifty years or so as part of the emergence of an 'economy of qualities'. In an economy driven by the ever-increasing specification of the particular qualities of innumerable, often basically very similar, competing products like, for example, shampoo, consumers are constantly prompted to pay attention, reflect upon, or 'qualify' and 'requalify' products with the aim of producing durable market attachments (see Chapter 1, Section 3 in this volume, and also **Muniesa, 2008**). In Callon et al.'s (2002) account, the work of business, retailing and marketing professionals is all about attaching individuals to products. Thus a 'free' children's book in a cereal box acts as a socio-technical device which, in coupling the persuasive force of children's 'pester power' with an ingeniously guilt-offsetting educational promise to parents, aims to prompt consumers to reconsider or 'requalify' products. These devices are socio-technical in that they combine an understanding of the social context in which shopping takes places with sophisticated technical tools including, for example, consumer profiling data through loyalty card schemes, specialised store and packaging design:

> In this economy, inhabited by actors who are real professionals in product qualification and the profiling of goods, consumers are constantly prompted to question their preferences and tastes and finally, through the explicit debates that that implies, their own social identity. ... Consumption becomes both more rational (not that the consumer is more rational but because (distributed) cognition devices become infinitely richer, more sophisticated and reflexive) and more emotional (consumers are constantly referred to the construction of their social identity since their choices and preferences become objects of deliberation: the distinction of products and social distinction are part of the same movement).
>
> (Callon et al., 2002, p. 212)

Of particular interest here is the emphasis upon 'reflexiveness'. This chimes with a much broader sociological preoccupation with the shifting characteristics of the individual in the social world of 'late modernity'. Late modernity, for sociologists like Anthony Giddens and Ulrich Beck, is characterised as a period of 'reflexive individualisation'. Reflexive individualisation calls attention to the ever-increasing emphasis placed on personal identity and its expression through consumption practices and 'psycho-therapeutic cultures' exemplified in the recent explosion of self-help manuals, life coaching and the wider availability and uptake of various forms of therapy and counselling (Beck et al., 1994). As we have seen, the idea of the individual as director of his/her own actions and centred in an inner, emotional core is a historically specific way of understanding the individual as possessing an inner 'self' (see Chapter 1 in this volume). The shift that sociologists like Giddens are pointing to is a spiralling obsession with this inner self; with reflecting upon, knowing, treating and expressing the self, particularly through consumption practices. Consumption and spending, accordingly, are best understood as personal and emotional, the 'objects of deliberation' (Callon et al., 2002, p. 212). Prudent conduct, in terms of the advice offered in programmes like *Spendaholics*, is similarly best achieved by coming to terms with, reflecting, deliberating upon the underlying psychological reasons behind spending patterns and working out how best to express your inner self through consumption without succumbing to pathological overspending.

This emphasis on consumption tempered by popular psycho-therapeutic ideas may seem like prima facie evidence of 'reflexive individualisation', but caution should be exercised in how such fragments of a much larger social world are interpreted. While the language of psycho-therapeutically inflected consumption and spending practices is clearly very distinctive, it constitutes only one part of a much broader tapestry of ideas about financial prudence. Within this tapestry, older and contradictory notions of prudence as dissimulation, as practised thrift and studied virtue, persist. That the financially prudent should act from Aquinas's 'right choice and not merely from impulse or passion' still to some extent underlies the ideals and norms expressed in contemporary self-help manuals. The emphasis may have shifted from Christian virtue to psychological wellness, but older traditions can be traced in the articulation of prudence as a normative ideal of conduct mobilised against emotional, passionate excesses.

4 Conclusion

This chapter has been concerned throughout with the long history of prudence as a virtue, habit and ideal of conduct in the management of personal finance. The discussion has attempted to uncover the variety of meanings which have attached to prudence over time, and how this relates, inextricably, to broader changes in the organisation of the social world and to changes in how the category of the human individual has been understood. In its passage from Christian virtue towards its contemporary currency as a behavioural ideal, prudence also reveals something about how the individual came to be understood as the proprietor of an 'inner self'. Financial prudence thus offers a substantial way of thinking through sociological questions about the nature of the relationship between the individual and the social. The underlying argument of this chapter is that this relationship is a contingent one in which individual practice cannot be meaningfully understood in isolation from the social world in which it is conducted.

This point is best illustrated by the examples of financial practices that have run through the chapter. If, for instance, prudent conduct in the early modern credit economy was about trust, character and candour, this was in part because credit chains were short and the participants were often known to each other. When nineteenth-century life insurance companies pushed thrift, self-denial and forward planning as prudent ideals, this in part reflected the needs of an emerging liberal market economy. Similarly, the late twentieth-century celebration of rational, responsible, choosing consumers makes sense only in the context of ascendant neo-liberal political rationalities which require high levels of individual consumption.

What these examples also show is the significance of material tools, technologies and practices in enabling prudent financial conduct. Financial prudence demands equipment. Whether in the forms of manuals, 'reckoning' books, household accounts, receipts, price lists, price-comparison websites or self-help books, financial prudence would be impossible without tools. At a bare minimum, prudence requires knowledge of income and expenditure. Even in the slower economies of early modern Britain, such knowledge required some form of material inscription. In contemporary economies, navigating the bewildering array of products and services on offer without the socio-technical devices described by Callon would be quite impossible. The fascinating thing about such devices is that our use of them is so ingrained and habitual that we are scarcely aware of their existence. So, when we move through a department store making purchases facilitated by technical devices like store layout, shelving, price labels, bar codes and chip-and-pin terminals, we are often aware of their necessity only when they fail (see also Chapter 1 in this volume).

It should also be clear by now that prudence has no timeless, essential core. Rather, its meanings shift over time and according to context such that, for example, prudence in financial matters may involve quite different priorities and judgements from, say, prudence in international relations. These shifting meanings offer a hint of the role of mediation in social worlds. At its simplest this means that we have no direct access to an unmediated existence, a sort of core, metaphysical essence of things. Instead, what we know about the world is always mediated. In the context of this chapter, then, what we know about financial prudence we know from what we have learned from a variety of intermediaries. The self-help gurus, insurance company promotions and early modern advice manuals can therefore be seen to mediate financial prudence by spelling out what it means in any given set of circumstances.

Despite the preponderance of tools and mediated advice, it should also be obvious that prudent financial conduct, for many people, remains a distant ideal rather than a description of existing practice. Engineering financial prudence is a project that, in certain respects, seems beset by failure. While tools and advice proliferate, the long-term trend is one in which debt continues to rise and saving to decline. Reversing this trend is a task of some magnitude, given the intricacy of the connection between consumption and the expression of the self. There is a dynamic and irresistible tension between the capacity of objects to capture desire, through their promise of expressing or 'propping' the self, and the prudent management of appetites, desires and passions. There is also an unavoidable contradiction, in that while objects of desire may make their appeal to all, satisfying such desire will cost some more than others. Lest this should be thought the inevitable result of a social world obsessed by consumption, one of the more important lessons to be derived from history is that the failures and contradictions of prudence have a considerable lineage. Whether mobilised as a virtue, a habit or as a behavioural ideal, prudence exists as an ethical technique, a way of gaining control over the unruly internal economy of passions. That fecklessness, impecuniousness and sheer disorganisation in financial matters prevail for many illustrates the difficulty of the project.

References

Aldridge, A. (1998) 'Habitus and cultural capital in the field of personal finance', *Sociological Review*, vol. 46, no. 1, pp. 1–23.

Aquinas, T. (1947) *Summa Theologica* (trans. Fathers of the English Dominican Province), 3 vols, New York, NY, Benziger Brothers.

BBC Three (2007) 'Spendaholics: Top Tips' [online], http://www.bbc.co.uk/bbcthree/programmes/spendaholics/spendaholics_tips.shtml (Accessed 29 July 2007).

Beck, U., Giddens, A. and Lash, S. (1994) *Reflexive Modernization, Politics, Tradition and Aesthetics in the Modern Social Order*, Polity Press, Cambridge.

Bourdieu, P. (1990 [1984]) *Distinction: A Social Critique of the Judgement of Taste* (trans. R. Nice), London, Routledge.

Callaghan, G., Fribbance, I. and Higginson, M. (eds) (2007) *Personal Finance*, Chichester, John Wiley/Milton Keynes, The Open University.

Callon, M., Meadel, C. and Rabeharisoa, V. (2002) 'The economy of qualities', *Economy and Society*, vol. 31, no. 2, pp. 194–217.

Elias, N. (1994 [1939]) *The Civilizing Process* (trans. E. Jephcott), Oxford, Blackwell.

Erturk, I., Froud, J., Solari, S. and Williams, K. (2005) *The Reinvention of Prudence: Household Savings, Financialisation and Forms of Capitalism*, CRESC working paper series, no. 11.

Hall, A. (2002) *Your Money or Your Life*, London, Hodder & Stoughton.

Hobbes, T. (1839 [1651]) 'Leviathan' in *The English Works of Thomas Hobbes of Malmesbury*, vol. III, London, John Bohn.

Hobbes, T. (1991 [1657]) *Man and Citizen: De Homine and De Cive* (ed. B. Gert), Indianapolis, IN, Hackett.

Machiavelli, N. (1964) *The Prince* (ed. and trans. M. Musa), New York, NY, St Martins Press.

Muldrew, C. (1993) 'Interpreting the market: the ethics of credit and community relations in early modern England', *Social History*, vol. 18, no. 2, pp. 163–83.

Muniesa, F. (2008) 'Attachment and detachment in the economy' in Redman, P. (ed.) *Attachment: Sociology and Social Worlds*, Manchester, Manchester University Press/Milton Keynes, The Open University (Book 2 in this series).

National Archives of Scotland (NAS) (*c*.1850) *The Elements of Success of a Life Assurance Agency*, GD294/29, Edinburgh, Register House.

Newton, T. (2003) 'Credit and civilization', *British Journal of Sociology*, vol. 54, no. 3, pp. 347–71.

O'Malley, P. (1996) 'Risk and responsibility' in Barry, A., Osborne, T. and Rose, N. (eds) *Foucault and Political Reason*, Chicago, IL, University of Chicago Press.

Scottish Widows Fund (1837) Pamphlet, Box 7, Insurance Series, John Johnson Collection of Printed Ephemera, Oxford, Bodleian Library.

Shepard, A. (2000) 'Manhood, credit and patriarchy in early modern England *c*.1580–1640', *Past and Present*, vol. 167, May, pp. 75–106.

Smith, A. (1976 [1759]) *The Theory of Moral Sentiments*, Oxford, Clarendon Press.

Vanden Houten, A. (2002) 'Prudence in Hobbes's political philosophy', *History of Political Thought*, vol. XXIII, no. 2, pp. 266–87.

Williams, Z. (2006) 'Bankruptcy by alcopop', *Guardian*, 19 July.

Chapter 3
Habit, freedom and the governance of social conduct

Tony Bennett

Contents

1   Introduction

Do you think **habit** is a good or a bad thing? Or is habit good in some circumstances but not others? Or are some habits good, and to be encouraged, while others should be discouraged? And do you see any difference between habit as such and particular habits? If so, how would you describe that difference? Can habits be freely chosen? Or is there always some element of compulsion about habit?

These questions have played a significant role in sociological debates about the nature and mechanisms of social change. They have also been central to debates about the regulation and governance of conduct in both sociology and political theory. These, then, are the issues that will concern us in this chapter. Before looking at what they entail in greater detail, however, let's look at a couple of examples where questions of habit and questions of governance are interrelated.

The first is the suggestion by a literary critic, John Carey, that reading literature might serve as an effective antidote to binge drinking (Carey, 2005). Discussing a report in *The Times* in May 2004 in which two 15-year-old schoolgirls account for their binge drinking as an attempt to escape the boredom of life in a small Gloucestershire village where there is nothing else to do but to get drunk, Carey recommends that they should read good literature in view of the opportunity it provides for a mind-enhancing and life-changing escape from boredom in contrast to the merely temporary escape offered by drugs, drinking and antidepressants. In short, to the bad habit of binge drinking he counterposes the good habit of reading literature and suggests that binge drinking may be partly a product of the fact that reading has declined significantly since the end of the Second World War and, particularly in recent years, that this reflects the declining role of the public library. You might, as I do, think that this is implausible. As we shall see, however, this kind of argument has a long pedigree in the varied history of attempts to get different sections of society to change their behaviour, but to do so freely and voluntarily, as a consequence of their exposure to the improving influence of 'culture'.

The second example concerns a public letter and accompanying do-it-yourself 'Family Communications Plan' (see Figure 3.1) that was circulated via newspapers and magazines by the newly created US Department of Homeland Security in February 2005. I take this from James Hay's discussion of the ways in which the programmes of the Department of Homeland Security have sought to mobilise what he calls the citizen-soldier in the 'war against terror' (Hay, 2006). Two aspects of Hay's discussion are relevant to my concerns here. The first is how this letter sought to make the 'war against terror' a regular aspect of everyday life, a daily habit – as in the suggestion that being prepared for emergencies should be as routine as wearing a seatbelt – by making the family responsible for its own safety and providing it with the resources (a template for a family communications plan) for carrying this responsibility into effect. It is, in this respect, similar to the ways in which retailers have trained customers in the techniques of self-service such that, as we saw from Paul du Gay's discussion in Chapter 1, self-service shopping is now a matter of routine habit rather than a challenge. The second relevant feature of this example concerns the ways in which the approach of the Department of Homeland Security builds on the earlier history of US cold war civil-defence drills in the 1950s and 1960s. The common thread connecting these two periods is that, in many crucial respects, the earlier programmes focused on making the private home safe and secure through the free actions of American citizens rather than aiming to provide public shelters against atomic attack. This was central to the tenets of American liberalism – shunning a state-sponsored militarisation of everyday life (through public bunkers and the like) and opting, instead, to make private citizens freely take responsibility for their own safety and security as a part of the struggle to defend liberalism against communist totalitarianism. Similarly, in 2005, citizens were enlisted in the war against terrorism by being made responsible for their own safety and security in the context of their individualised and private families and homes.

In both of these examples, questions concerning the relations between freedom, governance and habit are in play. So are questions of conduct and change – changing society by changing habits. And so also are questions about the relations between individuals and social worlds inasmuch as the concerns of this chapter will centre on those aspects of the conduct of individuals that are shaped by social processes through a wide variety of forces and agencies.

In exploring these questions in the rest of this chapter, I shall engage with three main issues. I look first, in Section 2, at the place occupied by the concept of habit and related concepts, like custom, in nineteenth-century social and political thought. I shall look here at the work of John Stuart Mill, the major English political theorist of liberalism, and at the respects in which the role he accorded habit exposed a fault-line in liberal political thought. Where a people were slaves to the yoke of custom, Mill argued that it was appropriate that they should be governed despotically – that is, in an authoritarian manner, without their consent or democratic participation. In considering why he said this and examining its consequences, we shall be well on our way to understanding some of the ambiguities and contradictions associated with the concept of habit.

In Section 3, I then look more fully at the differences between attempts which work to regulate conduct by changing habits through compulsory methods and those which, in presuming the freedom and independence of the individuals whose conduct they seek to change, work via more

YOU CAN BE READY FOR AN EMERGENCY

THERE ARE THINGS THAT YOU CAN DO NOW TO MAKE SURE YOUR FAMILY IS PREPARED.

MAKE A PLAN

FAMILY COMMUNICATIONS PLAN

USE THE FORM BELOW AND SIT DOWN WITH YOUR LOVED ONES TO FIGURE OUT
HOW YOU WILL GET IN TOUCH DURING AN EMERGENCY

| Out-of-state contact | Phone number |
| Email | Phone number |

FILL OUT THE FOLLOWING INFORMATION FOR EACH FAMILY MEMBER AND KEEP IT UP-TO-DATE

Name	Important Medical Information
Date of birth	Phone/Walkie-Talkie Number
Name	Important Medical Information
Date of birth	Phone/Walkie-Talkie Number
Name	Important Medical Information
Date of birth	Phone/Walkie-Talkie Number
Name	Important Medical Information
Date of birth	Phone/Walkie-Talkie Number
Name	Important Medical Information
Date of birth	Phone/Walkie-Talkie Number

WHERE TO GO IN AN EMERGENCY. WRITE DOWN WHERE YOUR FAMILY SPENDS THE MOST TIME: WORK, SCHOOL, AND OTHER PLACES YOU FREQUENT. SCHOOLS, DAYCARE PROVIDERS, WORKPLACES AND APARTMENT BUILDINGS SHOULD ALL HAVE SITE-SPECIFIC EMERGENCY PLANS.

HOME	**WORK**
Address	Address
Phone Number	Phone Number
Neighborhood Meeting Place	Neighborhood Meeting Place
Regional Meeting Place	Regional Meeting Place
SCHOOL	**OTHER PLACE YOU FREQUENT**
Address	Address
Phone Number	Neighborhood Meeting Place
Neighborhood Meeting Place	Regional Meeting Place
Regional Meeting Place	

IMPORTANT INFORMATION	NAME	TELEPHONE #	POLICY#
Doctor(s)			
Other			
Pharmacist			
Medical Insurance			
Homeowners/Rental Insurance			

Other useful phone #s   9-1-1 for emergencies   Police non-emergency phone #

EVERY FAMILY MEMBER SHOULD CARRY THE INFORMATION BELOW IN HIS OR HER WALLET

JUST LIKE WEARING A SEATBELT OR HAVING A SMOKE DETECTOR IN YOUR HOME, IT'S A SMART IDEA TO BE PREPARED FOR EMERGENCIES. MAKE A FAMILY COMMUNICATIONS PLAN AND PUT TOGETHER OR BUY AN EMERGENCY KIT. IT'S JUST COMMON SENSE.

MAKE A PLAN

FAMILY COMMUNICATIONS PLAN

Contact Name

Telephone

Out-of-state Contact

Telephone

Neighborhood Meeting Place

Meeting Place Telephone

DIAL 9-1-1 FOR EMERGENCIES!

OTHER IMPORTANT PHONE NUMBERS AND INFORMATION

_____

_____

_____

_____

_____

_____

_____

FAMILY COMMUNICATIONS PLAN

Contact Name

Telephone

Out-of-state Contact

Telephone

Neighborhood Meeting Place

Meeting Place Telephone

DIAL 9-1-1 FOR EMERGENCIES!

OTHER IMPORTANT PHONE NUMBERS AND INFORMATION

_____

_____

_____

_____

_____

_____

_____

_____

GET A KIT

USE THIS CHECKLIST TO MAKE SURE THAT YOUR KIT FITS YOUR FAMILY'S NEEDS

GET TOGETHER WITH YOUR FAMILY AND THINK ABOUT ITEMS YOU MIGHT NEED IF YOU HAD TO STAY IN THE SAME PLACE FOR UP TO THREE DAYS. FOCUS FIRST ON FOOD, WATER, SAFETY ITEMS AND OTHER NECESSITIES. YOUR READY KIT SHOULD CONTAIN THE FOLLOWING ITEMS:

☐ A backpack
☐ Battery operated radio
☐ Battery operated flashlight
☐ Extra batteries
☐ Water (40 fluid ounces for 3 days)
☐ Food (800 calories/day)
☐ Dust mask
☐ First aid kit
☐ Whistle
☐ Plastic sheeting
☐ Duct tape
☐ Plastic bags and ties
☐ Moist towelettes

YOU MAY WANT TO ADD SOME THAT ARE SPECIFIC TO YOUR OWN FAMILY'S NEEDS:

☐ Up-to-date Family Communications Plan
☐ Extra food and water
☐ A water container and container for unscented bleach (you can add 16 drops of bleach to a gallon of water to purify the water)
☐ Cotton fabric or a t-shirt if the dust mask won't fit snuggly
☐ Extra does of personal prescription medication
☐ Can opener if you add canned food to the kit
☐ Warm clothing/emergency blanket
☐ Rain gear/poncho
☐ Glow stick
☐ Identification
☐ Cash
☐ Baby or children's items
☐ Items for elderly
☐ Two way radio or walkie-talkie

BE INFORMED

Visit **WWW.READY.GOV** to find out about different emergencies and how to prepare for them.

Figure 3.1   US Department of Homeland Security's 'Family Communications Plan' (Source: Hay, 2006, Figure 1, p. 351)

voluntary mechanisms. My principal concerns here will be with the work of Michel Foucault, particularly the contrast between his account of the development of modern methods of **discipline** and those of liberal government. His concern in the first of these cases is with the methods through which, in institutions like schools, armies and prisons, habits are instilled or changed through compulsory training. Counterbalancing this, his work on liberal government has drawn attention to the parallel mechanisms, developed over roughly the same period, through which individuals are encouraged to govern themselves. Considering the different circumstances in which methods of discipline are judged to be more appropriate than those of liberal government will deepen our understanding of the contradictions associated with the notion of habit and its bearing on individual conduct.

Finally, in Section 4, I consider the place that habit has occupied in sociological accounts of the mechanisms of social change. My focus here is on the relations between the concept of habit and the related, but none the less different, concept of habitus. I look first at the role of habit in the work of one of the founders of sociology, Émile Durkheim. I then look at the notion of habitus. First introduced into sociological thought by Marcel Mauss, one of Durkheim's protégés, this concept was subsequently elaborated into one of the cornerstones of the sociology of Pierre Bourdieu. Interpreting habitus as 'history turned into nature' (Bourdieu, 2003 [1977], p. 78), Bourdieu uses the concept to explain how habits are acquired and transmitted from one generation to the next and how they are broken with, thus initiating a new cycle of habit formation. Habitus, in short, is the concept through which Bourdieu tries to account for both social continuity and social change. As we shall see, however, his account does not escape some of the contradictions associated with the role of habit in earlier social and political thought.

1.1 Teaching aims

The aims of this chapter are to:

- review the role that the concept of habit has played in the history of Western social and political thought

- examine the contradictions associated with the place that habit is accorded in relation to the mechanisms of discipline compared to those of liberal government

- consider the relations between the concept of habit and that of habitus in accounts of social change

- deepen your understanding of the relations between individuals and society.

2 Habit and government: the contradictions of liberalism

It will be useful, at this point, to define our terms a little more closely. The *Oxford English Dictionary* (OED) offers the following definition of habit as:

> Holding, having, 'havour'; hence the way in which one holds or has oneself, i.e. the mode or condition in which one is, exists, or exhibits oneself, (a) externally; hence demeanour, outward appearance, fashion of body, mode of clothing oneself, dress, habitation; (b) in mind, character, or life; hence, mental constitution, character disposition, way of acting, comporting oneself, or dealing with things, habitual or customary way (of acting, etc.), personal custom, accustomedness.
>
> (*OED Online*)

The entry goes on to indicate that the term is most used to refer to:

> A settled disposition or tendency to act in a certain way, esp. one acquired by frequent repetition of the same act until it becomes almost or quite involuntary; a settled practice, custom, usage; a customary way or manner of acting.
>
> (*OED Online*)

The strong link between the notion of habit and that of custom that is evident here is echoed in the OED entry for custom which defines it as a 'habitual or usual practice'.

We shall come back to this point later. Now, though, to get a sense of the role played by the concept of habit and its close cousin, custom, in modern social and political thought, let's look at a passage from Mill's essay *On Liberty* (1969 [1859]), the most important statement of the tenets of mid nineteenth-century classical liberalism.

You should now read the following excerpt from Mill's *On Liberty*. Pay particular attention to the effects of custom in Mill's schema.

Reading 3.1 John Stuart Mill, 'On liberty'

The despotism of custom is everywhere the standing hindrance to human advancement, being in unceasing antagonism to that disposition to aim at something better than customary, which is called, according to circumstances, the spirit of liberty, or that of progress or improvement. ... The progressive principle, however, in either shape, whether as the love of liberty or of improvement, is antagonistic to the sway of Custom, involving at least emancipation from that yoke; and the contest between the two constitutes the chief interest of the history of mankind. The greater part of the world has, properly speaking, no history, because the despotism of Custom is complete. This is the case over the whole East. Custom is there, in all things, the final appeal; justice and right mean conformity to custom; the argument of custom no one, unless some tyrant intoxicated with power, thinks of resisting. And we see the result. Those nations must once have had originality; they did not start out of the ground populous, lettered, and versed in many of the arts of life; they made themselves all this, and were then the greatest and most powerful nations of the world. What are they now? The subjects or dependants of tribes whose forefathers wandered in the forests when theirs had magnificent palaces and gorgeous temples, but over whom custom exercised only a divided rule with liberty and progress. A people, it appears, may be progressive for a certain length of time, and then stop: when does it stop? When it ceases to possess individuality.

Reading source

Mill, 1969 [1859], pp. 87–8

The key point I take away from this is the opposition between custom, as a set of politically enforced habits, and history: the greater part of the world, Mill says, and all of Asia, 'has ... no history, because the despotism of Custom is complete'. This opposition depends on a very modern sense of history: history as change, history as constant and restless movement forward in developmental time. This opposition between the free, progressive West on the one hand and a custom-bound, static or declining Orient on the other has proved a historically durable one in shaping colonial ideologies and practices. We can see this in the argument Mill goes on to make. His response to the 'despotism of custom' that he sees as the result of Asian despotism is to argue that, for the time being, this 'yoke' should provide the primary means through which the members of such societies should continue to be governed by their new British colonial governors. Christine Helliwell and Barry Hindess thus note that Mill viewed the vast mass of the population of India as so lacking the qualities of individuality and liberty that he did not think they were fitted to participate in representative government (Helliwell and Hindess, 2002, p. 145). What is at work here, they argue, is an 'orientalist syllogism' – a kind of catch-22 – according to which, because they have lacked any experience of the institutions of political democracy which nurture the qualities of liberty and individuality, Indians cannot be granted the freedom to govern themselves. Instead, they must be governed by their colonial masters until they have acquired enough experience of the spirits of liberty and improvement to be entrusted with this responsibility. These views, widely influential among colonial administrators as well as with the British Government, were put into effect with the paradoxical result that the very institutions that were held to be responsible for the 'yoke' of custom were the ones colonial rule sought to strengthen. This took the form in India, particularly after the Indian Mutiny of 1857, of strengthening the caste system as a means of resubmitting the Indian masses to the despotic grip of ancient habits and customs. This was a project which depended considerably on the embryonic social sciences – particularly, as Nicholas Dirks (2001) shows, on ethnographic surveys of the population, and, as Arjun Appadurai (1993) argues, on the census as a means of dividing the population into different castes for administrative purposes.

Here, then, we see an example of Mariana Valverde's (1996) argument that, in certain circumstances, habit functions as a despotic mechanism at the heart of liberal government. Where certain groups of people are not judged (by Western political theorists) to be ready for democratic self-government because they are too much subject to the influence of habit, one response has been to strengthen that influence as a mechanism of rule. Where this is so, the individual is denied any political voice in being subjected to forms of rule that work more coercively and through mechanisms that tend to be collective rather than individual. This is made clear in an earlier section of Mill's essay *On Liberty* where he states that his primary purpose is to assert the principle that the individual is absolutely sovereign over himself (or, for Mill, in some circumstances, herself) except insofar as his actions might adversely affect others. But he then immediately qualifies this 'absolute principle' by saying that it can only apply to 'human beings who are in the maturity of their faculties' (Mill, 1969 [1859], p. 15). Yet this, it turns out, excludes most of humanity: all children, all 'backward states of society in which the race itself may be considered as in its nonage' (1969 [1859], p. 15), all barbarians, for whom despotism is a legitimate mode of government provided it aims at their improvement, and all earlier societies 'anterior to the time when mankind have become capable of being improved by free and equal discussion' (1969 [1859], p. 16).

On Liberty was published in 1859, the same year as the publication of Charles Darwin's *The Origin of Species*. Over the course of the next forty years and well into the twentieth century, the perspective of natural selection as the mechanism of evolution was to have a profound influence on the development of both liberal thought and its translation into practices of government. An important aspect of this development consisted in the redefinition of the concept of habit that it brought in its tow. Under the influence of the biological sciences, habit came to be thought of as a more or less instinctual set of responses to the conditions of existence of an organism, affecting humans in much the same way as animals. Through constant repetition, these responses get hard-wired into the nervous system and are transmitted to the next generation as a more or less fixed set of behavioural codes which, however, are changed and adapted in response to changing conditions (natural as well as social).

The political theorist Walter Bagehot proposed such a view in his *Physics and Politics* (1873), in which he drew on contemporary developments in evolutionary thought to develop and qualify Mill's account in *On Liberty* (1969 [1859]). He did this by reinterpreting what Mill had described as the 'yoke' of custom in evolutionary terms. In liberal and democratic societies in which the spirits of liberty and improvement prevail, the habits that are acquired and hard-wired into the nervous system are transmitted to the next generation via what Bagehot calls 'the connective tissue of civilisation' (1873, p. 8). This inherited stock of habits then regulates the behaviour of the next generation, but is also partly changed by it in response to changing circumstances. This results in a progressive modification of 'the connective tissue of civilisation' as each generation builds on the accomplishments of the last one through this mechanism of 'inherited drill' in which the effects of social development become inscribed in the body for transmission across generations.

But social development is halted in its tracks if, for whatever reason, this mechanism for the transmission of acquired habits gets blocked. Then, Bagehot argued, placing an evolutionary gloss on Mill's account as to how once progressive societies – like China – come to ossify under the yoke of custom, the 'collective tissue of civilisation' gets stuck. Of the hill tribes of India, the Andaman Islanders, and the savages of Terra del Fuego, he thus argued that they had once 'made their little progress in a hundred different ways' and have consequently 'framed with infinite assiduity a hundred curious habits' with the result that they have 'screwed themselves into the uncomfortable corners of a complex life, which is odd and dreary' (Bagehot, 1873, p. 42). As to how such peoples might screw themselves out of such odd and dreary lives, Bagehot's answer, like Mill's, was that they couldn't. They could only be unscrewed out of them by imposing despotic forms of colonial rule through which, so to speak, the connective tissue of civilisation would eventually be grafted back into place, giving colonised societies a progressive momentum of their own again.

However, evolutionary thought opened up two further prospects that had not occurred to Mill. The first was that societies that were once progressive might become not just stationary but – in a prospect most forcibly expressed by the surgeon and naturalist Edwin Ray Lankester (1880) – degenerate or go backwards as the mechanisms for transmitting habits from one generation to the next broke down completely. The second prospect was that in some societies the 'connective tissue of civilisation' might never get started at all. These were the terms in which societies brought under the new concept of 'primitive' were increasingly viewed in the closing decades of the nineteenth and early twentieth centuries. This was particularly true of Australian Aborigines who, once viewed as noble savages unspoiled by civilisation, were redefined under the influence of evolutionary thought as 'primitive' in the sense of being throwbacks to earlier states of evolution. Interpreted as fossils of an earlier stage of social development, they were seen as remnants of prehistory within the present. This was the view of Baldwin Spencer, a Mancunian liberal who trained initially as a Darwinian biologist and subsequently, on moving to Melbourne, became one of the most important early ethnographers of the Aboriginal peoples of Central Australia. Viewing their ways of life as a kind of 'evolutionary ground zero', as the most primitive of the earth's peoples, Spencer interpreted this as a consequence of Australia's geographical isolation. This meant, he argued, that Aborigines had lacked any competition and had therefore failed to develop any spirit of improvement, with the consequence that customs and habits rooted in a stage of development that was only one level above the natural had been perpetuated across the generations (Spencer, 1914).

The political conclusions that Spencer, and the federal and state levels of government in Australia, drew from this were that Aborigines could not be treated as citizens. Deemed insufficiently developed to govern themselves, they could only be governed despotically until such a time as they might become sufficiently developed to be granted citizenship rights. And, for Spencer, this meant the forcible abduction of 'half-caste' Aborigines from 'full-blood' Aborigines – whom he viewed as doomed to extinction – in order that they might, through a programme of managed miscegenation, have their Aboriginal blood bred out of them, diluted from one generation to the next. This converted Bagehot's 'connective tissue of civilisation' into a bloodline through which the civilised habits acquired by 'half-caste' Aborigines when they were placed in white-run hostelries could be transmitted from one generation to the next.

Yet the primitive was not only to be found overseas. Here is Henry Cole, a nineteenth-century English liberal reformer and arts administrator, drawing on the currency of the Aborigine as the lowest level of human development to describe the phenomenon of working class male drunkenness:

> Now, if you want to see sights in Liverpool that reduce men to the nature of aborigines, you will see people that are allowed to get as drunk as they can, starve their wives and children, looking to others in the end to find coffins for themselves and feed them in the workhouse beforehand.
>
> (Cole, 1884, p. 364)

This takes us back to our opening example of binge drinking, except that 'the problem' here is defined not in terms of teenage girls and their drinking habits but those of the working man. The problems Cole was concerned with are brought into focus in a later passage where he says:

I have little hope for the class of people, forty years of age, that lay on straw drunk. I do not know what can be done with them; but if I were potent enough, I would take from their wages something for their wives and children before they had spent all, though that would be interfering with the liberty of the subject.

(Cole, 1884, p. 365)

The problem, then, is that during a period when, in the case of married couples, only men could be the legal heads of households, the only means for government to intervene in the conditions of life in working-class homes was via the working man whose freedom and autonomy had to be respected. Cole thus rehearses a number of possible solutions, only to reject them where they entail any trespass on the working man's freedom. He is tempted by the experiment of Sir Titus Salt in his custom-built Yorkshire town of Saltaire where public houses were banned, but rejects this as a solution that depended on the arbitrary despotism of a particular individual. Instead, Cole casts around for a voluntary mechanism of self-reform through which the working man might be induced to abandon drink and, thereby, cease to be an abusive husband and father. It was also believed that sobriety would help to stave off the Malthusian threat of overpopulation and misery which the working man's drunken promiscuity was believed to pose for society at large.

Cole's solution is to suggest that the working man might be weaned from drunkenness by being exposed to the influence of art, and to advocate government funding of public art galleries as the most effective means of accomplishing this. The rationale underlying this suggestion consisted in a view of art that had been developed over the course of the late eighteenth and early nineteenth centuries, according to which the appreciation of art and literature was seen as a significant means for developing the capacity of freedom. Since judging art was held to be an activity that was free from any compulsion to like this rather than that work of art, it followed that the more this faculty was exercised the more individuals would become used to judging freely for themselves. This would help them to develop a stronger capacity for reflecting on and changing their habits voluntarily. Art and culture, as poet and cultural critic Matthew Arnold put it, work by 'turning a stream of fresh and free thought upon our stock notions and habits' (Arnold; quoted in Rose, 2002, p. 8). Cole's suggestion thus reflected a common view at the time that the art gallery might serve as an antidote to the public house by leading the working man to reflect freely upon and change his habits in ways that would benefit both his wife and children as well as society at large (see Figure 3.2). When Cole's efforts resulted in evening openings at the South Kensington Museum, the precursor of the Victoria and Albert Museum, the newspaper *Lloyds* waxed lyrical about the social benefits this would bring:

> The anxious wife will no longer have to visit the different taprooms to drag her poor besotted husband home. She will seek for him at the nearest museum, where she will have to exercise all the persuasion of her affection to tear him away from the rapt contemplation of a Raphael.
>
> (quoted in Physick, 1982, p. 35)

Art, and the art museum, were thus thought of as a means of acting on society at a distance, of governing society indirectly, without the need for any compulsion that would trespass on the freedom of individuals.

This was a historically surprising development in reversing an earlier school of thought according to which art and the working classes should be kept as far apart as possible. This was the view of the eighteenth-century tradition of aesthetic theory known as civic humanism, perhaps most famously represented by Sir Joshua Reynolds, the first President of the Royal Academy. According to this tradition, those who worked in mechanical occupations – that is, artisans – were said to be so taken up with the routine and habitual nature of their tasks that they lacked any capacity to think freely and independently outside of the constraints of their occupation. Their freedom and independence was also constrained because of their dependence on their employers. Free and independent judgement in art as well as in politics was therefore regarded as something that could be exercised only by those who pursued liberal occupations – that is, the members of the professions – or by the landed gentry whose property made them economically and politically independent. Reynolds's prescription was therefore that everything should be done to keep rude mechanics out of art galleries so that they should not detract from the use of polite conversation about art as a means for forming judgements about the needs of society on the part of its free and independent citizens.

By advocating the exact opposite of this, Cole and his contemporaries give us a glimpse of two somewhat different perspectives on the concept of freedom and its relationship to liberal forms of government. On the one hand, the freedom of the working man is a limit which government must respect. On the other hand, however, freedom itself is envisaged as a mechanism of governing through the ways in which state support for the exercise of free judgement in public art galleries is envisaged as a means of indirectly intervening in working-class households.

Figure 3.2
Sunday Afternoon in a London Gin Palace, Drawn from Life, C. Gregory, *The Graphic*, 8 February 1879, p. 130 (*top*); *Sunday Afternoon in a Picture Gallery, Drawn from Life*, unattributed engraving, *The Graphic*, 8 February 1879, p. 134 (*bottom*)

These are questions I explore more fully in the next section. But let us first take stock of the ground we have covered so far. My purpose in this section has been to identify some of the contradictions that are bound up with the notion of habit and the place that it has occupied in the development of liberal theories and practices of government. These contradictions centre on the role of habit in distinguishing the circumstances in which the principles of liberal government should be applied and those in which they should be withheld in favour of more directive and despotic forms of government. As a rough summary, wherever and for whatever reason habit is held to hold an undue influence over the conduct of a particular population – the lower rungs of the Indian caste system, 'primitives', those whose work is purely mechanical – caveats are then entered to limit the extent to which liberal forms of government can or should be extended to include such groups. At the same time, we have seen that the notion of freedom is a somewhat ambivalent one: on the one hand, referring to freedom from government, placing freedom and government as opposites; and, on the other, placing freedom and government together by conceptualising freedom as a mechanism through which new forms of government should operate. Questions concerning the relations between individuals and society are centrally involved in these issues. As we have seen, the forms of despotic rule associated with colonialism tend to deal with populations as aggregates. Liberal government, by contrast, is individualising: it tries to transform individuals into a mechanism for the relay of government by making them responsible for managing their own conduct.

3 Discipline, freedom and the social regulation of conduct

I now want to pursue these questions further by looking at Michel Foucault's accounts of 'discipline' and 'governmentality'. These are the terms Foucault proposes for new ways of organising and exercising power which, from the eighteenth century, began in part to displace, and in part to complement, the power of 'sovereignty' – that is, the system of power that had been developed in association with the absolutist monarchies of Western Europe. What are the main differences between these three forms of power?

'Sovereign power', Foucault argues, aims to secure and extend the power of the sovereign *as an end in itself*. Treating Niccolo Machiavelli's *The Prince* (1964) as the paradigm account of this form of power, Foucault argues that sovereignty is dedicated to the task of securing and extending the power of the prince over and against both foreign enemies and his subjects. As such, it is exercised primarily via the law and other mechanisms of coercion through which obedience to the sovereign is secured. This is complemented by a politics of spectacle whereby the power of the sovereign is magnified in spectacular displays – the magnificence of royal palaces, for example, or the spectacle of punishment, discussed by Francis Dodsworth in Chapter 4, through which the power of the monarch is made publicly visible.

'Disciplinary power', incubated within the expanding state machineries of late eighteenth-century European societies, developed new ways of regulating conduct. These new ways centred upon the disciplined training of bodies in custom-built settings where those bodies are set apart from the rest of the population for specific periods of time during which they are subjected to exceptional forms of direction and control. The prison is one example. Others are the army, the initial incubator for the forms of disciplining and drilling bodies that were later extended to prisons, workhouses, asylums, orphanages, schools, and, of course, the factory.

'Governmental power', developing over roughly the same period as sovereign and disciplinary power, works differently from both sovereignty and discipline. Foucault differentiates governmentality from sovereignty in terms of its concern with population, or what he calls 'bio-power'. He clarifies what he means by this as follows:

> In contrast to sovereignty, government has as its purpose not the act of government itself, but the welfare of the population, the improvement of its condition, the increase of its wealth, longevity, health, etc.; and the means that the government uses to attain these ends are themselves all in some sense immanent to the population; it is the population itself on which government will act either directly through large scale campaigns, or indirectly through techniques that will make possible, without the full awareness of the people, the stimulation of birth rates, the directing of the flow of population into certain regions or activities, etc.
>
> (Foucault, 1991, p. 100)

The development of governmental forms of power, Foucault argues, is closely tied up with the emergence of *the* 'economy' and *the* 'social' as realms of behaviour which, for the first time, were clearly distinguished from the state. What mattered here was their conception as realms of conduct that were independent of the political authority of the state in the sense of having laws of their own. New and specific arts and techniques of government were needed to manage these realms, and these techniques in turn needed to be guided by new knowledges (economics and sociology), if economic and social behaviour was to be channelled in certain directions.

These, then, are the three major principles of power which Foucault sees as having been assembled by the end of the nineteenth century. Although sovereign power came first, discipline second, and governmental power third, Foucault urges that we should not interpret this historical development as one in which sovereignty is replaced by discipline which is then later replaced by governmental power. The logic is rather one of mutual adjustments between these three forms of power so as to form 'a triangle, sovereignty-discipline-government' (Foucault, 1991, p. 102).

With this general context in mind, let's now look a little more closely at what Foucault has to say about disciplinary power.

You should now read the following short excerpt from Foucault's *Discipline and Punish*, paying particular attention to *how* power is thought to operate.

Reading 3.2   Michel Foucault, 'Discipline and punish'

The classical age discovered the body as object and target of power. It is easy enough to find signs of the attention then paid to the body – to the body that is manipulated, shaped, trained, which obeys, responds, becomes skilful and increases its forces. The great book of Man-the-Machine was written simultaneously on two registers: the anatomico-metaphysical register, of which Descartes wrote the first pages and which the physicians and philosophers continued, and the technico-political register, which was constituted by a whole set of regulations and by empirical and calculated methods relating to the army, the school and the hospital, for controlling or correcting the operations of the body. ...

What was so new in these projects of docility that interested the eighteenth century so much? It was certainly not the first time that the body had become the object of such imperious and pressing investments; in every society, the body was in the grip of very strict powers, which imposed on it constraints, prohibitions or obligations. However, there were several new things in these techniques. To begin with, there was the scale of the control: it was a question not of treating the body, *en masse*, 'wholesale', as if it were an indissociable unity, but of working it 'retail', individually; of exercising upon it a subtle coercion, of obtaining holds upon it at the level of the mechanism itself – movements, gestures, attitudes, rapidity: an infinitesimal power over the active body. Then there was the object of the control: it was not or was no longer the signifying elements of behaviour or the language of the body, but the economy, the efficiency of movements, their internal organization; constraint bears upon the forces rather than upon the signs; the only truly important ceremony is that of exercise. Lastly, there is the modality: it implies an uninterrupted, constant coercion, supervising the processes of the activity rather than its result and it is exercised according to a codification that partitions as closely as possible time, space, movement. These methods, which made possible the meticulous control of the operations of the body, which assured the constant subjection of its forces and imposed upon them a relation of docility-utility, might be called 'disciplines'. Many disciplinary methods had long been in existence – monasteries, armies, workshops. But in the course of the seventeenth and eighteenth centuries the disciplines became general formulas of domination.

Reading source

Foucault, 1977, pp. 136–7

It is not difficult to see the close relationship between discipline and habit here. Recall the *OED* definition of habit as a 'settled disposition or tendency to act in a certain way, esp. one acquired by frequent repetition of the same act until it becomes almost or quite involuntary'. Discipline aims, through the mechanism of compulsory repetition, to make the forms of behaviour it prescribes into habits of the body so that they can be counted on to be repeated as a matter of routine. Here, then, dull, unthinking habit is counted a virtue. And you might also have noticed that disciplinary power is also 'individualising': that is, it targets individuals, exercising power over them through the work it makes them perform on themselves. But this is routine work aiming at installing habits that will make the bodies of the poor, or of prisoners, both docile and useful.

Liberal forms of government differ from disciplinary power in two main ways. The first concerns the respects in which their development has been tied up with what Foucault called 'the governmentalisation of the state' (Foucault, 1991, p. 103). Although this sounds formidable, what Foucault means by it is simple enough. If sovereign power is imposed on society from the top down, governmental power grows out of innumerable initiatives, developed by economic, social and cultural organisations in an attempt to regulate economic, social or cultural behaviour in specific ways that are later taken up, extended and generalised by the state. The development of insurance, discussed by Liz McFall in Chapter 2, is a good example. While it developed initially through the initiative of both private commercial insurance organisations and the forms of mutual support developed by cooperative associations, the later development of the principle of social insurance saw the state step in to extend and generalise similar arrangements to the whole population. Another example is the idea that art might be used as a means of bringing about changes of behaviour: this was advocated by a whole spate of voluntary, private, religious and philanthropic organisations in the early nineteenth century before it was taken up by the state as a reason for funding public art galleries.

The second point concerns the respects in which, unlike disciplinary power and the docility-utility effect it aims for, liberal government is obliged to respect the freedom and autonomy of those over whom it rules. This takes us back to Mill and his sense of the limits that government should not trespass beyond. As we have seen, these limits included, for Cole, the front door of the working man's home, even though Cole's earnest desire to improve the conditions of life for the working man's wife and children behind that door are clear evidence of a governmental concern with population. Yet this is a purpose which Cole is obliged to pursue indirectly rather than via direct intervention. However, the freedom and autonomy that governmental power has to respect and work with goes beyond this sense of a constitutional limit to its powers to include the notion that, in their daily economic and social lives, the members of liberal democratic societies and market economies conduct their affairs in realms that have significant degrees of autonomy and independence in relation to the state. If disciplinary power individualises to exercise control over bodies, the individual here is a value and limit that power must respect. The more complicated version of this argument, which I now want to consider, is that of Nikolas Rose (1999) who contends that liberal forms of government do not simply encounter the freedom and autonomy of those who are to be governed as a limit. Rather, he says, they more typically *work through* that freedom and autonomy, so that freedom itself becomes a part and parcel of particular ways of governing.

You should now read the following excerpt from Rose's *Powers of Freedom*.

Reading 3.3   Nikolas Rose, 'Powers of freedom'

The achievement of the liberal arts of government was to begin to govern through making people free. People were to be 'freed' in the realms of the market, civil society, the family: they were placed outside the legitimate scope of political authorities, subject only to the limits of the law. Yet the 'freeing' of these zones was accompanied by the invention of a whole series of attempts to shape and manage conduct within them in desirable ways. On the one hand, the 'public' activities of free citizens were to be regulated by codes of civility, reason and orderliness. On the other, the private conduct of free citizens was to be civilized by equipping them with languages and techniques of self-understanding and self-mastery. ...

...

The government of freedom can first be analysed in terms of the invention of technologies of spaces and gazes, the birth of calculated projects to use space to govern the conduct of individuals at liberty. We may see this in the multitude of programmes for governing urban space that emerged during the nineteenth century. Nineteenth-century thought was haunted by the spectre of the crowd, the mob, the mass, the riot, the multiplication of forces of rebellion which could be brought into being by the concentration of persons in space. These were not the exercises of freedom but its antithesis: the greatest challenge to a public order of liberty. One set of responses sought to use space against space, to transform towns from dangerous and unhygienic aggregations of persons into well-ordered topographies for maintaining morality and public health. This was the start of a series of dreams of the healthy 'liberal' city, in which the spatial forms – buildings, streets, public spaces – that had encouraged the agglomeration of masses outside the gaze of civilization would be reconstructed through town planning in order to produce health, happiness and civility. A whole diversity of inventions were involved which entailed opening space to visibility and locking each 'free' individual into a play of normative gazes. Police forces would patrol, map, inspect, supervise and know the moral character of each district of the town, operating not so much through terror and the certainty of apprehension, but by placing a grid of norms of conduct over urban space and regulating behaviour according to the division of the normal and the pathological. This work would be linked to that of medical practitioners, who would try to turn the town into a multi-faceted apparatus for fighting disease and securing health. Reform of dwelling houses and public institutions, planned patterns of boulevards and streets, public gardens and squares, sewers and running water, street lighting and pavements – this was not just a 'civilized architecture', but the calculated use of architecture in the service of well-regulated liberty.

...

...

Other spaces of well-regulated liberty were added: museums, exhibitions and department stores which ... operated both an explicit and an implicit pedagogy of civility. Their design explicitly sought to discipline and regulate the conduct of the masses they attracted. They were often accompanied by instructions as to proper forms of dress, conduct, cleanliness and deportment and the avoidance of liquor. And, within them, individuals were not only scrutinized by guards and attendants, but were scrutinized by one another, providing the spatial and visual means for self-education. ... These strategies govern all the more effectively because each individual is to play his or her part in the games of civility. Yet simultaneously they produce new spatial and topographical divisions between those within and those outside civility, and are linked to a whole set of new inventions for disciplining those whose transgressions are now seen as an affront to the order of proper comportment and propriety.

Reading source

Rose, 1999, pp. 69–74

The practice of government, as Rose discusses it, is partly concerned with the organisation of new spatial arrangements in which 'individuals at liberty' can regulate both their own conduct and the relations between themselves. But here, too, government is concerned with instilling habits. It does so, however, by engaging those who are to be governed as active participants in a process of self-transformation that, in some measure, involves their taking conscious responsibility for the new ways of behaving and acting that are enjoined upon them.

To summarise then, we have seen, in this section, that the relations between government, freedom and habit are organised in complex ways in modern societies, and that, as a part of this complexity, individuals are caught up in the exercise of different forms of power in different ways. Disciplinary power individualises in the sense that it targets individuals and makes them do things to and with themselves, but it does so largely in enclosed institutional contexts in which individuals are deprived of their liberty. Liberal forms of government, by contrast, take 'individuals at liberty' as both a constraint and a mechanism through which they operate. However, it is important to remember Foucault's caution against interpreting discipline and governmentality as different historical phases in the development of modern forms of government. Disciplinary and liberal techniques of regulating conduct have coexisted alongside one another, the former being applied to sections of the population which, for a variety of reasons, are denied the freedom and autonomy that liberal forms of government both take account of and work through. Depending on the time and circumstances, these sections of the population have included, and in many cases continue to include, the colonised, children, those with disabilities, the insane, criminal offenders, the work-shy, young offenders, etc.

4 From habit to habitus: the problem of social change

I now go on to consider the role that the concept of habit has played in accounts of social change. This will involve an examination of its relationship to the concept of 'habitus' and, as we shall see, questions concerning the relationships between habit, freedom and individuals will still claim our attention. We begin by delving straight into an excerpt from Charles Camic's (1986) account of the role played by habit in the concerns of classical sociology as these are exemplified by the work of Durkheim.

You should now read the following excerpt from Camic's 'The matter of habit'.

Reading 3.4   Charles Camic, 'The matter of habit'

[Durkheim's] speculations on social and cultural change repeatedly harked back to habit, which he viewed as one of the greatest impediments to progress of any sort. 'It is always a laborious operation to pull up the roots of habits that time has fixed and organized in us' [...]; operating outside the 'sphere of the clear consciousness, ... habits ... resist any change [since] what cannot be seen is not easily modified' [...].

... In his last new lecture course, Durkheim brought into the open a fundamental claim that had long been in the recesses of his work [...]. This was the idea that, by its very nature, human action, whether individual or collective, oscillates between two poles, that of consciousness or reflection on the one side, and that of habit on the other side, with the latter pole being the stronger. Durkheim wrote that as long as 'there is an equilibrium between our dispositions and the surrounding environment, [action occurs by] merely skim[ming] over [our] consciousness'; 'consciousness and reflection [only awaken] when habit is disrupted, when a process of nonadaption occurs' [...] But to say this is obviously to imply that most actors proceed most of the time under the sway of their habits [...] And this is precisely the position that Durkheim forthrightly embraced, declaring that 'it is not enough to direct our attention to the superficial portion of our consciousness; for the sentiments, the ideas which come to the surface are not, by far, those which have the most influence on our conduct. *What must be reached are the habits*' – '*these are the real forces which govern us*' [...].

[...]

[...] It is well known that, in Durkheim's view, modern secular society requires a moral code emphasizing (a) group attachment, or devotion to collective ideals; (b) regularity, or 'behaving similarly under like circumstances'; (c) authority, or dutiful submission and self-restraint in accord with obligatory rules; and (d) autonomy, or reflective consciousness concerning ethical principles [...] What has never been appreciated is the place of habit in this whole affair. But, for Durkheim, certain components of morality are inherently matters of habit: to become attached to collective ideals, 'one must have developed the habits of acting and thinking in common'; 'to assure regularity, it is only necessary that habits be strongly founded' [...]. Furthermore, while something more than habit is required, in his view, to produce submission to rules and reflective consciousness [...], even this something more develops from the base of early habits, particularly 'the habit of self-control and restraint' and 'the habit of lucid thought' [...]. This fact, along with the postulate that children are 'creature[s] of habit', led Durkheim to argue that educational institutions could go far in laying the groundwork for *all* elements of his secular morality: by offering the example of common classroom life, the school could 'induce[e] in the child the habits of group life' and attachment; by enforcing a regimen of rules and discipline, it could 'accustom [the child] to regularity' and 'develop ... the habit of self-control'; and by teaching natural science, it could encourage 'the child to acquire wholesome intellectual habits, which will strengthen his moral conduct' [...].

... It should be noted, though, that when advancing this position, Durkheim's focus was principally on primary education [...] In his analysis of secondary education, a very different spirit seems to be at work. In Durkheim's judgement, secondary schooling is not, and should not be, a process revolving about 'the acquisition of certain specific abilities or habits' [...]. This contention is an outgrowth of two aspects of his moral theory mentioned, but not elaborated, above: first, his insistence [...] that insofar as it involves dutiful conformity to rules, morality necessarily transcends habit, since 'a rule ... is not only a habitual means of acting, it is, above all, an obligatory means of acting' – a means of acting that is imperative [...]; second, his belief that, under the dynamic conditions of the modern age, any viable morality entails as well continual reflection at the upper reaches of the social order [...]. It was in hopes of fostering these obligatory and reflective features of moral life that Durkheim's writings on secondary education set aside the issue of cultivating particular habits of conduct. Moral education, in his view, clearly required more than this.

Reading source

Camic, 1986, pp. 1051–55

For Durkheim, like Mill, whose work he knew well, habit is a problem because it stands as an obstacle to progress by dimming the force of free action. And, again like Mill, Durkheim also operates with a distinction between behaviour that is consciously regulated as a result of reflection, and behaviour that is entirely subject to the influence of habit.

Durkheim also follows Mill in translating this distinction into a division between those sections of the population whose conduct is to be regulated entirely by means of habit and those whose capacity for conscious self-regulation is accorded a role in this process. The secular social morality provided by the primary school is thus based entirely on an enforced regime of rules and discipline through which wholesome habits are to be formed. But note then the further contention that the acquisition of a higher level of morality, one which Durkheim preserves for those who go on to secondary schooling (a tiny minority at the time), involves going beyond habit to govern oneself by means of self-reflection. Here too, then, we find another version of those distinctions we have seen between different levels of society, one of which is to be governed entirely by means of habit while the other has a privileged claim to governing because of its capacity to be lifted above the routines of habit and to engage with questions of social morality in a more reflective way. This recalls the distinction between the liberal and mechanical occupations that we found in eighteenth-century civic humanism, and it has the same effect: it produces a distinction between those who are seen as being capable both of governing and governing others because they have acquired the capacity to govern themselves through self-reflection, and those who, lacking this capacity, must be governed by habit.

I shall return to this point when considering Bourdieu's account of the relationships between different class habitus. First, though, a few words are in order about the concept of habitus itself. The concept is one that Bourdieu derived from Mauss, so let's take a quick look at how Mauss defined the term and how he distinguished it from habit in his discussion of techniques of the body.

You should now read the following excerpt from Mauss's essay 'Techniques of the body'. An extract from the same essay featured in Chapter 1; on this occasion, pay close attention to how the habitus is constituted.

Reading 3.5   Marcel Mauss, 'Techniques of the body: the habitus'

An example will put us in the picture straight away ... Previously we were taught to dive after having learnt to swim. And when we were learning to dive, we were taught to close our eyes and then to open them under water. Today the technique is the other way round. The whole training begins by getting the children used to keeping their eyes open under water. Thus, even before they can swim, particular care is taken to get the children to control their dangerous but instinctive ocular reflexes; before all else they are familiarized with the water, their fears are suppressed, a certain confidence is created, suspensions and movements are selected. Hence there is a technique of diving and a technique of education in diving which have been discovered in my day. And you can see that it really is a technical education and, as in every technique, there is an apprenticeship in swimming. On the other hand, here our generation has witnessed a complete change in technique: we have seen the breast-stroke with the head out of the water replaced by the different sorts of crawl. Moreover, the habit of swallowing water and spitting it out again has gone. In my day swimmers thought of themselves as a kind of steam-boat. It was stupid, but in fact I still do this: I cannot get rid of my technique. Here then we have a specific technique of the body, a gymnic art perfected in our own day.

...

Hence I have had this notion of the social nature of the 'habitus' for many years. Please note that I use the Latin word – ... habitus. ... These 'habits' do not vary just with individuals and their imitations; they vary especially between societies, educations, proprieties and fashions, prestiges. In them we should see the techniques and work of collective and individual practical reason rather than, in the ordinary way, merely the soul and its repetitive faculties.

Reading source

Mauss, 1973 [1935], pp. 71–3

There are three main aspects to Mauss's argument here. The first concerns the respects in which techniques of the body are socially learned habits which – through repetition – come to seem natural. Second, when he talks about the habitus, he has in mind the ways in which a number of different ways of thinking and doing interact with one another to add up to a whole – in the habitus – that is greater than the sum of its various parts. The habitus is a collection of different ways of thinking and doing which derives a degree of unity from its relationship to, for example, a particular society, level of education, or prestige group. And third, a habitus is not simply the result of unthinking repetition (referred to here as 'the soul and its repetitive faculties'). It is also the result of 'collective and individual practical reason' – that is, of ways of thinking and doing that individuals imbibe from the social collectives they belong to.

These three aspects of the concept of habitus were more fully elaborated by Bourdieu, particularly in his *Outline of a Theory of Practice* (2003 [1977]).

You should now read the following excerpt from Bourdieu's *Outline of a Theory of Practice*. Bourdieu's style is a little convoluted, so you might find it useful to summarise what you think are his main points in two or three sentences each.

Reading 3.6   Pierre Bourdieu, 'Structures, habitus and practices'

In short, the habitus, the product of history, produces individual and collective practices, and hence history, in accordance with the schemes engendered by history. The system of dispositions – a past which survives in the present and tends to perpetuate itself into the future by making itself present in practices structured according to its principles, an internal law relaying the continuous exercise of the law of external necessities (irreducible to immediate conjunctural constraints) – is the principle of the continuity and regularity which objectivism discerns in the social world without being able to give them a rational basis. ...

...

The habitus is the product of the work of inculcation and appropriation necessary in order for those products of collective history, the objective structures (e.g. of language, economy, etc.) to succeed in reproducing themselves more or less completely, in the form of durable dispositions, in the organisms (which one can, if one wishes, call individuals) lastingly subjected to the same conditionings, and hence placed in the same material conditions of existence. Therefore sociology treats as identical all the biological individuals who, being the product of the same objective conditions, are the supports of the same habitus: social class, understood as a system of objective determinations, must be brought into relation not with the individual or with the 'class' as a *population*, i.e. as an aggregate of enumerable, measurable biological individuals, but with the class habitus, the system of dispositions (partially) common to all products of the same structures. Though it is impossible for *all* members of the same class (or even two of them) to have had the same experiences, in the same order, it is certain that each member of the same class is more likely than any member of another class to have been confronted with the situations most frequent for the members of that class. ...

...

Since the history of the individual is never anything other than a certain specification of the collective history of his group or class, *each individual system of dispositions* may be seen as a *structural variant* of all the other group or class habitus, expressing the difference between trajectories and positions inside or outside the class.

Reading source

Bourdieu, 2003 [1977], pp. 82–6

In his many discussions of the concept of habitus, Bourdieu has argued that, while clearly related to the concept of habit, it is not to be simply equated with it. One key difference consists in his contention that a habitus is a structure – that is, a systemically connected set of practices, values and beliefs that are governed by similar principles. A habitus, then, is a patterned whole, a closely related set of ways of thinking and doing which derives its coherence and consistency, its underlying unity, from its association with a particular social class. It is a way of translating that class's position in the social world, and particularly its relations to other classes, into a set of beliefs, tastes, values and everyday practices that has a patterned unity.

A second key aspect of Bourdieu's discussion here is his somewhat enigmatic contention that the habitus is 'the product of history' which, in its turn, produces history 'in accordance with the schemes engendered by history'. What does he mean by this? A little earlier in the book from which this excerpt is taken, Bourdieu (2003 [1977], p. 78) argues that the habitus is 'history turned into nature' – that is, a history which is denied as history (in the sense of being limited to a specific time and set of circumstances) in being accepted as the natural way of doing things. But the habitus is also the mechanism through which new history is engendered as it is adjusted to take account of changing class circumstances. It is the mechanism by and through which particular ways of thinking and doing become habitual, and are then transformed to be replaced by other ways of thinking and doing that, in their turn, become habitual – another cycle of history turned into nature.

Since this is all a little abstract, it will be useful to consider a specific example. Bourdieu's most influential application of the concept of habitus is in *Distinction* (Bourdieu, 1984) where he argued that people's cultural tastes and interests are determined by their class habitus. There is, he argued, a systematic unity governing the tastes of members of the same class such that they share a similar logic whether they are literary, musical, or artistic tastes, or tastes for food or drink, clothes, or sport. He says of this logic that:

It is to be found in all the properties – and property – with which individuals and groups surround themselves, houses, furniture, paintings, books, cars, spirits, cigarettes, perfume, clothes, and in the practices in which they manifest their distinction, sports, games, entertainments only because it is in the synthetic unity of the habitus, the unifying, generative principle of all practices.

(Bourdieu, 1984, p. 173)

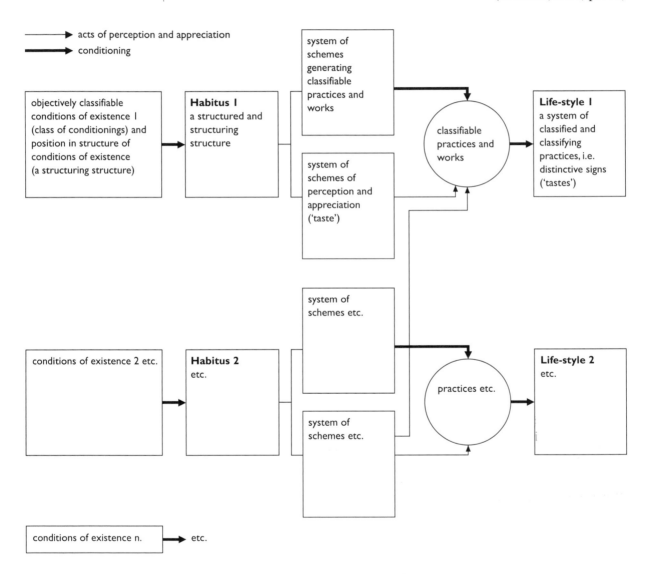

Figure 3.3   Conditions of existence, habitus and lifestyle

(Source: Bourdieu, 1984, Figure 8, p. 171)

This contention that cultural tastes can be related systematically to different class-based habitus was one that Bourdieu set out to prove in *Distinction*. He makes his intentions clear enough in the diagram that is reproduced as Figure 3.3. If we read this from left to right, what he is saying is that particular social positions – and positions of social class are the ones he has in mind – serve as the seedbeds for particular habitus comprised of particular ways of doing and thinking. His reference in the next box to habitus as a 'structured and structuring structure' indicates that a habitus is not just shaped by particular conditions of class existence but is dynamically reshaped by the ways in which people in those classes respond creatively to those conditions. This habitus is then, as we move across the diagram, connected to particular schemes of classification and systems of perception and appreciation – ways of classifying, judging, and liking or not liking particular kinds of food, drink, reading, art and sport – which add up to a whole set of distinctive tastes comprising a class lifestyle.

The value of Bourdieu's study consists in the degree to which, by analysing the results of a large-scale survey of the cultural tastes and practices of a sample of the French population in the mid 1960s, he is able to show strong correlations between particular bundles of tastes and particular class positions. Figure 3.4 offers an insight into how he does this. The figure shows the statistical distribution of tastes for different kinds of music which Bourdieu interprets as representing different musical tastes associated with different class habitus. *The Well-Tempered Clavier*, he argues, represents legitimate taste – taste validated by the education system and the institutions of high culture – and is accordingly most liked by members of the professional and managerial classes whose class habitus is strongly related to educational success and cultural achievement. He interprets *Rhapsody in Blue* as middlebrow culture and notes its greatest popularity among the intermediate classes: junior administrative and commercial executives, secretaries and technicians. Finally, *Blue Danube* is interpreted as an example of popular musical taste, most liked by skilled and semi-skilled sections of the working class.

It is not such tastes considered in isolation that point to the existence of habitus, however, but the fact that Bourdieu is able to show, for each of the three classes he is concerned with – the professional and managerial sections of the bourgeois class, intermediate classes, and the working class – that whole sets of related tastes congregate together. If the upper sections of the managerial and professional classes like *The Well-Tempered Clavier* more than do other classes, so they are also the classes who most like opera, books on art, paintings by Goya, Duchamp and Kandinsky, going to art galleries and museums, drinking whisky and champagne. Similarly, as well as liking *Blue Danube* more than the other

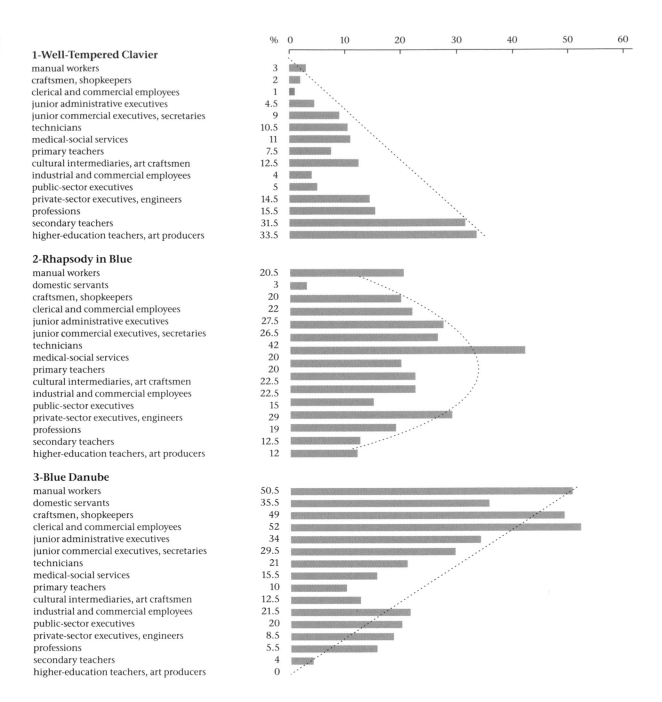

% 0   10   20   30   40   50   60

1-Well-Tempered Clavier

manual workers	3
craftsmen, shopkeepers	2
clerical and commercial employees	1
junior administrative executives	4.5
junior commercial executives, secretaries	9
technicians	10.5
medical-social services	11
primary teachers	7.5
cultural intermediaries, art craftsmen	12.5
industrial and commercial employees	4
public-sector executives	5
private-sector executives, engineers	14.5
professions	15.5
secondary teachers	31.5
higher-education teachers, art producers	33.5

2-Rhapsody in Blue

manual workers	20.5
domestic servants	3
craftsmen, shopkeepers	20
clerical and commercial employees	22
junior administrative executives	27.5
junior commercial executives, secretaries	26.5
technicians	42
medical-social services	20
primary teachers	20
cultural intermediaries, art craftsmen	22.5
industrial and commercial employees	22.5
public-sector executives	15
private-sector executives, engineers	29
professions	19
secondary teachers	12.5
higher-education teachers, art producers	12

3-Blue Danube

manual workers	50.5
domestic servants	35.5
craftsmen, shopkeepers	49
clerical and commercial employees	52
junior administrative executives	34
junior commercial executives, secretaries	29.5
technicians	21
medical-social services	15.5
primary teachers	10
cultural intermediaries, art craftsmen	12.5
industrial and commercial employees	21.5
public-sector executives	20
private-sector executives, engineers	8.5
professions	5.5
secondary teachers	4
higher-education teachers, art producers	0

Figure 3.4
Distribution of preferences for three musical works by class fraction

classes, members of the working class are the most likely to watch sport on television, to drink beer and ordinary red wine, to eat bread, pasta and potatoes, and to play belote, rugby or football.

It is, however, the terms that Bourdieu uses to describe the working-class habitus as being governed by what he calls the 'choice of the necessary' that I want to focus on in concluding. Since, he argues, the working classes are materially deprived, they tend, in their cultural preferences, to like what they have to. The habitus in which they are shaped is one that makes a virtue out of necessity through its commitment to the pragmatic and the functional, and its eschewal of any interest in aesthetic form that is not strongly informed by an interest in usefulness. This is related to a tendency towards conformist views on political and ethical questions that is connected to an inability to abstract from particulars in order to engage in general principles of reasoning. Another way of putting this is to say that, for Bourdieu, the working-class habitus is more strongly habitual than that of the middle classes, and it is so because the working classes are placed on the losing side of the way in which the education system distributes people between roles preserved for those who are regarded as having the intellectual skills of conception and those who have the purely practical skills of execution.

It is useful, at this point, to recall our earlier discussion of the division between liberal and mechanical occupations, of the distinction within civic humanism between those whose occupations mired them in necessity and so bound them to routine and repetitive tasks that they were denied any active role in government and those whose freedom from necessity entitled them to govern as well as to be governed. We might also recall the distinction Durkheim draws between the role of habit in the development of morality in primary schooling and the need for secondary schooling to develop more self-reflexive capabilities for future elites. Bourdieu's position differs from these earlier ones in the crucial respect that his purpose is to draw attention to the mechanisms which produce these unequal outcomes and to support actions that would bring such inequalities to an end. However, while applauding this objective, Bourdieu's critics have argued that his characterisation of the working-class habitus as being governed by the 'choice of the necessary' remains caught up in the ways in which distinctions have been drawn, in earlier phases of social and political theory, between those whose lives are entirely governed by habit and those whose conduct is liberated from its constraint. This is the view of Jacques Rancière who argues that Bourdieu's account of the working-class habitus portrays a 'working-class world more sunk in nature than the "primitive" universe of the ethnologists since objects there have only the value of utility and foods only the function of filling oneself up' (Rancière, 2003, p. 196).

5 Conclusion

This chapter has covered a lot of ground both historically and theoretically. Our historial concerns here range across eighteenth-century aesthetic theory through nineteenth-century debates about liberalism and government to accounts of the social organisation of cultural tastes in post-war France. Our theoretical concerns have encompassed the relations between two major social and political theorists of the nineteenth century – Mill and Durkheim – and two of the most influential social theorists of the late twentieth century: Foucault and Bourdieu. The concept of habit has provided an organising focus for these concerns in offering a dual point of entry into questions concerning the social organisation of conduct. As we have seen, the concept of habit provides one answer to such questions in pointing to the role of repetition and routine training in shaping social conduct. Bourdieu's concept of habitus offers a more nuanced and complex account of this view, one which seeks to explain how forms of social conduct are both perpetuated through time and subject to change. But the concept of habit has also focused questions of conduct in a second way by representing forms of behaviour which, from a variety of perspectives, have been seen as needing to be changed, managed or regulated. In exploring these questions, we have considered the different ways, in different contexts, in which the mechanisms of discipline and those of liberal government have been brought to bear on the management of conduct. This has entailed a consideration of the different ways in which these mechanisms either work on individuals to make them docile and useful, or seek to enlist individuals in managing themselves in ways which respect and work through their autonomy and freedom. We have seen, finally, how these different strategies for managing conduct have been, and continue to be, connected to ways of dividing societies into different categories of persons who are accorded different kinds of freedom, autonomy and individuality, and different positions and responsibilities in relation to the governance of conduct.

References

Appadurai, A. (1993) 'Number in the colonial imagination' in Breckenridge, C.A. and van der Veer, P. (eds) *Orientalism and the Postcolonial Predicament: Perspectives on South Asia*, Philadelphia, PA, University of Pennsylvania Press.

Bagehot, W. (1873) *Physics and Politics: Or Thoughts on the Application of the Principles of 'Natural Selection' and 'Inheritance' to Political Society*, London, Henry S. King & Co.

Bourdieu, P. (1984) *Distinction: A Social Critique of the Judgement of Taste* (trans R. Nice), London, Routledge.

Bourdieu, P. (2003 [1977]) *Outline of a Theory of Practice* (trans. R. Nice), Cambridge, Cambridge University Press.

Camic, C. (1986) 'The matter of habit', *American Journal of Sociology*, vol. 91, no. 5, pp. 1039–1087.

Carey, J. (2005) *What Good Are the Arts?*, London, Faber and Faber.

Cole, Sir H. (1884) *Fifty Years of Public Work of Sir Henry Cole, K.C.B., Accounted for in his Deeds, Speeches and Writings*, 2 vols, London, George Bell and Sons.

Darwin, C. (1968) *The Origin of Species by Means of Natural Selection*, Harmondsworth, Penguin.

Dirks, N.B. (2001) *Castes of Mind: Colonialism and the Making of Modern India*, Princeton, NJ, Princeton University Press.

Foucault, M. (1977) *Discipline and Punish: The Birth of the Prison*, London, Allen Lane.

Foucault, M. (1991) 'Governmentality' in Burchell, G., Gordon, C. and Miller, P. (eds) *The Foucault Effect: Studies in Governmentality*, London, Harvester Wheatsheaf.

Hay, J. (2006) 'Designing homes to be the first line of defence: safe households, mobilisation, and the new mobile privatisation', *Cultural Studies*, vol. 20, nos 4–5, pp. 349–77.

Helliwell, C. and Hindess, B. (2002) 'The "empire of uniformity" and the government of subject peoples', *Cultural Values*, vol. 6, nos 1–2, pp. 139–52.

Lankester, E.R. (1980) *Degeneration: A chapter in Darwinism*, London, Macmillan.

Machiavelli, N. (1964) *The Prince* (ed. and trans. M. Musa), New York, NY, St Martins Press.

Mauss, M. (1973 [1935]) 'Techniques of the body', *Economy and Society*, vol. 2, no. 1, pp. 70–88.

Mill, J.S. (1969 [1859]) 'On Liberty' in *On Liberty, Representative Government, The Subjection of Women: Three Essays by John Stuart Mill*, London, Oxford University Press.

Physick, J. (1982) *The Victoria and Albert Museum: The History of Its Building*, London, Victoria and Albert Museum.

Rancière, J. (2003) *The Philosopher and His Poor*, Durham, NC, and London, Duke University Press.

Rose, J. (2002) *The Intellectual Life of the British Working Classes*, London and New Haven, CT, Yale University Press.

Rose, N. (1999) *Powers of Freedom: Reframing Political Thought*, Cambridge, Cambridge University Press.

Spencer, B. (1914) 'The Aboriginals of Australia' in Knibbs, G.H. (ed.) *Federal Handbook Prepared in Connection with the Eighty-fourth Meeting of the British Association for the Advancement of Science Held in Australia, August 1914*, Melbourne, Commonwealth of Australia.

Valverde, M. (1996) '"Despotism" and ethical liberal governance', *Economy and Society*, vol. 25, no. 3, pp. 357–72.

Chapter 4
Governing conduct: violence and social ordering

Francis Dodsworth

Contents

1 Introduction

When speaking about the way 'society' or 'the social' is formed it is common to use terms such as 'the social order' or 'social relations'. This draws our attention to the fact that 'society' is not just an abstract structure of 'classes' or 'socio-economic groups', but a field of human interaction, one that is not random, but which takes an ordered, regular and generally comprehensible form. This chapter will explore the ways in which this interaction shapes both the individual and the social and the relationship between the two. In particular, it focuses on various ways in which individuals and groups have tried, either explicitly or implicitly, to establish or enforce on society at large a particular vision of order through direct or indirect attempts to influence certain aspects of public behaviour.

The concern of this chapter, then, is with what Michel Foucault called 'the conduct of conducts'; that is, the ways in which people are made or encouraged to regulate their behaviour according to particular norms or established values. Conduct has a dual meaning in Foucault's work: 'To "conduct" is at the same time to "lead" others (according to mechanisms of coercion that are, to varying degrees, strict) and a way of behaving within a more or less open field of possibilities' (Foucault, 2000a, p. 341). It is this double sense of the term that will be the focus here. More particularly, the chapter will examine the ways in which sociologists have tried to explain the regulation of conduct and its relation to wider social change. As will become clear, the way in which people conduct themselves has often been linked by sociologists to the development of particular kinds of personality and analysis of this type has been related to the nature of the social order more broadly. It is perhaps because of this link between conduct and its implications for wider society that public behaviour has been the target of such concern from social reformers and indeed government generally. Further, as we shall see, an examination of public conduct relates directly to the emergence of the idea that there is something distinct called 'society' at all – that is, something that is separate from both the state and the individual, not just equivalent to the sum of individuals, or reducible to a particular community or communities, but that has aspects irreducible to these, governed by 'social laws' which can be understood by scientific investigation.

Because conduct has been identified as so important in defining the nature of both the individual and the social, a diverse range of institutions has been mobilised to act upon people's conduct and form it according to the desired norm. This chapter will therefore explore the way in which particular institutions have been used to enforce social norms or guide and delimit the conduct of conduct. Sociologists and historians have identified a wide array of such institutions which sought to affect public behaviour. These have included religious, philanthropic and welfare organisations, as well as schools and the more obvious structures of the criminal justice system – the police and the prison or reformatory specifically designed to reform the character of 'deviants' to a socially acceptable model. We might say that these institutions mediate between the individual and the social by transmitting and enforcing social values.

What do I mean here by 'mediate'? I employ the term in the sense given to it by Régis Debray (2000) in his study of how meanings are materially transmitted. The material dimension of structure and practice, Debray argues, is fundamental to the solidification and perpetuation of a culture and, we might add, society. When Debray talks about mediation he means the transmission of cultural (or social) values from one generation or one group to another through particular structures, technologies or systems of practice. The question addressed in this chapter is how particular values, in the form of cultural norms relating to conduct, are generated, reproduced and transformed through the mediation of particular social institutions and certain forms of practice. The creation of highly visible institutions for the mediation of social values, such as the police, can be seen as central to the emergence of the distinction between 'the state' and 'society', the latter being formed in part through the actions of state institutions, but at the same time establishing the values on the basis of which those institutions act.

Within most social worlds there is normally some expectation that people will behave according to certain norms; that is to say, we expect others to conduct themselves in predictable ways in given situations. There is often surprise, offence or confusion when people behave in ways contrary to these expectations. In situations where behaviour steps outside these norms we often feel threatened or perhaps repulsed, and sometimes we may even call upon the relevant authorities, such as the police, or other representatives of the state to enforce adherence to those norms, ultimately by force if necessary. These social norms are often codified in laws written for the purpose and they are maintained by organised bodies created with the express purpose of ensuring the law is adhered to.

It should be clear even from a very basic understanding of anthropology that these values and this system of government are not universal, but culturally and historically specific, although they have been widely exported through imperialism. The particular focus in this chapter is Britain and its transformation in the modern period (roughly since the 1750s), when such a system for the government of conduct was legitimised and made central to Britain's social organisation. It will become clear throughout the chapter that the creation of mediating institutions, such as the police, principally controlled by the state, whose task is to regulate conduct so as to reproduce the desired social order, is of relatively recent provenance in Britain. However, their effects had a powerful influence on the way Britons understood themselves and others, becoming linked to claims that British society was 'civilised', a value seen to inhere in the modes of conduct and the form of order brought about by the institutions of police, prisons and so on. The definition of certain societies or parts of society as 'civilised' and those of other individuals, communities or societies as 'uncivilised' or even 'savage' or 'barbaric' has been, and in some areas still is, used as a tool to legitimise punitive action or forceful intervention in particular interpersonal, social or political situations, ranging from the suppression of customary practices, the criminalisation of 'deviance', or the imposition of hygiene inspections on working-class families, to imperialism and conquest. Accepted codes of conduct and how they are regulated, then, have implications far beyond their immediate context, relating to the ways in which states are judged to be legitimate or in which peoples or regions are considered fit for military or humanitarian intervention by international bodies operating according to 'Western' value systems.

One of the things that supposedly marks out 'modern', Western society as 'civilised' is the notion that one particular form of conduct, violence – that is, the use of significant force so as to cause (generally physical) harm – should be the preserve only of particular institutions of the state, sanctioned by law. Only the executive institutions of justice have the power of physical coercion, and then only in very limited circumstances, generally in order to prevent violence between individuals or sections of the community. The overall intention of this chapter is to analyse the way in which what has been called 'modern' or 'civilised' society and the forms of institutionally mediated violence associated with it emerged historically in the particular – though by no means unique – case of Britain through the definition of particular relationships and forms of behaviour as acceptable or unacceptable and the elaboration of new systems of government and law in order to enforce these ideals.

The particular focus of this chapter, then, will be on the history of violence and its increasing government by the state. There was a pronounced shift in attitudes towards – and practices for 'dealing with' – this subject between the late eighteenth and the late nineteenth centuries. During the nineteenth century, violence came to be seen as a 'social problem' which threatened the social order and therefore required government action to remedy it. From the 1780s to the 1830s many parts of England and Wales instituted police forces, in part, to deal with just such problems of 'disorder'. In contrast, in previous generations, customary modes of communal life had relied upon violence in order to define and maintain their society. John Carter Wood (2004) has defined this period as the one in which 'violence' with all its modern meanings and implications was 'invented' – defined as a social problem with particular causes that needed to be tackled. We might extend this and suggest that it was through analysis of the relationship between dominant modes of conduct and individual personality that the very idea of 'society' emerged.

1.1 Teaching aims

The aims of this chapter are to:

■ explore the historical shift from a conception that violence was a way of governing society to its construction as a social problem itself

■ engage with three different sociological explanations for this transformation: 'social control', the 'disciplinary society' and the 'civilising process'

■ analyse the connections understood by different authors to obtain between modes of interpersonal and public conduct, the structure of the human psyche, and the formation of the wider social order

■ consider the significance of the emergence of the state as an institution for the mediation of violence and its consequences for the nature of the modern social order.

2 Violence and the state in modern society

This section will explore the classic definition of the place of violence in modern society before, in the next section, contrasting this to the role violence played in early modern culture and the way in which it was increasingly problematised and governed by the state. The rest of the chapter will examine sociological explanations for this transformation in the status and use of violence, paying particular attention to the significance of conduct in the mediation of the relationship between the individual and the social through certain institutions.

In 1922 Max Weber argued in *Economy and Society* (1978 [1922]) that modern society is peculiarly characterised by the restriction of legitimate violence to the institutions of the state. The fact that the agencies of the state hold a monopoly on violence has been linked to the growth of civility and a general decline of violence in society at large. The use of violence, particularly as a means to govern the conduct of others, is removed from wider society and reserved for specific agencies, which punish its use among others. Indeed, the very threat of punishment by these agencies is usually enough to prevent the use of violence.

The task of these governing agencies, we might argue, is to act as mediators between the individual and society, enforcing individuals to act according to the norms generally considered desirable which make predictable social interaction possible. The social institutions of criminal justice, education and so on, act to delimit the conduct of individuals, establishing a peaceable 'civilised' norm of conduct. If you find it difficult to think of law enforcement as connected to social norms, consider the fact that the law deals not only with situations such as theft and criminal damage, but violence, indecency, obscenity and even such loose categories as 'disorderly behaviour' or 'disturbance of the peace'. Dealing with any of these constitutes enforcement of an expected standard of behaviour, many of which have changed over time and which vary from culture to culture.

What agencies does the state use in order to enforce social norms? Is Weber correct that in modern society violence is the preserve of the state? Police and prison officers are the most obvious groups possessing the legitimate use of violence for the enforcement of the laws relating to public and private conduct. In extreme cases this can even extend to the use of lethal force if a situation presents an immediate threat to the lives of members of the public. Some democratic states – for example, at the time of writing the USA, Japan and India, and many undemocratic states, continue to impose the death penalty on those who contravene particular laws (usually murder). The military are likewise allowed to use violence, but generally in liberal or democratic regimes this is not permitted against members of their own society and even this use of violence is regulated by a particular code of conduct, the Geneva Convention. There are also many private security organisations, extending from the shop security guard to private prison wardens, which have the power to use force in particular circumstances, legitimising the use of significant force during apprehension of thieves or controlling order at public events or in prisons.

Other individuals or bodies are able to use force in modern society; for example, in Britain any citizen is allowed to perform a citizen's arrest if they see a felony in progress, likewise in many places parents have the power to physically discipline their children and schools are allowed to do the same. However, the level of force parents are entitled to use is much lower than that of the agencies of the state and as soon as the force used causes harm to the child it is by definition beyond the sphere of legitimacy and constitutes abuse. Certainly, then, although there are small areas of modern life where individuals can exercise legitimate force, they are severely curtailed and the state closely regulates their use. Of course, this is not to say that modern society does not witness significant violence between its members, or that all members of society accept these conditions, but nonetheless such acts are prohibited by law and those who commit acts of violence are liable to control and punishment by the state.

At the same time it is clear, as Weber argues (1978 [1922]), that most of the time the state either cannot or does not need to coerce people into obeying the law; people simply act according to the social norm without being coerced into doing so. Why do they do this? In part, as Weber suggests (1978 [1922]), it is because they know that if they did contravene these boundaries of acceptable behaviour, they would be liable to discipline by the authorities; in other words, they police themselves, because they know that otherwise someone will police them. But they also follow the social rules because, in many cases, they have internalised the values of society through education and imitation. Many sociologists have seen a link between forms of social discipline, the internalisation of these values by individuals and the nature of the social order. Some of these links will be explored in the section on 'social control', but first I will contrast, in the next section, the place of violence in modern society with its early modern precursor.

3 Violence and social ordering

Writing in 1605, Sir Edward Coke, England's Attorney General, offered a detailed consideration of the method of public execution normally used for traitors. The person convicted of treason was to be:

> drawn to the place of execution from his prison as being not worthy any more to tread upon the face of the earth whereof he was made: also for that he hath been retrograde to nature, therefore is he drawn backward at a horse tail. And whereas God hath made the head of man the highest and most supreme part, as being his chief grace and ornament, ... he must be drawn with his head declining downward, and lying so near ground as may be, being thought unfit to take the common air. For which case also he shall be strangled, being hanged up by the neck between heaven and earth, as deemed unworthy of both, or either; as, likewise, that the eyes of men may behold, and their hearts condemn him. Then is he to be cut down alive, and to have his privy parts cut off and burnt before his face as being unworthily begotten, and unfit to leave any generation after him. His bowls and inlay'd parts taken out and burnt, who inwardly had conceived and harboured in his heart such horrible treason. After, to have his head cut off, which had imagined the mischief. And lastly his body to be quartered, and the quarters set up in some high and

eminent place, to the view and detestation of men, and to become a prey for the fowls of the air.

(Amussen, 1995, pp. 6–7)

Figure 4.1
Execution of Guy Fawkes and other Gunpowder Plotters, 31 January 1606

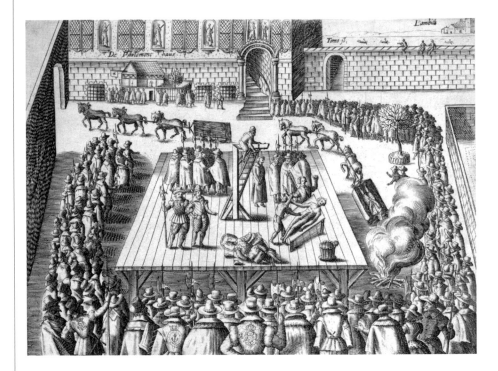

In contrast to contemporary society, where violent conduct is driven to the margins of life, restricted to certain agencies of the state only for the purpose of restoring social order (that is the general condition of orderly, non-violent conduct), early modern society used violence regularly and visibly as a means to enforce social norms and particular patterns of conduct. The passage above describes one of the clearest examples of this. The purposes of this public violence were various. First, of course, it acted as punishment of the offender. There is no sense here that it is the purpose of the law to reform the criminal; rather, its function is to sanction and meet out the appropriate penalty. The more serious the crime, the more serious the penalty. In this case, for treason, a symbolic assault on the basis of society itself and its centrepoints the King and Parliament, an exceptionally severe penalty was deemed fitting. This not only signified the gravity of the offence, but provided a terrible warning to those who might consider attempting something similar. In fact, this exemplary notion of punishment was widespread.

Many crimes before the nineteenth century carried the death penalty; indeed, by the early 1800s there were more than 200 separate capital offences, including going through a forest, chase, park or paddock with a blackened face, cutting down hop binds, damaging Westminster Bridge, breaking down the head or mound of a fish-pond or cutting down trees in a garden, orchard or plantation (Gilmour, 1992, p. 147). All of these offences carried the death penalty. But this did not mean that anyone convicted of such offences would automatically be executed; rather, only a proportion would be, the rest would have their sentences commuted to a lesser form, usually transportation to a penal colony. Nonetheless, execution was part of the routine of public life, being conducted in the open, usually with the presence of a large crowd. Although execution of women was rarer than that of men, it was not unheard of and could be particularly brutal: murdering one's husband was classed as petty treason until 1790 and, given that drawing and quartering women would have offended 'decency', the penalty was burning alive, although in practice they were usually strangled first. There was little discrimination regarding age either: teenagers and the aged were frequently executed. The whole rationale of the system, then, was to provide a few, terrible examples which would deter others from following in their footsteps.

In fact, taken as a whole, the use of violence as a tool of government in the early modern period extended far beyond Weber's definition of its modern equivalent, not only because the focus here is on exemplary and symbolic punishment, but also because the state was far from being the only body with the power to carry out legitimate violence. There were many circumstances in which those in authority in a given situation felt that it was both their right and duty to use violence to discipline others, particularly those subordinate to them. As Susan Dwyer Amussen (1995, p. 4) puts it, 'Not only did discipline – legitimately – include the use of violence, but most people saw violence as a way to discipline or punish those by whom they felt wronged'. As such it was often felt legitimate for the head of the household to discipline physically his children, wife and even servants. The level of violence meted out was not random, it was governed by customary rules and assumptions about proportion to the offence (rules which could, of course, be breached). This is strikingly different from the position of legitimate violence in contemporary society. Rather than violence being a form of conduct that is outlawed, violence itself was used to enforce particular modes of conduct, religious, moral, political and so on. Of course, it must be recognised that this remains the case on an informal level in the present day, but such violence is not regarded as legitimate, particularly in the eyes of the law.

Violence was a major feature of social, religious and political disputes in the early modern period, as late as the eighteenth century. Food riots were a common feature of public life, rural and urban. When the price of bread or corn was high, agricultural and urban labourers would express their discontent in a ritualised, but nonetheless violent, manner. Such outbursts were considered a part of the routine of public life, were generally accepted as a form of legitimate protest, and were themselves regulated by customary rules (Thompson, 1993, pp. 185–258). At the same time, anti-Catholic riots were relatively common in seventeenth- and eighteenth-century England. Although the status of these was more uncertain, with the authorities more divided over their legitimacy, such events formed a part of the pattern of popular protest. Politics itself was riddled with violence. Election contests were commonly accompanied by violent clashes between partisan mobs and intimidation was used to prevent people voting or to discourage candidates from standing. At Coventry in 1705, a mob of 600 men captured the town for three days, controlling the voting and assaulting voters (Gilmour, 1992, pp. 207–23). The role of the politician and the elector, particularly before the secret ballot in 1870 meant that votes were no longer declared in public, often involved a demonstration of physical masculinity.

Beyond this, it was common for whole communities to admonish those members who stepped outside the commonly accepted code of conduct. Those 'guilty' of upsetting the social order, be it wives who scolded or beat their husbands, husbands who beat their wives too harshly, or were beaten by them, those guilty of infidelity, prostitution, re-marriage and so on, were regularly the subject of public punishments or elaborate shaming rituals, often termed 'rough music', something which united all classes or groups in society. These rituals could include the use of the ducking stool or bridling for women who were perceived to be 'scolds', or might result in the burning of effigies or symbolic mock stag hunts for those suspected of adultery (Amussen, 1995; Thompson, 1993, pp. 467–531). At the same time, duelling, boxing and other forms of fighting were common ways of settling disputes without recourse to legal process (Wood, 2003). In such situations the violence was often real, but also ritualised and formal in nature, with rules governing its use and extent, and rapid reconciliation was common in the less serious cases. In all these situations, physical force was often used as a way of enforcing social norms, disciplining the unruly or righting a perceived wrong, and such methods were common to many different social groups, not only the poor. It was important that the whole community observe or participate in these events. The public nature of this ritual-but-real violence was central to its purpose, which was to act both in an exemplary manner, as a warning to others not to commit such acts themselves, and as a symbolic restoration of the social order. As such, violence was the most important tool in the maintenance of the early modern social world through enforcement of the norms that bound it.

In this situation, violence is not reserved to particular institutions whose task is to mediate the relationship between the individual and the social; rather, the character of the individual and the community are bound up together and the conduct of individuals is regulated directly by the

Figure 4.2
Sabre duel between
German students,
c.1900; painting by
Georg Mühlberg
(1863–1925)

actions of the whole community. In this sense we might say that there is
no 'social' here at all. That is not to say that there is no sense of a
collective group or communal identity, for clearly there was. But there is
no sense here of a space between the individual, the community and
government which needed to be acted upon. The community considered
it their right and duty to mould the conduct of its members according to
their norms, and violence, which was both real and symbolic, was one
of the principal ways in which this was effected.

But over the course of the late eighteenth and early nineteenth centuries,
this situation underwent a dramatic change. Violence ceased to be the
means of enforcing order and came to be seen as one of the problems of
disorder. Violence was associated with a lack of self-control, a lack of
humanity and cultivation. In particular, violence became associated with
the poor, who became subject to intervention from other parts of the
community. From the 1770s onwards, a series of interconnected social
and political movements sought to problematise and prevent the use of
violence in social relations. In tandem with legal reform, the movements
for the reformation of manners and reform of the system of policing and
punishment attempted, in different ways, to restrict public violence and
ultimately to limit its commission to officers of the state.

From the 1770s and 1780s there was a series of attempts to reform the
system of police, the prisons, and more generally to effect a reformation
of manners in the British population. Some of this was directed at the
life and leisure of the poor, but much of this was directed at aristocratic
conduct and the reform of rakes and libertines like the infamous Earl of
Rochester. In addition, John Howard and others sought to create a new

more humanitarian prison system focused on the reformation of prisoners rather than their detention before punishment. At the same time the criminal code itself was reformed so that imprisonment and reform replaced execution and transportation for the majority of offences. Simultaneously, a series of moral reformers formed associations which produced pamphlets outlining the importance of proper conduct and which sought to prosecute offences involving immorality or irreligion. This coincided with reform of the systems of policing from a system of parish constables, unpaid gentlemen who served in the office for a year in rotation, assisted by watchmen, to a new body of paid, uniformed officers regularly patrolling the towns and cities of the country. The most famous of these 'new' police bodies was the Metropolitan Police, introduced in London in 1829 under Sir Robert Peel's tenure as Home Secretary, but in fact the improvement in policing took place gradually over many years, spread across the whole country. Policing institutions comparable to London's Metropolitan Police were established in many boroughs in the 1830s and were made mandatory in all counties and boroughs in 1856 (Emsley, 1996).

The consequences of this change from regulation of conduct by community and custom to institution and legalisation were significant. The onus was no longer on the member of the community to draw the attention of the authorities to crimes committed against them. Under the 'old' system of police, constables did not patrol the streets seeking out offenders (although watchmen did do this to some extent); their task was simply to apprehend offenders when a complaint was made to them by a member of the public. Often, people did not resort to the use of the constable at all: either matters were dealt with in the customary manner by the community if the offender was known, or, if not, individuals resorted to private thief-takers to recover their property for them. By the mid nineteenth century most towns possessed a regular system of patrolling constables whose task was to seek out offenders and initiate prosecutions against them. In less serious cases the police would caution those stepping outside the acceptable realms of behaviour and, if the case was more serious, arrest them and remove them to a reformatory, where they would learn to obey the governing norms through repetitive discipline. Why did this change take place? Sections 4 to 6 will proceed to examine three different kinds of sociological explanation for this transformation which all posit a distinct understanding of the nature of the modern social order.

4   Social control

For Robert Storch (1976), the key function of the 'new police' introduced by Peel was to act as an instrument of 'social control', not simply preventing crime but enforcing a particular set of moral and social codes on the working class. The purpose of these codes was to make individuals diligent and proper, to force them to act in such a manner as to render themselves fit for work and a life lived in a socially productive mode. The poor, the particular targets of this discipline, were to be rendered capable of working in the new system of factory labour which had recently emerged through the industrial revolution and which required punctuality and diligence from each individual:

> The police had a broader mission [than the prevention of crime] in the nineteenth century, however – to act as an all-purpose lever of urban discipline. The imposition of the police brought the arm of municipal and state authority directly to bear upon key institutions of daily life in working-class neighbourhoods, touching off a running battle with local custom and popular culture which lasted at least until the end of the century. Riots and strikes are by nature ephemeral episodes, but the monitoring and control of the streets, pubs, racecourses, wakes, and popular fêtes was a daily function of the 'new police.' It was in some part on this terrain that the quality of police-community relations in the second half of the nineteenth century was determined. In northern industrial towns of England these police functions must be viewed as a direct complement to the attempts of urban middle-class elites – by means of Sabbath, educational, temperance, and recreational reform – to mold [sic] a laboring class amenable to the new disciplines of work and leisure. The other side of the coin of middle-class voluntaristic moral and social reform (even when sheathed) was the policeman's truncheon.
>
> (Storch, 1976, p. 481)

At the same time as learning to conduct themselves in a disciplined manner, everyone had to be able to conduct their lives according to a pattern that would prevent them from falling into indigence through gambling, drinking or other improvidence (see Chapter 3 of this volume), which would render them a burden on the useful members of society. This had to be done despite isolation from the rest of society through the urbanisation and fragmentation of community which was thought to accompany industrialisation. Urbanisation not only detached individuals from the idealised rural community in which it was believed conduct was regulated through the close hierarchical and mutual observation characteristic of orderly rural life, absent when they moved to the city for work, but it also saw the growth of entire working-class districts, separated from middle- and upper-class housing and their guiding influence. The new police, then, are seen as the agents of the middle classes, entering into and governing the working-class districts in which the new generation of suburban commuters feared to tread, spreading the values of the bourgeoisie (the owners of the industries in which the poor worked) throughout society.

The sociological concept of **social control** proceeds on the premise that 'social order is maintained not only, or even mainly by legal systems, police forces and prisons, but is expressed through a wide range of social institutions, from religion to family life, and including, for example, leisure and recreation, education, charity and philanthropy, social work and poor relief' (Donajgrodzki, 1977a, p. 9). This concept has a long sociological heritage, extending back to the work of E.A. Ross in 1901, through Paul Landis in the 1950s, and is particularly associated with the work of Talcott Parsons, but it reached its heyday in the 1970s in work uniting historical and sociological studies.

Donajgrodzki (1977b) identifies a phenomenon he terms 'social police' which emerged in the early Victorian period and which, he argues, was reflected in an understanding of the role of the police shared by most middle-class traditionalists and utilitarian reformers. What he means by 'social police' is that, for Victorians seeking to reform society, 'social order was the product of a common morality, which was sustained and expressed by its general diffusion throughout the institutions of society' (Donajgrodzki, 1977b, p. 52). This meant that attempts to preserve order had to involve not only the law, police and reformatories, but also religion, education, appropriate forms of leisure and public health. These social reformers were particularly concerned with the poor 'whom it was assumed, were normless, or at least insufficient [sic] if left to themselves; liable to be led astray by agitators or to form "perverted" social systems'. This 'social police' was not so much a system designed to oppress or suppress the poor; rather, it was assumed that for common morality to exist, it was the duty of the rich to guide the poor and for the poor to follow the rich. Indeed, it was the right of the poor to expect such government (Donajgrodzki, 1977b, p. 52). The rich, then, were to establish the principles of conduct for the poor to follow and equip them with the capacity to do so. In the generalised moral government that characterised early Victorian social reform, 'Teachers, clergymen, poor law officials and distributors of charity were to some extent policemen. It followed that even the "specialised" police function was indeterminate; the policeman a moral guide, lay preacher and social worker as well as thief-taker' (Donajgrodzki, 1977b, pp. 54–5). It is this generalised function of the 'specialised' police that Storch is concerned with above.

Figure 4.3
Duty and Pleasure: a policeman on duty on a snowy night in a fashionable London square, while some of the residents set off for an evening of leisure; C. Gregory, *The Graphic*, 21 December 1872

The moral codes that the new police were to enforce were those established by the new urban elites – the middle class – whose increased wealth had allowed them to dominate and direct local government and so to shape the social into their desired form. That form was the capitalist system of wage labour and its associated cultural values of temperance, industriousness and propriety. Storch sees the emergence of the modern social order, produced through the disciplinary actions of the new police, as a manifestation of the values of the new middle class, whose power can itself be seen as a consequence of their new economic power as the urban commercial class. Modern, 'civilised' social order, then, is a consequence of economic change.

From this perspective, then, the police were acting as the agents of the bourgeoisie who had risen to control of the state with the emergence of the capitalist mode of production. The police were used by the bourgeoisie to maintain the conditions of their dominance and to create a labouring class who would produce their profit for them. In order to do so it was necessary not only to instil a new kind of discipline into the population, but also to eradicate practices and customs that offered competing alternatives to the capitalist model of wage labour. The police were not invented simply to control the working class, but to create them, to transform the world of custom, mutual assistance and barter into one where individuals worked for wages set at market rates and where disputes were arbitrated, not between the disputants themselves, but by the higher authority of the legal process. The police became the main instigators of prosecutions and often created trials between disputants who would happily have considered the matter settled by their brief conflict (Wood, 2003, p. 121). The fight was no longer the means to settle a dispute, but was a criminal act which required the apportioning of blame and reform of the guilty party.

One aspect of this transformation of popular culture was the eradication of violence which was perceived to be disorderly, immoral and contrary to the (often evangelical Christian) bourgeois values that drove capitalist expansion, but which also mitigated against efficient working practices. Among the chief targets of such forms of 'urban discipline' were the popular shaming rituals and 'rough music' that were such a feature of the customary mode of social ordering. Theorists of social control would argue that this was because in the same process the bourgeoisie not only took control of the state, but, having done so, they extended the power of this institution so that it came to monopolise all other forms of authority that had previously been dispersed throughout the social body. Having made the state the only legitimate location of force, since they were in control of the state the bourgeoisie were able to legislate against any mode of social action, any form of social ordering, that was not contributory to their (economic) interests.

Ultimately in this account it is economic change (the emergence of capitalism) and class interest and conflict that drive this transformation in conduct and therefore society. Police institutions and prisons, the mediating agencies of this change, are seen as a manifestation of the economic transformation that saw power shift from land, which underpinned the aristocratic feudal order, to capital, which underpinned the new strength of the metropolitan middle class. Much is made here of the apparent coincidence in time of the emergence of capitalism and police in the late eighteenth and early nineteenth centuries. According to this scheme, conduct is shaped by the institutions of the law so as to form personalities that are productive, not wasteful or lazy, and capable of working in the new industrial economy. Conduct in modern society is shaped to meet the requirements of the capitalist economy and labour structure by institutions that are themselves an epiphenomenon of that economic structure.

5 Disciplinary society

For Foucault, the emergence of new disciplinary mechanisms is also seen as the defining feature of modern society. In his book *Discipline and Punish*, first published in France in 1975, Foucault (1991 [1977], pp. 135–94) charts the ways in which what he calls the 'micro-physics of power' came to diffuse themselves silently throughout society. From the school to the army or police barracks, bodies were worked on, not through extreme pain, but through constant assessment and adjustment. Paying minute attention to detail, the deportment and conduct of people was assessed and disciplined through habituation to follow particular guidelines. These new disciplinary techniques were not aimed at the social body as a whole, in the way that 'rough music' sought to produce general conformity to social norms by the whole population through the disciplining of one individual. Rather, all individuals were subjected to the eye of power, whose aim was to make the body conform to an 'economy of movement'. Hierarchical observation and the correction of minute deviations from the norm were the key features of this mode of government. The habits of discipline would be internalised to the point where hierarchical observation was no longer required. Instead, the individual would become self-governing, habituated to monitor in detail and correct their own conduct. In this sense, through discipline, order would be produced from within the individual, rather than imposed from outside. The emergence of the disciplinary society (see Chapter 3, Section 3 in this volume) was nowhere clearer than in the displacement of violence by reform in the system of punishment:

> By the end of the eighteenth and the beginning of the nineteenth century, the gloomy festival of punishment was dying out ... In this transformation, two processes were at work. They did not have quite the same chronology or the same *raison d'être*. The first was the disappearance of punishment as a spectacle. ... And whatever theatrical elements it still retained were now downgraded, as if the functions of the penal ceremony were gradually ceasing to be understood, as if this rite that 'concluded the crime' was suspected of being in some undesirable way linked with it. It was as if the punishment was thought to equal, if not to exceed, in savagery the crime itself, to accustom the spectators to a ferocity from which one wished to divert them, to show them the frequency of crime, to make the executioner resemble a criminal, judges murders, to reverse roles at the last moment, to make the tortured criminal an object of pity or admiration. ... The public execution is now seen as a hearth in which violence bursts again into flame.

> Punishment, then, will tend to become the most hidden part of the penal process. This has several consequences: it leaves the domain of more or less everyday perception and enters that of abstract consciousness; its effectiveness is seen as resulting from its inevitability, not from its visible intensity; it is the certainty of being punished and not the horrifying spectacle of public punishment that must discourage crime ...

The disappearance of public executions marks therefore the decline of the spectacle; but it also marks a slackening of the hold on the body. ... One no longer touched the body, or at least as little as possible, and then only to reach something other than the body itself. It might be objected that imprisonment, confinement, forced labour, penal servitude, prohibition from entering certain areas, deportation – which have occupied such an important place in modern penal systems – are 'physical' penalties: unlike fines, for example, they directly affect the body. But the punishment–body relation is not the same as it was in the torture during public executions. The body now serves as an instrument or intermediary: if one intervenes upon it to imprison it, or to make it work, it is in order to deprive the individual of a liberty that is regarded both as a right and as property. The body, according to this penalty, is caught up in a system of constraints and privations, obligations and prohibitions. ... [P]unishment has become an economy of suspended rights.

(Foucault, 1991 [1977], pp. 8–11)

For Foucault, then, violence ceased to be an appropriate form of punishment partly because it called forth passions that were contrary to those it was desired to effect. Violence itself came to be understood not only as terrifying and off-putting, but also as brutalising through engendering an eagerness to resort to violence and bloodshed. Violence called forth undisciplined passions and encouraged people to abandon their restraint and forget their self-government. But violence also ceased to be central to the system of punishment because the target ceased to be the exemplary body and became the individual mind. In switching from the exemplar to the individual, the 'micro-techniques' of power Foucault describes were less extreme, less forceful than the symbolic torture of the early modern period, but at the same time they were more pervasive, more relentless.

This is not to say that techniques of public shaming were absent from this mode of discipline, for, as Andy Croll (1999) has demonstrated, these remained central to the disciplinary project in practice. However, the techniques used to administer this were very different from the 'rough music' of the preceding century, involving surveillance by the uniformed body of the police and other agents, not always those of the state. These techniques of discipline extended into the home and school, through pedagogy and the self-help manual. In this sense Foucault's account of disciplinary power is comparable to the notion of social control in its pervasiveness, involving many agencies acting in diverse fields of life in order to act on individuals in particular ways. Yet it is also different in other respects. What Foucault is talking about here is a change in the 'mentality' of punishment. This is not change that is necessarily driven by a particular social, political or economic agenda.

Neither is it necessarily dependent upon a transformation in economic conditions, nor upon the assumption of social power by a new group. Rather, it represents a gradual change in the way the nature and purpose of punishment is understood. This is a change in the concept of punishment, but also in its practice. We do not need to understand this as a deliberate programme of change or reform, comparable with the eighteenth-century movements for the reformation of manners, or the 'social police' of early Victorian Britain, although there were explicit programmes of rational reform. For Foucault, these changes happened as much through the gradual dissemination of ideas about discipline from the military to the educational and other spheres as they did through the actions of enlightened statesmen or intellectuals. These were practical techniques which were transmitted, learned and improved for specific, local reasons, but underlying which was an (often unacknowledged) principle of government.

Foucault spoke principally about the state here, particularly changes in the nature of criminal justice, the prime site for the legitimate deployment of force. But, as Croll (1999) and others have made clear, Foucault's ideas have much wider implications for the social order in general. Indeed, Foucault goes on to detail not simply the birth of the prison, but the emergence of 'disciplinary society'; that is, a social form whose central element is the disciplinary mentality he described. Proper conduct in the disciplinary society was restrained, efficient; indeed, Foucault speaks of a 'bodily economy'. In the disciplinary society spontaneous or extreme violence represents the very opposite of the disciplined self-control idealised in these practices and in a very visible manner, rendering the violent individual a prime target for disciplinary intervention and correction. Spontaneous or random violence was outlawed in general; violence was to be used only in targeted form, with a specific end.

This mentality of government was characterised by a concern for reason, order and regularity. Economy is included in this concern, but more in the sense of the economy of movement, in contrast to wasteful, expansive or violent gesture. In this sense, the introduction of a particular form of reason into the government of conduct might imply that customary behaviour, 'rough music' and shaming rituals, ancient folk customs and the use of violence as a system of social regulation are problematised as modes of conduct, not principally because they are 'immoral' or subversive, but precisely because they are customary and irrational, not logical.

This 'rationalisation' of government extended beyond the 'micro' level of disciplinary practices to the 'macro' level of the structure and conceptualisation of government more broadly, what Foucault (2000b)

Figure 4.4
Newgate Prison
galleries, *c*.1900: the
nineteenth-century
prison, emblematic of
the emergence of the
'disciplined society'

termed the 'governmentality' – that is, the way of thinking about how government should be exercised (see Chapter 3, Section 3). One particularly prominent aspect of the rationalisation of government was an attempt to eradicate the ancient, fragmented systems of authority, local privilege and customary rules which characterised most systems of European government, replacing them with a consolidated, unitary system of power organised on a rational basis. This involved the codification of law, institutional reform, centralisation and the establishment of uniformity within political units. According to the Foucauldian argument, the eighteenth century witnessed a new way of thinking about how government should be conducted. Traditionally, government had been understood in terms of the exercise of particular local or individual rights and privileges and questions of sovereignty, essentially who had the right to exercise power in particular places or circumstances. Gradually, however, the dynastic conflicts and wars of religion that had plagued the sixteenth and seventeenth centuries were replaced with increasing political stability, and the concern became the most effective conduct of government and the maximisation of national resources in the context of interstate competition. The concern of this 'reason of state' was to devise a mechanism for organising public life so as to best promote these ends. A necessary part of this cultivation of state power was the health, wealth and well-being of its members, a subject termed 'bio-power' by Foucault.

As part of this concern with maximising the 'bio-power' of populations, governments began to regulate forms of conduct which were seen to detract from the well-being of the state. At the same time, governments started to think in terms of populations and demographics, rather than individuals, regions or communities (Dean, 1999, pp. 73–112). In doing so, it has been argued, they were in the process creating the idea of 'the social' itself. 'The social' emerged as a concept over the late eighteenth and early nineteenth centuries through an understanding that human relations were shaped by processes and forces that were beyond the individual or group (Rose, 1999, pp. 101–19). Populations were subject to norms of death, birth, disease and so on that were regular, whatever the fortunes of particular individuals within them. The task of government was increasingly seen as ensuring the conditions under which these processes could enfold according to their 'natural' laws, interfering in them as little as possible. This was both efficient, requiring less investment from government, and effective.

This new 'mentality' of government, or 'governmentality' as it is often termed in sociological literature influenced by Foucault, not only implied a new structure of government, but a new relationship with the governed (Rose, 1999, pp. 40–7; see Chapter 3, Section 3). If government was to operate according to the principles of reason, then the governed would have to do so as well, otherwise the logical structure of rule would fail and would have failed in its duty. Further, if rational and particularly efficient government were to be possible, it would mean that people would to a large extent have to be capable of governing themselves. This would release government from the expensive and difficult task of directly governing every form of interaction, while ensuring that society acted as fruitfully as possible. The shaping of rational, independent individuals, then, was as much related to making people governable, and thus a certain form of government practical, as it was to instilling specific cultural values in the population. The institutions of education and criminal justice that mediated these values sought to transmit rationality throughout society.

6   The civilising process

Whereas the advocates of 'social control' saw the emergence of disciplined, restrained and non-violent conduct as a product of government 'from above', enforcing the logic of capital, Norbert Elias, writing in the 1930s, envisioned the transformation in conduct as something that emerged as part of a *civilising process* within social relations. For Elias, the modern social form emerged through a process of differentiation and imitation, whereby individuals and groups sought to alter their conduct to distinguish themselves from their social inferiors, who in turn imitated the new models of 'refined' behaviour to claim access to the world of privilege. This process of change in conduct, increasing 'refinement' and 'civility', Elias (2000 [1939]) argues, is directly related to the structure of the personality and the form of society more broadly. But although the logic driving this transformation is largely 'internal' to particular groups, it is not totally dissociated from institutional change. As will become apparent in this section, this increasing civility depends upon the monopolisation of force within the modern state and the emergence of stable conditions of life. It is only this stability that allows the emergence of the modern, 'civilised' personality and its associated modes of conduct.

Elias contrasts the form of the modern personality with its early modern and medieval counterparts. Whereas the modern personality is characterised by restraint, the early modern world was characterised, he argues, by greater extremes of emotion and forceful expression:

> Much of what appears contradictory to us – the intensity of their piety, the violence of their fear of hell, their guilt feelings, their penitence, the immense outbursts of joy and gaiety, the sudden flaring and the uncontrollable force of their hatred and belligerence – all these, like the rapid changes of mood, are in reality symptoms of one and the same structuring of the emotional life. The drives, the emotions were vented more freely, more directly, more openly than later.
>
> (Elias, 2000 [1939], p. 168)

The modern personality, by contrast, is restrained, both in expression and experience. These different forms of personality have distinctive modes of conduct associated with them, again characterised by expression and restraint. The wildness, boisterousness and indulgence of early modern life is contrasted to the closely (self-) regulated, cautious, restrained behaviour of modernity. Elias goes on to chart this transformation in detail, exploring ways in which conventions in eating, dress, deportment, interaction and so forth changed across Europe.

For example, Elias quotes from a series of conduct manuals that emerged in the early modern period and sought to proscribe previously common behaviour. The following injunctions (Elias, 2000 [1939], pp. 111–12) were given in relation to bodily functions: '[I]t does not befit a modest, honourable man to relieve nature in the presence of other people' (1588); 'One should not, like rustics who have not been to court or lived among refined and honourable people, relieve oneself without shame or reserve in front of ladies, or before the doors or windows of court chambers or other rooms' (1570); 'Let no one, whoever he may be, before, at, or after meals, early or late, foul the staircases, corridors or closets with urine or other filth, but go to suitable, prescribed places for such relief' (1589). Likewise, not only should one control one's bodily functions and only carry them out in privacy, but one should also control the way in which one displayed and addressed one's own body more directly:

> It is a part of decency and modesty to cover all parts of the body except the head and hands. You should care, so far as you can, not to touch with your bare hand any part of the body that is not normally uncovered. ...

> It is never proper to speak of the parts of the body that should be hidden, nor of certain bodily necessities to which Nature has subjected us, nor even to mention them. (1729)
>
> (Elias, 2000 [1939], pp. 112, 113)

In these ways people were encouraged to govern their conduct, limiting the expression or performance of natural bodily functions when in the presence of others (and even, in certain circumstances, when alone). Given the existence of such instructions in conduct manuals, it is likely that these forms of conduct could not be taken for granted, they required instruction. What came to be considered 'civilised' behaviour had to be learned. At the same time, this was not necessarily a matter of direct government; rather, these conduct manuals were written to assist those who desired to engage in 'civilised' society to act upon themselves in order to fit in to the 'honourable' circle.

civilised behaviour learned

Elias argued that there was a direct relationship between the extremes of personality and uninhibited conduct characteristic of medieval and early modern people and the nature of early modern society, one that depended upon the likelihood of violence: 'In the social spaces where violence is an unavoidable and everyday event, and where individuals' chains of dependence are relatively short, because they largely subsist directly from the produce of their own land, a strong and continuous moderation of drives is neither necessary, possible nor useful'

Figure 4.5
The governing of
conduct and the
requirement to carry
out bodily functions
in private led to a
programme of public-
toilet building in the
nineteenth century

(Elias, 2000 [1939], p. 370). Elias is arguing here that the self-governing, restrained personality served no purpose in early modern society: there was nothing to be gained by careful and prudent conduct, by a restriction of immediate gratification for long-term goals, because early modern life was so precarious that these aspirations would very likely be upset by the intrusion of some calamitous, probably violent event, either from within or without the community. The satisfaction of desires could not be deferred, or they might never be realised. It was only once there was some security for their realisation in the future that it began to make sense for people to restrain some emotional or physical drives in favour of greater benefits which they could reasonably expect to obtain at a later time as a consequence of resisting immediate gratification. This weighing of the satisfaction of physical or emotional desires or drives in relation to their likely outcomes is what Elias calls the 'drive economy'.

The link to violence is central to Elias's account. In the early modern world, violence was an ever-present threat between individuals and communities, and the greater this level of direct threat, the more chance that the desires of particular individuals could be thwarted by others, or that they could be subjected to pain and violence by them. It is clear that Elias considers that violence was one of the principal means through which the various desires of people were fulfilled. This was a double-edged sword, because this situation provided the possibility for immediate and extensive fulfilment of desire, while at the same time opening up the possibility of being entirely subjected to the desires of another:

In this social structure the victorious have a greater possibility of giving free rein to their drives and affects, but greater too is the direct threat to one man from the affects of another, and more omnipresent the possibility of subjugation and boundless humiliation if one falls into the power of another.

(Elias, 2000 [1939], p. 371)

This had a specific impact on the structure of the personality and therefore on how people conducted themselves: 'The greater spontaneity of drives and the higher measure of physical threat, that are encountered whenever strong and stable central monopolies have not yet formed are, as can be seen, complementary' (Elias, 2000 [1939], p. 371).

It is the generalised, dispersed nature of violence that gives this social form its characteristic mode of existence and which defines the personality structure common in the early modern period:

To the structure of this society with its extreme polarisation, its continuous uncertainties, corresponds the structure of the individuals who form it and of their conduct. Just as in the relations between person and danger as well as the possibility of victory or liberation arise more abruptly, more suddenly and incalculably before the individual, so he or she is thrown more frequently and directly between pleasure and pain.

(Elias, 2000 [1939], p. 371)

In such situations, 'The personality, if we may put it thus, is incomparably more ready and accustomed to leap with undiminishing intensity from one extreme to the other, and slight impressions, uncontrollable associations are often enough to induce these immense fluctuations' (Elias, 2000 [1939], p. 372).

How did this situation change, and the modern personality and 'civilised' modes of conduct emerge? It is the restriction of the right to use violence, Elias argues, that generates the stability which leads to the development of 'civility'. It is only once there is a certain degree of stability and the expectation of a reasonable chance of seeing them come to fruition that long-term plans and the deferral of immediate gratification of desire in favour of greater long-term gain become a sensible course of action because, 'Through the formation of monopolies of force, the threat which one person represents for another is subject to stricter control and becomes more calculable. Everyday life is freer from sudden reversals of fortune' (Elias, 2000 [1939], p. 372).

Just as social life becomes more predictable and less subject to random fluctuation, so does the personality and its attendant modes of conduct:

> As the structure of human relations changes, as monopoly
> organizations of physical force develop and the individual is held no
> longer in the sway of constant feuds and wars but rather in the more
> permanent compulsions of peaceful functions based on the
> acquisition of money or prestige, affect-expressions too slowly
> gravitate towards a middle line. The fluctuations in behaviour and
> effects do not disappear, but are moderated. The peaks and abysses are
> smaller, the changes less abrupt.
>
> (Elias, 2000 [1939], p. 372)

It is important to note that the way in which desires are gratified
changes here. Violence and physical domination cease to be quite so
central, while the accumulation of money and prestige, only possible
with stability, assume greater significance. It is significant that the
acquisition of money and prestige has often been linked to the
emergence of 'civilised' modes of conduct. Trade, in particular, has been
associated with a form of conduct which necessitates a degree of
measured and civilised behaviour, where inspiring the trust of one's
trading partner depends upon one's own predictability and connections
to respectable society.

However, this does not mean that violence is no longer central to the
nature of the social form:

> Even in this form as a control organization ... physical violence and
> the threat emanating from it have a determining influence on
> individuals in society, whether they know it or not. It is, however, no
> longer a perpetual insecurity that it brings into the life of the
> individual, but a peculiar form of security. ... [A] continuous, uniform
> pressure is exerted on individual life by the physical violence stored
> behind the scenes of everyday life, a pressure totally familiar and
> hardly perceived, conduct and drive economy having been adjusted
> from earliest youth to this social structure.
>
> (Elias, 2000 [1939], p. 372)

The presence of violence in the background of society, through the
instruments that monopolise force, defines the mode of conduct. We
might say that the presence and visibility of society's instruments of
coercion provide the reassurance and security that (perhaps
unconsciously) give individuals confidence to regulate their own drive
economy and thus perpetuate a pacific social order, as well as acting
directly to prevent serious contraventions of the non-violent code.

This is not to say that the regulation of conduct here is entirely coercive,
acting from outside the individual; rather:

> This operates to a considerable extent through the medium of his or
> her own reflection. It is normally only potentially present in society,

as an agency of control; the actual compulsion is one that the individual exerts in himself or herself either as a result of his knowledge of the possible consequences of his or her moves ... or as a result of corresponding gestures of adults which have helped to pattern his or her own behaviour as a child.

(Elias, 2000 [1939], pp. 372–3)

The 'drive economy' is modified in the following way:

As the monopolization of physical force reduces the fear and terror one person must have for another, but at the same time reduces the possibility of causing others terror, fear, or torment, and therefore certain possibilities of pleasurable emotional release, the constant self-control to which the individual is now accustomed seeks to reduce the contrasts and sudden switches in conduct, and the affective charge of all self-expression. The pressures operating upon the individual now tend to produce a transformation of the whole drive and affect economy in the direction of a more continuous, stable and even regulation of drives and affects in all areas of conduct, in all sectors of life.

(Elias, 2000 [1939], pp. 373–4)

Drawing upon the work of Elias, Wood (2003) has called this the 'civilising bargain', where individual or communal power is ceded to the state (principally the police) on the condition that it monopolises violence, preventing its occurrence between individuals and groups. Wood relates this directly to the transformation of conduct in Britain. Middle- and working-class communities in nineteenth-century Britain, Wood argues, gradually acquiesced to the intrusion of police and their role in regulating conduct, relinquishing the right to order their own communities through exemplary violence, in return for effective maintenance of general conditions of peace, order and security in daily life. The emergence of the modern 'civilised' mode of conduct is not seen as the imposition of bourgeois values for the construction of industrial culture, nor is it seen as the march of discipline. Rather, civility emerges as a bargain in which the right to force is traded for the effective provision of security.

From the Eliasian perspective, then, there is a reciprocal relationship between the nature and location of violence and the social order. The less that random violence becomes a feature of everyday life through increasingly effective government of peace and security, the more people develop a psychology of self-control, leading to less tolerance for violence and less propensity to commit acts of violence. This is a self-driving process whereby the degree of 'civility' increases inexorably through this reciprocal structure. Its only precondition is the effectiveness of the security provided by the authorities who claim the monopoly on violence. It is here, Wood (2003) argues, that most conflicts arise, as expectations of security and intolerance of violence rise inexorably to a level where the degree of security expected from the state is almost impossible for it to meet.

Elias suggests that the civilising process works through increasing differentiation in conduct, with greater and greater attention being applied to the minutiae of everyday life. This process of differentiation is central to the formation of psychological structure and identity. Particularly fine judgement was reserved for certain modes of interpersonal conduct. In contrast to some positions on the subject, that saw modern state-controlled violence as the imposition of middle-class values on the working class, Wood (2004, pp. 31–2) argues: 'The emergence of a "civilised" mentality of violence was concurrent with a foundational period in middle-class identity. Rather than a pre-formed middle-class identity clashing with violence, new attitudes toward violence contributed to the formation and maintenance of a fractious and unstable middle-class identity.' Self-restraint and control became the hegemonic values around which nineteenth-century notions of masculinity and respectability were anchored, and both middle- and working-class men often worked hard to conform to these ideals. As such, it was often the respectable working class who acted most forcefully to discipline the 'rougher' elements of their own communities in order to maintain their respectability in the face of wider public scrutiny. Violence ceased to be a means of ordering these communities and became problematic for the 'respectable' members of both the working and middle classes. Violence became a problem not only because it undermined stability and unsettled the expectations upon which fulfilment of immediate drives was deferred, but also because it undermined the claims of these communities to the civility that was taken as a marker of membership of 'respectable' society. In order to achieve this condition of respectability or civility these communities ceded the right to mediate these values to the state which, through the institutions of police and criminal justice, was to provide the order that was a condition of civility and to patrol its boundaries.

7   Conclusion: violence, institutions and the social

You have been presented with a series of explanations for the transformation of violence from a mechanism of ordering to a social problem over the late eighteenth and early nineteenth centuries. For advocates of the social control thesis, violence was monopolised by the state, dominated by the middle class, in order to shape the conduct of individuals so as to enable the most effective operation of the capitalist economy. For Foucault, violence and the customary behaviour of which it was a part was problematised by the emergence of new ways of thinking about government and conduct, which prioritised the rational, economic deportment of the individual body and the organisation of resources. For Elias, the emergence of civility was a process of differentiation and aspiration, whereby people sought to regulate their conduct so as to assure their status as part of the 'respectable' population, in doing so necessarily distancing themselves from those who failed to do so. At the same time, however, civility was only able to emerge, and to survive, through the monopolisation of violence by the state.

It is common to see these as competing explanations for change and to attempt to critique them and adjudicate between them according to their relative merits. But do we need to view them in these terms? Perhaps rather than dwell on the various possible critiques of each position, we might conclude by reflecting more on the broader implications of these arguments. First, in all these explanations in this chapter a direct relationship was understood to exist between forms of (largely public) conduct and the nature of the social order, which shifted from a disorderly one characterised by extremes of expression and violence, to an orderly one characterised by restrained civility, where violence was the monopoly of the state and only used to prevent breaches in civil conduct. The location of violence within society, then, has generally been seen to determine its nature. The assumption in all these academic accounts, and of many of the contemporary commentators in the periods discussed, was that the way people conduct themselves, and the way they are themselves conducted or governed, is one of the primary ways in which both the social order and the character of the individual are defined. There is a reciprocal relationship between the two: the nature of the individual personality is felt to be heavily influenced by the modes of conduct dominant in society and to which individuals are exposed. At the same time, in order to change society, it was increasingly felt that one must act upon individuals and particular transgressions and encourage them to act upon themselves, rather than perform communal restorations of the social order or exemplary punishment.

Beyond this, it is argued in the Foucauldian literature that it was precisely in the process of thinking about how conduct should be governed, and in the process of its government, that the very idea of 'society' as a discrete entity, a domain characterised by demographic regularities of birth, disease, crime, violence and death, separate from the economic, the political, the religious or the individual, came to be conceptualised and acted upon. If the government of conduct was one way in which 'the social' itself came to have an independent existence, this cannot be dissociated from a second facet of all these accounts: the mediating role of institutions of the state. In contrast to the early modern world, where communities acted directly upon their own members to enforce the norms they valued, modern society is characterised by the existence of mediating institutions (police forces, welfare networks and so on) acting as an interface between one individual and another, between different groups and between the individual or particular groups and society at large. These institutions are responsible not only for directly administering the normative values determined by the society (or those sections of society in a position to direct these institutions), through discouraging, preventing or punishing acts which contravene those values, but also, particularly for Elias, for providing the conditions under which it may be possible for people to mould their own conduct according to new sets of values, without the threat of interference from others. The establishment of mediating institutions between individuals, groups and society at large must be seen as central to the definition and production of the social as a discrete domain.

References

Amussen, S.D. (1995) 'Punishment, discipline and power: the social meanings of violence in early modern England', *Journal of British Studies*, vol. 34, no. 1, pp. 1–34.

Croll, A. (1999) 'Street disorder, surveillance and shame: regulating behaviour in the late Victorian British town', *Social History*, vol. 24, no. 3, pp. 250–68.

Dean, M. (1999) *Governmentality: Power and Rule in Modern Society*, London, Sage.

Debray, R. (2000) *Transmitting Culture* (trans. E. Rauth), New York, NY, Columbia University Press.

Donajgrodzki, A.P. (1977a) 'Introduction' in Donajgrodzki (ed.) (1977).

Donajgrodzki, A.P. (1977b) '"Social Police" and the bureaucratic elite: a vision of order in the age of reform' in Donajgrodzki (ed.) (1977).

Donajgrodzki, A.P. (ed.) (1977) *Social Control in Nineteenth-Century Britain*, London, Croom Helm.

Elias, N. (2000) [1939] *The Civilizing Process: Sociogenetic and Psychogenetic Investigations* (trans. E. Jephcott, revised edn), Oxford, Blackwell.

Emsley, C. (1996) *The Police: A Political and Social History*, London, Longman.

Faubion, J.D. (ed.) (2000) *Power: The Essential Works of Foucault, 1954–1984*, vol. 3, London, Penguin.

Foucault, M. (1991) [1977] *Discipline and Punish: The Birth of the Prison* (trans. A. Sheridan), London, Penguin.

Foucault, M. (2000a) 'The subject and power' in Faubion (ed.) (2000).

Foucault, M. (2000b) 'Governmentality' in Faubion (ed.) (2000).

Gilmour, I. (1992) *Riots, Risings and Revolutions: Governance and Violence in Eighteenth-Century England*, London, Hutchinson.

Rose, N. (1999) *Powers of Freedom: Reframing Political Thought*, Cambridge, Cambridge University Press.

Storch, R.B. (1976) 'The policeman as domestic missionary: urban discipline and popular culture in northern England 1850–1880', *Journal of Social History*, vol. 9, no. 4, pp. 481–509.

Thompson, E.P. (1993) *Customs in Common*, London, Penguin.

Weber, M. (1978 [1922]) *Economy and Society: An Outline of Interpretive Sociology*, Berkeley, CA, University of California Press.

Wood, J.C. (2003) 'Self-policing and the policing of the self: violence, protection and the civilizing bargain in Britain', *Crime, Histoire & Sociétés/Crime History & Societies*, vol. 7, no. 1, pp. 109–28.

Wood, J.C. (2004) 'A useful savagery: the invention of violence in nineteenth-century England', *Journal of Victorian Culture*, vol. 9, no. 1, pp. 22–42.

Chapter 5
Human conduct in extreme situations

Charles Turner

Contents

1   Introduction

In his autobiography, *Goodbye to All That*, the poet Robert Graves recalls the following incident from the First World War:

> Beaumont had been telling how he had won about five pounds' worth of francs in the sweepstake after the Rue de Bois show: a sweepstake of the sort that leaves no bitterness behind it. Before a show, the platoon pools all its available cash and the survivors divide it up afterwards. Those who are killed can't complain, the wounded would have given far more than that to escape as they have, and the unwounded regard the money as a consolation prize for still being here.
>
> (Graves, 1999 [1929], p. 118)

Scenes and practices like this, in which the seemingly normal rules of behaviour are suspended (and in which a bombardment and massed charge towards enemy machine guns is described as 'a show') occur repeatedly in the memoirs of those who have fought in wars, and they raise for us the question of how we are to make sense of human conduct in the kind of extreme situations that wars exemplify. This is a challenge for sociology because, while such material continues to fascinate historians, psychologists, and historians of literature, sociology has traditionally been about the regularity and orderliness of human conduct in what we might call normal circumstances. You have studied examples of such conduct in the previous chapters.

The term **extreme situations** appears in a famous essay by the psychologist Bruno Bettelheim, published in 1943 and based on his experiences in the Dachau concentration camp:

> We find ourselves in an extreme situation when we are suddenly catapulted into a set of conditions where our old adaptive mechanisms and values do not apply any more and when some of them may even endanger the life they were meant to protect. Then we are, so to say, stripped of our whole defensive system and thrown back to rock bottom – whence we must carve out a new set of attitudes, values, and ways of living as required by the new situation.
>
> (Bettelheim, 1979 [1943], p. 11)

In this chapter I will try to find ways of thinking sociologically about human conduct in extreme situations. My examples will be drawn from the scholarly, literary and autobiographical writing that has grown up in the twentieth century around two substantive areas: war and totalitarianism. There are two main reasons for this choice. First, an almost unimaginable number of people had their lives changed forever or simply destroyed by these phenomena in the twentieth century. Second, the conduct of human beings in war and in the Nazi and Soviet camps has been seen as more than something of intrinsic interest. For some philosophers, it tells us something about the nature of morality; for some psychologists, something about human motivation; and for some sociologists, something about the dynamics of group life and about the nature of modernity. I say 'some' because there is an unresolved question of just how much continuity there is between conduct in these circumstances and conduct more generally. The word 'extreme' leaves this question open in ways that words like 'exceptional' or 'unique' do not. As the Bulgarian psychologist Tzvetan Todorov put it:

> My intent is to use the extreme as an instrument, a sort of magnifying glass that can bring into focus certain things that in the normal course of human affairs remain blurry ... I think the camps and the experiences of those interned in them represent a double extremity, which is to say, they are extreme in two distinct senses of the word: the camps are the extreme manifestation of the totalitarian regime, itself the extreme form of modern political life.
>
> (Todorov, 2000 [1986], pp. 27–8)

Here I am interested less in Todorov's diagnosis of modernity than in the first part of the quotation: if the extreme situation is a magnifying glass, then we must assume that the thing which it brings into focus was there all along, in other words that there are possibilities and tendencies which exist in all human affairs but which come to the surface only in situations which prompt them to do so. Now we know, from the literature of warfare and of the camps, of numerous examples of conduct in which the veneer of civilisation slipped away and human beings were left in what we might call their raw state, competing with one another in a battle for survival and pushing familiar ethical concerns to one side. But Todorov puts the matter as he does because he wishes to impress upon us that the opposite was equally true. As the Spanish writer and Buchenwald survivor Jorge Semprun put it in *The Long Voyage*: 'In the camps man becomes a creature capable of stealing a mate's bread, or propelling him towards death. But in the camps, man becomes that invincible being capable of sharing his last cigarette butt, his last piece of bread, his last breath, to sustain his fellow man' (Semprun, 1964 [1963], p. 60). Primo Levi too, who experienced a more extreme situation still in Auschwitz, wrote that in the camps one could observe the same range of moral behaviour as one might anywhere else, only with heightened intensity and with more direct consequences (1987 [1958]). A fellow survivor even described Auschwitz as 'my university'.

Against this stands the argument that life in the camps or in the trenches, life lived in the proximity of death, represents something unprecedented, something that requires us to develop entirely new categories in order to make sense of it. It is unique and so shocking that nothing can properly describe it. According to this view, the thousands of books of literature and testimony that have been written on the subject are attempts to get to the bottom of something that remains unfathomable even to those who participated in it. The direct and straightforward language in which many of these books are written – Levi (1987 [1958]) said that when writing *If This Is a Man* 'questions of style never occurred to me' – does not make the reality of what happened any more available to the reader.

There is truth in both positions. Indeed, the same author will often oscillate between them. I will suggest that the extreme situations considered in this chapter are qualitatively different from 'normal' situations, but that if we make use of categories of sufficient generality and scope, we may be able to make some sense of them. This will involve either moving a little beyond some of the sociological categories deployed in previous chapters, or showing the points at which they run up against the limits of their usefulness. For instance, sociologists studying the 'arts of government' (see Chapter 3 in this volume) or the state's role in the management of violence (see Chapter 4 in this volume) or ideas about 'insurance' (see Chapter 2 in this volume) will readily talk of the relationship between 'the individual and society'. But what if human beings have been placed in situations in which society in any meaningful sense of the term appears to be absent, or temporarily suspended? To do justice to this, I think that we need to be hesitant in our use of standard sociological terminology and to supplement it with terminology drawn from other disciplines, and also to allow the voices of witnesses – many of whom were, in any case, philosophers and writers – to be heard.

1.1 The self and the world

In much of what follows I will talk not of 'the individual and society' but of the self and the world. This might not sound like a significant distinction but I make it because the scholarly literature on what we might call selfhood and worldhood is often more sensitive to the vulnerabilities and uncertainties which can affect our sense of self and our sense of external reality. The term 'self' is probably familiar enough to you (see Chapter 1 in this volume), but there are philosophical and psychological and sociological views of selfhood. The one that informs this chapter is derived largely from the work of the sociologist Erving Goffman, and its main claim is that, regardless of whether we say that the self is something we have or something we are, something which is on display before others or hidden behind surface appearances, all human beings face the problem of how a sense of self is sustained. Further, and this is the focus of Goffman's work, a sense of self depends crucially upon what he calls 'props'. Props include such things as one's clothes, one's haircut, one's characteristic mode of bodily comportment – posture and gesture – and one's use of language, including the stories one tells about oneself. Goffman showed that without these external markers of selfhood, without the 'matter' or material resources that the social world makes available, the individual is deprived of the means with which he or she can sustain a sense of self over time. Take these props away from a person, Goffman says, and the self becomes an unstable thing, something that, as he put it in *Asylums*, 'can be seen as something outside oneself that can be constructed, lost and rebuilt, all with great speed and with some equanimity' (Goffman, 1963, p. 151). He called this process 'the mortification of self'. Goffman believed that, in the case of the mental institution, this process took time, so much so that he referred, ironically, to 'the moral career of the mental patient'. The individual undergoes a series of mortifying experiences, beginning with betrayal by an 'alienative coalition' of friends and relatives who have her or him admitted, passing through the removal of external markers of identity and their substitution by institutional ones, such as a haircut and uniform, and ending with 'the ward system', the division of the hospital into a series of wards whose conditions vary considerably. The most important feature of the ward system is its arbitrariness and lack of rigidity – even if an individual reaches an improved or privileged position within the ward system, this is provisional and may be removed at will by the authorities. Goffman believed that the effect of this process was not to instil in the individual a respect for rigid rules and procedures, but to induce a 'civic apathy' in which one's own self was not to be taken seriously and in which individuals became indifferent towards their own fate. Conduct in such an institution becomes what he calls 'a shameless game', and displays 'moral loosening'.

Goffman's theory of the mortification of self also implies that nobody sustains a sense of self in isolation from others. In her fine meditation on war and torture, *The Body in Pain* (1985), subtitled, significantly, 'the making and unmaking of the world', the literary theorist Elaine Scarry argues that everyday objects, whether or not we have produced them ourselves, are a means by which we project ourselves into the world, and through which we demonstrate our social membership beyond the limits of our own bodies. The everyday markers of identity that extreme forms of incarceration take away are not only markers of selfhood but are a means of communication with others and hence markers of a social world sustained in common. However individual is our way of speaking, for instance, it draws upon a shared repertoire of expressive possibilities, a tradition of speaking. The stories we tell about ourselves are only comprehensible to others if they share to some extent the way of life in which our biographies are rooted, just as the way we hold our bodies during conversation is a marker of a certain cultural and political belonging (see the discussion of Marcel Mauss's views in Chapters 1 and 3 in this volume):

> The extent to which in ordinary peacetime activity the nation-state resides unnoticed in the intricate recesses of personhood, penetrates the deepest layers of consciousness and manifests itself in the body itself is hard to assess; for it seems at any given moment 'hardly' there, yet seems at many moments ... *there* in the learned postures, gestures, gait, the ease or reluctance with which it breaks into a smile; *there* in the regional accent, the disposition of the tongue, mouth, and throat, the elaborate and intricate play of small muscles that may also be echoed and magnified throughout the whole body, as when a man moves across the room, there radiates across his shoulder, head, hips, legs, and arms the history of his early boyhood years of life in Georgia and his young adolescence in Manhattan.
>
> (Scarry, 1985, pp. 108–9)

1.2 World and worldlessness

Use of the term 'world' has a philosophical heritage as complex as that of 'self'. It is a more general term than 'society' and I use it here because we are trying to make sense of situations in which there is frequent reference to the inhuman, not to say 'animal' conditions in which people were having to conduct themselves. One useful idea for our purposes comes from the tradition of philosophical anthropology. The main claim here is that human beings are distinguished from all other creatures by virtue of the fact that they have no natural environment, no niche into which they fit. Accordingly, they have no natural survival instinct, and are 'eccentric' and 'artificial' creatures who instead, and uniquely, have to construct their own means of survival, shelter and so on. What they have instead of an environment, is a world (Gehlen, 1988 [1940]), and they are 'world open' in so far as they are, potentially, constantly confronted with the need to make a decision about how to operate in this world, a decision which other creatures do not have to make because they act on instinct. This basic human lack is the point at which culture and society come in. Abstracting from the variety of cultures and societies which have existed throughout history, we can say that the most basic rationale for culture – social institutions, belief systems, forms of symbolisation and so on – is to act as a mediator between the self and the world, to turn our world openness into something we can cope with. Institutions and traditions, rules and customs, make a world liveable in by putting a potentially hostile reality at a distance, shielding us from it. Without them we would all be left alone, overwhelmed by the need to make decisions that our instinctual equipment does not provide for. We would face what Ernst Jünger (whose views will be discussed in more detail in Section 3.2) called 'the absolutism of reality' (Blumenberg, 1985, p. 3). Institutions, belief systems and customs relieve us of the burden of having to work out the difference between the things in the world we have to attend to and those we can disregard; they ensure that we are not, as Freud put it, overwhelmed by stimuli (Freud, 1984 [1920], p. 299).

I have put matters in these fairly philosophical terms because so much of the literature on the camps refers to such phenomena as the breakdown of civilisation, the reduction of human beings to the status of animals, inhuman conditions and so on. In other words, it refers to situations in which the accoutrements of a liveable life, the basis for any sort of human conduct, were placed in jeopardy. Having a sense of what was placed in jeopardy will also enable us to understand some of the means of survival that did remain available to those caught up in extreme situations.

1.3 Teaching aims

The aims of this chapter are to:

- appreciate the distinctiveness and intrinsic interest of those extreme situations that arose within twentieth-century politics

- consider extreme situations as challenges to the sociological understanding of conduct

- suggest a terminology with which to make sense of them, centring on the tools and techniques for sustaining a sense of self and world

- appreciate the efforts that people make to sustain a sense of self and of the world even in circumstances in which the tools and techniques available for this task are either absent or radically restricted.

2 Concentration and labour camps

I referred earlier to Goffman's idea of a 'mortification of self' as it occurs in total institutions such as the mental hospital of the 1950s. In his Auschwitz memoir, *If This Is a Man*, Levi (1987 [1958]) expresses a similar idea in more dramatic and urgent tones:

> [F]or the first time we became aware that our language lacks words to express this offence, the demolition of a man. In a moment, with almost prophetic intuition, the reality was revealed to us: we had reached the bottom. It is not possible to sink lower than this; no

human condition is more miserable than this, nor could it conceivably be so. Nothing belongs to us anymore; they have taken away our clothes, our shoes, even our hair; if we speak, they will not listen to us, and if they listen, they will not understand. They will even take away our name: and if we want to keep it, we will have to find in ourselves the strength to do so, to manage somehow so that behind the name something of us, of us as we were, still remains.

(Levi, 1987 [1958], pp. 32–3)

Even if you have read very little about the Nazi concentration camps, the chances are that you will have seen images of prisoners with shaven heads, a striped uniform and a number looking blankly into the camera through barbed wire. Such images alone, however, tell us little about the manner in which prisoners conducted themselves in the world – or non-world – they inhabited. Levi refers at the end of the passage to 'something of us, of us as we were' remaining even after the obvious external markers of identity have been removed. We might refer here to the idea that an individual's 'character' remains, or that people retain a core sense of self inside them, a soul perhaps, regardless of the hardships inflicted on them. But a different approach invites us to consider something else 'of us' that prisoners sought to retain in the face of this process of the mortification of self.

2.1 *Moralität*, *Sittlichkeit* and hunger

The subtitle of Todorov's book, to which I referred earlier, refers to 'moral life in the concentration camps'. In trying to understand whether extreme situations reveal or do not reveal something about moral life under normal circumstances we may be tempted to ask whether life in the camps was subject to the same sort of 'rules'. But here we should be aware that much of our sense of right and wrong is not derived from a set of explicit and abstract rules which we could formulate and which we constantly have to consult, but is the product of repeated and learned forms of conduct, of sensibility, a set of dispositions – what the French sociologist Pierre Bourdieu called 'habitus' (see Chapters 1, 2 and 3 in this volume), and what the philosopher Georg Wilhelm Friedrich Hegel called *Sittlichkeit*. *Sittlichkeit* is usually translated into English as 'ethical life', but it is related to *Sitte*, the German word for custom. It refers to our involvement in the family, in associations and organisations, in our place of work, in our membership of a nation. All of these involvements help to shape the manner in which we conduct ourselves, and they often do so in ways that are not easy to express through an explicit set of rules or instructions (what Hegel called *Moralität*, morality).

The topic of conduct in extreme situations offers an interesting perspective on this. For instance, here is another passage from *If This Is a*

Man, in which Levi describes an incident that occurred early on in his incarceration:

> I must confess it: after only one week of prison, the instinct for cleanliness disappeared in me. I wander aimlessly around the washroom when I suddenly see Steinlauf, my friend aged almost fifty, with nude torso, scrub his neck and shoulder with little success (he has no soap) but great energy. Steinlauf sees me and greets me, and without preamble asks me severely why I do not wash. Why should I wash? Would I be better off than I am? Would I please someone more? Would I live a day, an hour longer? I would probably live a shorter time, because to wash is an effort, a waste of energy and warmth. Does not Steinlauf know that after half an hour with the coal sacks every difference between him and me will have disappeared? The more I think about it, the more washing one's face in our condition seems a stupid feat, even frivolous: a mechanical habit, or worse, a dismal repetition of an extinct rite. ...
>
> But Steinlauf interrupts me. ... And without interrupting the operation he administers me a complete lesson ... that precisely because the Lager [camp] was a great machine to reduce us to beasts, we must not become beasts; that even in this place one can survive, and therefore one must want to survive, to tell the story, to bear witness; and that to survive we must force ourselves to save at least the skeleton, the scaffolding, the form of civilization. We are slaves, deprived of every right, exposed to every insult, condemned to certain death, but we still possess one power, and we must defend it with all our strength for it is the last – the power to refuse our consent. So we must certainly wash our faces without soap in dirty water and dry ourselves on our jackets. We must polish our shoes, not because the regulation states it, but for dignity and propriety. We must walk erect, without dragging our feet, not in homage to Prussian discipline but to remain alive, not to begin to die.
>
> (Levi, 1987 [1958], pp. 46–7)

Levi then points out that Steinlauf's response to these circumstances, though expressed as though it conformed to a universal principle of civilisation, was the product of his background as an officer in the Austro-Hungarian army; Steinlauf's habitus, his *Sittlichkeit*, his sense of civilised bodily comportment, is peculiar to his class, education and nation, and Levi doubts whether he himself could carry on in this way in the face of the reduced circumstances which confront him, in view of the fact that his own habitus is the product of a different milieu from that of his officer friend. And what is true for Levi is true for every inmate. Tens of thousands of people with a wide range of habitus, custom or tradition are thrown together in one place. This means that if there is an order to the camp, if there are rules, a way of behaving, a code of conduct if you like, it is one that is peculiar to the camp itself, it is not part of the inherited behavioural repertoire of any of the inmates. It belongs to no recognisable tradition of practices. Indeed, so different is it that a failure to adapt, to grasp the reality of one's situation, even within a matter of minutes, may be enough to condemn a person to death. The suddenness of the transition from normal member of society to camp inmate distinguishes the concentration and forced-labour camps – and war – from the protracted and laborious processes of the mortification of self described by Goffman in *Asylums* (1963). Goffman demonstrated that it takes time to become a mental patient, and the more general claim of the symbolic interactionist tradition with which Goffman's work is often associated is that becoming a member of any subculture requires the individual to learn the ways of talking and behaving peculiar to it. It is also assumed by this tradition of enquiry that social learning requires the efforts of a significant number of other people responsible for the initiation of new members. Becoming a prisoner at Auschwitz – which meant knowing what version of a world operated there – was almost instantaneous. In a way, it had to be, and this may explain the phenomenon which Levi repeatedly returns to, the fact that bewildered new arrivals would be greeted with a beating, with blows, kicks and screaming, not only from the SS guards but from the existing inmates. One interpretation of this is that, regardless of the intentions of those who administered the beating, it functioned as a kind of tertiary socialisation, impressing upon the new arrivals the seriousness of their situation and the irrelevance of their inherited cultural baggage, and enabling them to 'become' an inmate in the shortest possible time.

This removal of props, and of inherited modes of conduct associated with them, provides an important contrast to the cases studied so far in this book, in many of which an attempt is made by political and economic institutions to develop the everyday skills of individual agents, so that the governance of modern society depends partly on providing individuals with the capacity and the tools to govern their own conduct (see Chapters 1 to 3 in this volume). The logic of the concentration camps is to remove such tools. Hence Bettelheim's use of the phrase 'rock bottom' (1979 [1943], p. 11).

But the state of being at 'rock bottom' was brought about not only by the 'policy' of concentration camp administrators. It also arose from the overwhelming presence of hunger. The situation into which individuals were thrown in the camps was so extreme, the possibility of death was so proximate, that the accumulated wisdom of any version of 'culture' or 'tradition' became irrelevant to the need that dominated everything, the need to survive. The prisoners' days would consist of seemingly endless hours of meaningless, uncreative labour, queuing for meagre rations of soup or bread, and vigilantly hanging on to whatever material possessions they were able to acquire, primarily a bowl or spoon and some bearable footwear. In his account of his time in a Soviet forced-labour camp near Archangel, *A World Apart*, dissident Polish author Gustav Herling writes:

> An orthodox Marxist would say that there is no such thing as absolute morality, since individual experience is conditioned by material surroundings. ... The experiences of the past twenty years in Germany and Soviet Russia confirm this to a certain extent. There it has been proved that when the body has reached the limit of its endurance, one cannot, as was once believed, rely on strength of character and conscious recognition of spiritual values; that there is nothing, in fact, which man cannot be forced to do by hunger and pain.
>
> (Herling, 2005 [1951], p. 131)

Numerous accounts confirm this observation. 'Who could imagine a time with no hunger? The camp is hunger. We ourselves are hunger, living hunger' (Levi, 1987 (1958], p. 80). 'My only interest was my daily soup and my piece of bread. Bread and soup – that was my whole life. I was all body, and perhaps even less: an emaciated body' (Wiesel, 1960, pp. 63–4). For Scarry, this reduction of the self to the body can be observed in more overt forms of torture; and this has implications for what it means for the individual's sense of 'world':

> As the body breaks down, it becomes increasingly the object of attention, usurping the place of all other objects, so that finally, in very old and sick people, the world may exist only in a circle two feet out from themselves; the exclusive content of perception and speech may become what was eaten, the problem of excreting, the progress of pains, the comfort or discomfort of a particular chair or bed.
>
> (Scarry, 1985, pp. 32–3)

She goes on to observe that self-inflicted physical pain has been central to many religious traditions in which asceticism, or self-denial, plays a role:

> The self-flagellation of the religious ascetic ... is not (as is often asserted) an act of denying the body, eliminating its claims from attention, but a way of so emphasizing the body that the contents of the world are cancelled and the path is clear for the entry of an unworldly, contentless force. It is in part this world-ridding, path-clearing logic that explains the obsessive presence of pain in the rituals of large, widely shared religions ... that partly explains why the crucifixion of Christ is at the centre of Christianity, why so many primitive forms of worship climax in pain ceremonies, why ... the

metaphysical is intensely coupled with the physical with the equally insistent exclusion of the middle term, world.

(Scarry, 1985, p. 34)

It is something like such an exclusion of the world that is described by numerous survivors of the camps. The difference, however, is that most of them agree that the physical was not coupled with the metaphysical at all, that physical deprivation did not enable them to see clearly where material comforts had once clouded their vision.

The truth here is that we know less about whether bodily deprivation and withdrawal of the material accoutrements of a civilised life created a space for faith than about the effects of hunger and deprivation on other aspects of camp life. One of those is social hierarchies, which all testimony and witnessing has been compelled to discuss.

2.2 Social hierarchies in the camps

All social organisations and institutions in which there is a measure of continuity over time display characteristic social hierarchies. In this respect the concentration camps were unexceptional. Nevertheless, some of the forms of social division they produced appear peculiar to them, arising no doubt from the conditions of hunger referred to in Section 2.1. Consider the following passage from Levi:

> We do not believe in the most obvious and facile deduction: that man is fundamentally brutal, egoistic and stupid in his conduct once every civilized institution is taken away, and that the *Häftling* [prisoner] is consequently nothing but a man without inhibitions. We believe, rather, that the only conclusion to be drawn is that in the face of driving necessity and physical disabilities many social habits and instincts are reduced to silence.

> But another fact seems to us worthy of attention: there comes to light the existence of two particularly well differentiated categories among men – the saved and the drowned. Other pairs of opposites (the good and the bad, the wise and the foolish, the cowards and the courageous, the unlucky and the fortunate) are considerably less distinct, they seem less essential, and above all they allow for more numerous and complex intermediary gradations.

> This division is much less evident in ordinary life; for there it rarely happens that a man loses himself. A man is normally not alone, and in his rise or fall is tied to the destinies of his neighbours; so that it is exceptional for anyone to acquire unlimited power, or to fall by a succession of defeats into utter ruin. Moreover, everyone is normally in possession of such spiritual, physical and even financial resources

that the probabilities of a shipwreck, of total inadequacy in the face of life, are relatively small. And one must take into account a definite cushioning effect exercised both by the law, and by the moral sense which constitutes a self-imposed law; for a country is considered the more civilized the more the wisdom and efficiency of its laws hinder a weak man from becoming too weak or a powerful one too powerful.

But in the Lager things are different: here the struggle to survive is without respite, because everyone is desperately and ferociously alone.

(Levi, 1987 [1958], pp. 93–4)

This division between the drowned and the saved, although it looks like a definition arrived at by Levi when reflecting at a later date on all that has befallen him, was part of the prisoners' knowledge of how to conduct themselves, and was essential to survival: 'In history and in life one sometimes seems to glimpse a ferocious law which states: "to he that has, will be given; from he that has not, will be taken". In the Lager, where man is alone and where the struggle for life is reduced to its primordial mechanism, this unjust law is openly in force, is recognized by all' (Levi, 1987 [1958], pp. 94–5). Tadeusz Borowski, another Auschwitz inmate, makes the same point in one of his stories: 'The capo points his cooking spoon at those who are to be given a second helping. Only the better workers, the stronger and healthier prisoners receive it. A sick, weak person has no right to a second bowl of nettle soup. Not a drop of it can be wasted on people who will go through the chimney anyway' (Borowski, 1976 [1959]; quoted in Langbein, 2004 [1975], p. 11). In the most extreme of the camps, these figures – the weak – were not distinguished from others by degrees, as they might be in normal society. Once one has passed beyond a certain point – and the testimonies are agreed on this – there is no turning back. The person who has reached this point has no world, not even the denuded version of one. Levi again:

To sink is the easiest of matters; it is enough to carry out all the orders one receives, to eat only the ration, to observe the discipline of the work and the camp. Experience showed that only exceptionally could one survive more than three months in this way. All the musselmans [camp slang – literally, 'Muslims', but the term was used 'by the old ones of the camp to describe the weak, the inept, those doomed to selection'] who finished in the gas chambers have the same story, or more exactly, have no story; they followed the slope down to the bottom, like streams that run down to the sea. On their entry into the camp, through basic incapacity, or by misfortune, or through some banal incident, they are overcome before they can adapt themselves; they are beaten by time, they do not begin to learn German, to disentangle the infernal knot of laws and prohibitions until their body is already in decay, and nothing can save them from selections or from death by exhaustion. Their life is short, but their number is endless; they, the *Muselmänner*, the drowned, form the backbone of the camp, an anonymous mass, continually renewed and always identical, of non-men who march and labour in silence, the divine spark dead within them, already too empty to really suffer. One hesitates to call them living: one hesitates to call their death death, in the face of which they have no fear, as they are too tired to understand.

(Levi, 1987 [1958], p. 96)

These are clearly extreme versions of social division that develop in extreme situations such as those of the camps. However, even those forms of social hierarchy that bore a resemblance to those in certain recognisable organisations took on their own characteristics in the camps. On this, if on nothing else, Bettelheim and Levi agree:

Practically all prisoners who had spent a long time in the camp took over the attitude of the SS toward the so-called 'unfit' prisoners. Newcomers presented the old prisoners with difficult problems. Their complaints about the unbearable life in the camp added new strain to the life in the barracks, as did their inability to adjust to it. Bad behavior in the labor gang endangered the whole group. ... Old prisoners were therefore sometimes instrumental in getting rid of the 'unfit' – in this way incorporating Nazi ideology into their own behavior. This was one of many situations in which old prisoners would demonstrate toughness, having moulded their treatment of these 'unfit' prisoners to the example set by the SS. ...

Old prisoners who identified themselves with the SS did so not only in respect to aggressive behaviour. They would try to acquire old pieces of SS uniforms. If that was not possible, they tried to sew and mend their uniforms so that they would resemble those of the guards.

(Bettelheim, 1979 [1943], pp. 78–9)

The fact of being an old prisoner here is not enough; one needs a marker, an outward sign, in order that this version of a social world can be made to work. The old prisoners – regular criminals who were often placed in positions of privilege in the pre-war concentration camps such as Dachau – even aped the SS leisure-time activity of seeing who could be hit the most without falling down. At Auschwitz, which was both a concentration camp and a death camp, there were even Jewish prisoners who found their way to the top of a hierarchy of sorts. The psychological mechanism was different, the cruelty the same:

They [the Jewish prominents] are the typical product of the structure of the German Lager (camp): if one offers a position of privilege to a few individuals in a state of slavery, exacting in exchange the betrayal of natural solidarity with their comrades, there will certainly be someone who will accept. He will be withdrawn from the common law and will become untouchable; the more power that he is given, the more he will be consequently hateful and hated. When he is given the command of a group of unfortunates, with the right of life or death over them, he will be cruel and tyrannical, because he will understand that if he is not sufficiently so, someone else, judged more suitable, will take over his post. Moreover, his capacity for hatred, unfulfilled in the direction of the oppressors, will double back, beyond all reason, on the oppressed; and he will only be satisfied when he has unloaded on to his underlings the injury received from above.

(Levi, 1987 [1958], p. 97)

So inherited habits of conduct were made irrelevant, both because of the logic of the camp and because of the fact of hunger. Moreover, the reduction of the human being to a hungering body did not generate any of the metaphysical compensations associated with ascetic self-denial in religious contexts; it contributed instead to the emergence of the kind of social hierarchies that we have just considered and that occur nowhere else.

Despite this, the literature on the camps is replete with stories, and we may say that, in so far as those who survived the camps have thought it worthwhile to tell those stories, there must have been aspects of camp life that were comprehensible to the reader who did not experience it. This is not so much a matter of saying that human beings are human beings wherever they are alive – the point of the title of Levi's (1987 [1958]) most famous book from which I have been quoting is to question this easy conclusion – but one of being ready to ask whether there were any practices at all that carried over from normal life into the camps. One possibility is that inmates might have preserved the semblance of a liveable world by means of formal, ritual practices. But even here, as we shall see in Section 2,3, the record is bleak.

2.3 Desocialisation of death

In all societies, transitions from one period of life to another are marked by rites of passage – ceremony, ritual, oath taking, gift giving, and so on. All of these are ways of making a social world work and confirming our membership in that world. People do not simply marry, they go through a set of procedures which constitute the act of getting married and, increasingly, divorce by means of corresponding procedures; they may be baptised or confirmed; they take exams, they graduate from university. And of course they die, and this too is never mere annihilation, but rather surrounded by ritual. Death means different things in different cultures, and is made to mean these different things through the social procedures which surround it. In the camps, the most common transition from one state to another was that from life to death. There were other transitions: Bettelheim, for instance, argued that prisoners regressed to a state of childhood; and an inmate's status within the camp hierarchy might be transformed, in the Soviet camps, for instance, when a woman became the (albeit unwilling) 'wife' of one of the prominent non-political prisoners. But death was all-pervasive. Levi writes that one hesitates to call the death of the 'musselman' death, but we may add that the death of everybody in the camps – those who perished on arrival in the Nazi death camps, those who died of disease and exhaustion in both Nazi and Soviet camps – was such an everyday event that it almost ceased to be noticed. I will discuss indifference towards the death of others in connection with war in Section 4, but note here the social psychological mechanism at work in the camps, as described by Herling:

> Death in the camp, because it threatened constantly and struck suddenly and unexpectedly, seemed to break the laws of time and acquired a metaphysical inscrutability which placed it outside the rhythm of our material existence. ...
>
> A second reason of our fear of that death which we imagined as lurking behind the night's dark curtain was the very quality which in normal conditions usually robs it of its irresistible terror – its community to all mankind. ... Only healthy men, secure in their own lives, can be moved by a sudden call for help from a dying man. In the barrack, where all prisoners were equally vulnerable, where all hearts were beating with the same difficulty, an agonised cry could only remind us of our own sickness, and pass unheeded. ... We recalled moments when, without making the slightest movement, we had watched from under drooping eyelids as dead bodies were being carried out of the barrack at night and we knew that our own shrieks for help would fail to rouse the others from their defensive apathy.
>
> (Herling, 2005 [1951], pp. 147–8)

Herling adds a final terror which death possessed: despite the fact that people died every day, nobody in the camp knew where the dead were buried, or whether a death certificate was issued. He regularly saw a sledge being dragged along a rarely used path and eventually disappearing from view, but more than this he could not say. The thought that nobody would know of their last resting place, that relatives would not be able to mark their passing with the usual social forms, that there would be no material trace to prolong their memory – no prop for the self in death if you like – 'was one of the prisoners' greatest psychological torments' (Herling, 2005 [1951], p. 149). But in the face of this death shorn of the usual trappings which make it part of a social world, prisoners were drawn together in a spirit, if not of altruism, then of cooperation: 'There were secret, many-sided agreements which laid on the party who survived the duty of informing the others' families of the date of death and the approximate place of burial; the barrack walls were covered with the names of prisoners scratched in the plaster, and friends were asked to complete the data after their death by adding a cross and the date' (Herling, 2005 [1951], p. 149).

2.4 Summary and transition

The material discussed in this section suggests three tentative conclusions:

■ Prisoners in concentration and labour camps were placed in situations of extreme material deprivation such that inherited or learned modes of comportment became subservient to the business of survival.

■ In so far as these modes of comportment – be they habitual (Levi's washing example) or ritual (such as ceremonies marking rites of passage) – are the means by which social worlds are routinely sustained, conditions in the camps considerably undermined the basis for such worlds.

■ Although 'worldlessness' would be too strong a term to use here – there were basic but recognisable social hierarchies as well as known codes of behaviour – individuals caught up in these extreme situations were placed face-to-face with matters that in 'ordinary peacetime activity' (Scarry, 1985, p. 108) they would be shielded from through forms of institutional (rules, norms, habits) and material (tools and props) mediation.

In the next section I will examine a second type of extreme situation, war. Here, there is more variation in the extent to which standards of ordinary peacetime conduct have been perceived to enter into the conduct of people caught up in war. Once again, the aim will be to appreciate some of the peculiarities of conduct in war, and, the interest will be in forms of mediation between self and world that war either fosters or undermines.

3 War

Few periods in history have been free from warfare. The first half of the twentieth century only confirms this grim image. Yet despite the ubiquity of war, relatively few attempts have been made, in both the social sciences and in military history, to make confident generalisations about the experience of war. One reason for this is that that experience is so disparate – conditions vary enormously, from the intensity and inescapability of the Eastern front in the Second World War, or the experience of the trenches, through the more ritualised forms of warfare of the eighteenth century, to the brutalities of civil war in which the division between civilians and soldiers breaks down.

This is clearly an enormous topic, and so we will think about it under two separate headings.

3.1 Forms of sociability and group solidarity

One of the differences between the experience of the most extreme concentration camps and that of, say, the First World War, lay in the extent to which an individual's inherited ethos or tradition prepared them for what they were faced with. It has been observed that the backgrounds of the British officers were different at different stages of the First World War. The early officers were often men from the landed aristocracy who saw the war as a version of hunting and who took part in cavalry charges. Conduct in war (in 1914) displayed continuities – in their imaginations – with conduct in peacetime. For a later class of officers from a middle-class background, the technologisation of warfare and the absence in their own upbringing of overtly martial leisure pursuits made for a greater discrepancy between peacetime perception and wartime reality. The Vietnam War has been called the rock and roll war because of the role played by popular music in the efforts of American soldiers to make sense of it. Finally, in societies like ours in which, as Norbert Elias says, acts of everyday violence are far less common than in the past (Elias, 2000), the training of soldiers has often involved the deliberate and systematic brutalisation of individuals in order to make them 'battle ready'.

We also need to think about the difference between wars in terms of the length and intensity of the fighting which a soldier was expected to engage in. American soldiers in Vietnam, for instance, never served more than a year. One peculiarity of the Western front in the First World War was that time in the trenches – generally a few weeks – was interspersed with time spent only a few miles from the trenches yet in a position of complete safety. This was particularly true of the officer class:

Officers on the Somme could ride back to Amiens for dinner in a restaurant with linen and silver on the table; enlisted men could find a village *estaminet*, get drunk on cheap wine and talk to a French woman, or fall in line at a government brothel and go a bit further. That interweaving of ordinary, pleasurable life and life in the trenches was one of the war's strange differences.

(Hynes, 1997, p. 54)

In contrast to this, *Wehrmacht* soldiers on the Eastern front in the Second World War became stranded in trenches for months on end with no hope of taking a break in the nearby towns and villages, not least because they themselves had often destroyed them.

These observations imply that there is a range of relationships between human conduct in peace and war, between their associated relationships between self and world. Despite this, one relatively durable theory of social cohesion in battle is that proposed by Edward Shils and Morris Janowitz in 1948. Shils and Janowitz were seeking to explain the tenacity of the German *Wehrmacht* towards the end of the Second World War when it was clear that the war was lost. They argued that, regardless of political or ideological beliefs, regardless of their inherited or learned habitus, soldiers in battle owed their loyalty to, oriented themselves towards, their immediate military unit. Such a unit might be a platoon or a mere handful of men, certainly nothing larger than a battalion (Ashworth, 1980). Shils and Janowitz theorised this through the idea that the soldier's military unit functioned as a kind of substitute family. The technical term for this is 'primary group', meaning that group which is primarily responsible for the socialisation and the protection of human beings who are just beginning their membership in society:

In the army, when isolated from civilian primary groups, the individual soldier comes to depend more and more on his military primary group. His spontaneous loyalties are to its immediate members whom he sees daily and with whom he develops a high degree of intimacy. For the German soldier in particular, the demands of his group, reinforced by the officially prescribed rules, had the effect of an external authority. It held his aggressiveness in check; it provided discipline, protection and freedom from autonomous decision.

(Shils and Janowitz, 1948, p. 285)

In the case of the *Wehrmacht* on the Eastern front this thesis has been disputed. But the general idea that what binds soldiers together in situations of extreme danger is not a grand sense of national pride or a belief in certain political values, but something small scale, local and very basic, has been affirmed by numerous memoirs and accepted by many historians. Rather than being driven by patriotism, suggested war poet Siegfried Sassoon in 'Dreamers', soldiers are 'citizens of death's grey land'. Graves concurs:

> [W]e all agreed that regimental pride remained the strongest moral force that kept a battalion going as an effective fighting unit; contrasting it particularly with patriotism and religion.
>
> Patriotism, in the trenches, was too remote a sentiment, and at once rejected as fit only for civilians, or prisoners. A new arrival who talked patriotism would soon be told to cut it out.
>
> (Graves, 1999 [1929], p. 196)

The historian John Keegan has gone further than Graves: 'Ordinary soldiers do not think of themselves, in life and death situations, as subordinate members of whatever formal military organisation it is to which authority has assigned them, but as equals within a very tiny group – perhaps no more than six or seven men' (Keegan, 1976, p. 53). As the literary scholar Samuel Hynes has argued, 'The first thing to be said of comradeship is that it is accidental. Comrades in war are not chosen: they are simply the men picked by the system to stand beside you ... They share no common past (which is the glue of ordinary friendship); their ties are all in the present, in the war culture they share ... But though comradeship is accidental, it is intense beyond the likelihood of back-home life' (Hynes, 1997, p. 9). Confirmation of these ideas – about the irrelevance of inherited authority and tradition, and about alternative forms of human attachment – can be found in German writer Erich Maria Remarque's *All Quiet on the Western Front*: 'In our minds the idea of authority ... implied insights and a more humane wisdom. But the first dead man that we saw shattered this conviction' (Remarque, 1994 [1929], p. 9). Compensation is found in 'the best thing that the war produced – comradeship' (Remarque, 1994 [1929], p. 19). But so localised is this comradeship that 'if your own father came across with those from the other side you wouldn't hesitate to hurl a hand grenade straight at him' (Remarque, 1994 [1929], p. 82).

3.2 The empire of the senses: the sensations of warfare

For Remarque, the best thing produced by the First World War, in all its extraordinariness and horror, in the oscillation between boredom and sudden intense danger, was comradeship, a localised form of solidarity that bore no resemblance to the conventional forms of membership and belonging in civilian life. *All Quiet on the Western Front* (1994 [1929]) is frequently contrasted with German novelist Jünger's memoir *Storm of Steel* (2003 [1920]). One reason for this is that Jünger points towards experiences in war that are even further removed from the regularities of peacetime conduct. When he asked what was more sublime than to face death at the head of a hundred men, he did not mean that a confrontation with death would enable him to put his life into some sort of perspective. On the contrary, the idea here is that, after a relatively long period without conflict, the thoughts of a generation of (mostly aristocratic) Germans produced a genuine craving for the abnormal, a craving stimulated partly by literature. This is something more than a glorification of war; it is, rather, the expression of a desire to be placed in an extreme situation, a situation which takes the individual completely out of the world of social relations – the vertical relations of command and obedience, but also the horizontal relations of comradeship, all of which are hedged about with moral prohibition and the cumbersome accoutrements of civilisation, all of them at least a part of the war experience of people like Remarque – and allows him to enter the vertiginous, amoral abysses of something entirely at the limit of imaginable experience. Central to the danger, the intensity that he said he craved, is the suddenness with which the extreme situation, the moment of danger, manifests itself (Bohrer, 1994). Jünger describes, for instance, the moment during a night patrol when it is clear that the English have heard him and his comrades no more than ten metres away:

> 'Such moments on the prowl by night are unforgettable. Eyes and ears are stretched to their utmost. The sound of the enemy's feet coming nearer through the tall grass assumes a remarkable and portentous distinctness that takes almost entire possession of one ... The fray will have to be short and murderous. You are aquiver with two violent sensations – the tense excitement of the hunter and the terror of the hunted. You are a world in yourself ...'
>
> (Jünger, 2003 [1920], pp. 69–70)

Questions of conduct, of how to behave and not to behave, of the shaping or forming of experience, even in a minimal sense, are entirely out of place here. The art of having a world or of making a world in common with others is sacrificed to the raw and individual experience of danger, so much so that Jünger can say that the outside world is, if you like, excluded completely.

However, if Jünger has described such extremes as well as anyone, we should beware of seeing them as typical or as representative of trench warfare itself. If for him there was a distinction between long periods of boredom and suddenly apparent danger, for scholars of trench warfare such as Tony Ashworth, a more accurate and less stark distinction is that between 'quiet and active sectors' (Ashworth, 1980, p. 17). In other words, it would be wrong to define trench warfare as something that consisted of spectacular battles and that contrasted with periods spent away from the front-line. Trench warfare itself consisted mostly of the quiet periods in which soldiers, rather than being deprived of the means of sustaining a world in common, developed a modus vivendi that was common to both sides and that Ashworth dubs, ironically enough, 'the live and let live principle'. Here, 'soldiers strove with success for control over their environment and thereby radically changed the nature of their war experience' (Ashworth, 1980, p. 15) In other words, they succeeded in creating a kind of social world in a situation that otherwise threatened to undermine it:

> The 'profound difference' between the quiet sector and the active sector was ... the exchange of peace, according to the rules of live and let live on the former, and the exchange of aggression according to the rules of kill or be killed – the high command policy for trench warfare – upon the latter. The quietness of a sector did not signify either a social void or a vacuum between enemies but the replacement of one form of exchange with the enemy by another, which trench fighters found more consistent with their needs.
>
> (Ashworth, 1980, p. 19)

The point here is that, almost regardless of official policy, one sector was quiet because the soldiers of the units stationed there were disposed to live and let live, while another was active because the soldiers there wanted to fight.

3.3 Summary and transition

In this section, then, we have seen that:

- War may be memorable as an individual's only means of involvement in affairs of world historical import.

- Paradoxically, war generates forms of group solidarity and loyalty that are intense precisely because they are only tangentially related to the large ideas – such as patriotism – that motivate decisions to go to war.

- War provides for the possibility of extreme experiences in which the individual's awareness of surrounding reality is at its height.

- War may also feature sustained periods of inactivity in which the threat of extreme conduct can be actively placed at a distance by soldiers themselves.

So far, conclusions about the camps and about war have been based on the fate of individuals facing extreme situations which place them in a position of vulnerability, either from hunger or from death at the hands of a prison guard or an enemy; and I have considered the effect this has both on the individual's capacity to sustain a sense of self and on the efforts of groups of people to build a world in common. In the final section we will return to a topic with which we began, namely the effect of extreme situations on the ability of human beings to maintain standards of civilised conduct. I will reconsider war, and end with an example that combines themes from Sections 2 and 3.

4 Ordinary men and extraordinary conduct

We cannot avoid the fact that throughout the history of warfare soldiers have not only loosened the boundaries of civilised behaviour but have gone well beyond them. Beyond its connection with geopolitics and patriotism, and beyond the frequent reference that is made in the literature to clean and dirty wars, the point of war is injuring and killing the enemy. Perhaps, then, we should not be surprised by the frequency, not so much of atrocities, but rather of disdain, contempt or indifference displayed by soldiers towards enemy corpses. We may speculate here on whether war releases in all of us – or in all men – a desire to harm and kill others, but the record is sufficiently varied for it to be worth seeking some explanation for the variation in the conduct of soldiers and in their sense of the world of war in which they are caught up. Here is Graves on British atrocities in the First World War:

> Nearly every instructor in the mess could quote specific instances of prisoners having been murdered on the way back. The commonest motives were, it seems, revenge for the death of friends or relatives, jealousy of the prisoner's trip to a comfortable prison camp in England, military enthusiasm or fear of being suddenly overpowered by the prisoners, or, more simply, impatience with the escorting job. In any of these cases the conductors would report on arrival at headquarters that a German shell had killed the prisoners; and no questions would be asked.
>
> (Graves, 1999 [1929], p. 135)

The historical record is replete with instances of this maltreatment of prisoners.

A second phenomenon is the taking of war trophies from among the possessions of the enemy dead. This may include body parts of mutilated corpses. Historian Joanna Bourke (1999) reports a grim series of cases, including the very common practice of removing an ear. In Vietnam it was not unknown for American soldiers to string a set of enemy ears together to form a decorative chain. Such practices continue today. They were not unknown in the British campaign in the Falkland Islands in 1982, and they will have taken place in the Iraq conflict that began in 2003. Since the advent of portable camera equipment the somewhat less gruesome practice of taking photographs of enemy corpses has become common. Members of the *Wehrmacht* did this in the Second World War, and with the internet and digital cameras, images of enemy dead now circulate around the world. Explanations for these kinds of practice are not easy to come by. One is that willingness to commit atrocities is a result of a training in brutalisation received before the conflict, an attitude towards the enemy already in place before the enemy is encountered. As for photographs, they are sometimes seen as a coping mechanism, a way for some individuals to come to terms with an experience of extreme danger by finding a mediated way of relating to it subsequently. Another explanation, one that suggests continuities between normal and extreme situations, is that war trophies function as 'souvenirs' or memento mori in much the same way that they would in any other branch of human experience. After all, part of the art of making social worlds work is to use devices not only to mark our identity but also to mark events in the past which have shaped our character or confirmed our membership in a certain collectivity. The photographs of family events that we keep in an album or in a drawer perform this function. Peculiar though it may seem, the photographs taken by soldiers of the evidence of their soldiering might be said to play the same role.

A third feature of conduct in war, which all who have written about it have struggled to make sense of, is atrocities committed on civilians. Here again, general explanations are hard to come by. For instance, it has been argued that part of the amorality/brutality of Vietnam was influenced by the fact that it was neither a war of position (with armies stuck in trenches) nor a war of movement (such as that in North Africa during the Second World War). There was no discernible front, so that soldiers out on patrol were in constant danger of ambush from any direction; the theatre of war contained Vietnamese villages, and for this reason villagers had to be treated as, at best, collaborators with the enemy. On this account, the extremity of the situation, the constant danger to which the soldiers were exposed, accounts for the extremity of conduct. However, we know from the conduct of Japanese soldiers in Manchuria in the 1930s, and from that of German soldiers on the Eastern front in the Second World War, that such situation-specific explanations need to be supplemented by consideration of the role played by inherited perceptions and beliefs. This is what historian Omer Bartov (1992) tries to do in his study of the brutalisation – he calls it 'demodernisation' – which characterised the conduct of *Wehrmacht* soldiers on the Eastern front during the Second World War. After the initial successes of 1941, the German army in the East became bogged down in trench warfare reminiscent of the First World War. The extreme conditions it faced included not only the possibility of imminent death at the hands of the enemy, but also extreme physical conditions, in this case not only rain and mud, but also freezing temperatures, lack of food supplies and the impossibility of escaping to somewhere in the surrounding countryside for relief. The relentlessness of this experience contrasts with that of soldiers in the First World War, as we have seen. Bartov argues that the *Wehrmacht*'s fighting spirit in these conditions had less to do with the structure of primary groups (which was constantly being destroyed through heavy losses and reorganisation) than with a deeply instilled ideological fear of the consequences of a Russian victory – the triumph of Eastern barbarism – and the harsh internal army discipline which was a response to the harsh conditions. And so, 'under permanent threat of draconian punishment by his superiors if he shrank away from the lethal realities of the front, the individual soldier's compensation was his ability to wield the same destructive power against enemy civilians and POWs' (Bartov, 1992, p. 71).

The precise weight accorded to the extremity of the situation, to strength of belief and to discipline as factors governing conduct continues to exercise historians and social scientists alike. It is part of a more general problem – the explanation of behavioural patterns – that all enquiry has to face. I will end this chapter with an example that complicates the image of conduct in extreme situations presented so far. In many ways it is the most troubling of all, because it involves neither hunger nor a mere struggle for survival nor the danger of being killed. And it ties together the broad themes of war and concentration camps that we have been examining.

Reserve Police Battalion 101 was a German police unit based in the Lublin region of Poland during Germany's wartime occupation. It was made up of men who were either unfit or (the majority of cases) too old for military service. They had no connection with the *Wehrmacht*, or with the SS or the Waffen SS or the Gestapo. One morning in July 1942 their commanding officer, Major Trapp, had them rise early, and announced that he had an unpleasant task for them. They were to go to the nearby town of Jozefów, round up all the Jews, take them to a nearby forest, and shoot them. He then made them what historian Christopher Browning, in his book of 1992 about the case, calls 'an extraordinary offer'. Anyone wishing not to participate was free to stay behind. Browning then relates how very few of the men did refuse, how they were plied with alcohol and carried out the task, and how they repeated their actions over the course of the next fifteen months at a series of locations all over the Lublin region. These actions involved accompanying individual Jews, walking with them to the forest and then dispatching them with a single bullet to the back of the head from close range. If we recall that Bettelheim's definition of an extreme situation includes the phrase 'we are suddenly catapulted into a set of conditions where our old adaptive mechanisms and values do not apply any more' (1979 [1943], p. 11), we may be tempted to see the situation faced by the members of Reserve Battalion 101 as extreme, even though they faced neither hunger nor cold nor death at the hands of an enemy. The material in Browning's book raises the question of what made these ordinary middle-aged men carry out such extraordinary actions. Browning's own answer is what has come to be known in the historical literature as a 'functionalist' one: the primary motivating factor was a combination of a well-entrenched sense of duty and peer group pressure. Browning draws here on the famous 'experiments with authority' carried out by US psychologist Stanley Milgram in the 1960s, in which subjects were persuaded to administer ever fiercer electric shocks to individuals who failed to give correct answers to simple logical questions, and who would cry out when the shock was administered. The individuals were actors and nobody was hurt, but the subjects were not to know this, and Milgram's point is that there are conditions in which people will accept the authority of a superordinate to the point of being prepared to take their conduct beyond the limits of what was hitherto thought acceptable. Indeed, the idea of such experiments had been suggested to Milgram by the trial of Adolf Eichmann in 1961, at which the architect of the final solution declared that he was 'only following orders'.

For Browning, the members of Police Battalion 101 were 'ordinary men' like you or me, and we too, finding ourselves in that situation, might well have done the same. Four years after Browning's book was published, and using the same archive material as Browning had, US political scientist Daniel Goldhagen's *Hitler's Willing Executioners* (1996) argued that the reason these men carried out these acts was that they were not 'ordinary men' but 'ordinary Germans', imbued with what he calls 'eliminationist anti-Semitism'. It was this ideological factor, not their (German) sense of duty or spirit of obedience, and certainly not the pressures induced by the situation they found themselves in, which prevented them from raising objections to what they were being asked to do. An extensive and often acrimonious debate ensued.

There is an aspect of the Browning–Goldhagen debate which is of interest to us and which cuts across disputes of this sort. In *The Civilising Process*, Elias (2000) argues that the less pervaded a society is by everyday violence or the more attuned it is to the importance of hygiene and other factors of propriety, the lower will be what he calls the threshold of shame, and the more easily will people take offence or recoil with horror. This chapter has been about extreme situations in which this threshold was, or had to be, raised. The fate of Reserve Battalion 101 is no exception. As one of its members put it at his trial in 1964:

> The shooting of the men was so repugnant to me that I missed the fourth man. It was simply no longer possible for me to aim accurately.

I suddenly felt nauseous and ran away from the shooting site. I have expressed myself incorrectly just now. It was not that I could no longer aim accurately, rather that the fourth time I intentionally missed. I then ran into the woods, vomited, and sat down against a tree. To make sure that no one was nearby, I called loudly into the woods, because I wanted to be alone. Today I can say that my nerves were totally finished. I think that I remained alone in the woods for some two or three hours.

(Browning, 1992, p. 65)

Browning suggests, somewhat speculatively, that one of the reasons why the Nazis developed industrialised methods for the killing of Jews on a mass scale was that those doing the rounding up and shooting of Jews in forests were unable to raise the threshold of shame to the requisite level, that they were unable to cope with having repeated and immediate contact with their victims. Faced with the absolutist character of the reality of what they were doing, they needed to be given a means of putting it at a distance, shielding themselves from it. The ultimate cruelty of the Nazis was that at Auschwitz and elsewhere they were able to construct such a set of procedures. People were not only herded onto trains all over Europe, but through a complex set of financial arrangements they were made to pay for the journey; the people were referred to in official documents not as people but as *Stücke*, or pieces/ items; at the death camps, once the victims had been herded into the gas chamber and rendered invisible, the contents of gas canisters were dropped in through openings in the roof. The death of victims had been rendered impersonal and anonymous, placed at a distance from the perpetrator, the task of physically removing the corpses and burning them falling to Jewish prisoners, themselves destined to be disposed of in the same way. Through these and other mediating procedures, an extreme situation was turned into a social world that, for the perpetrators, could be made to work.

5 Conclusion

I began by referring, in the Introduction, to Todorov's idea of the concentration camp as a magnifying glass for bringing into focus matters that would remain blurry under normal conditions. Todorov was interested in what concentration camp behaviour might tell us about the moral life of human beings, the extreme forms of cruelty and of kindness they fostered perhaps teaching a broader, philosophical lesson. The thrust of this chapter has been that the extreme situations considered here do not lend themselves easily to such conclusions concerning morality. If they do teach us a lesson, it is perhaps less about the human capacity for evil than about something more technical, something that has hovered over much of this book. It is that wherever there is a self and wherever there is a world for that self to inhabit, there is work to be done in their maintenance, and that without the requisite equipment and settings, equipment through which our relationship to reality is mediated, a common social world as well as a defensible image of self can atrophy. When this happens, the very idea of 'conduct' in any of the recognisable sociological senses of the term that have been deployed in this book is placed under threat. It is this simultaneous loss of self and loss of the capacity to make social worlds that is described in much of the literature on the concentration camps. Bettelheim (1979 [1943]) sums it up with the phrase 'rock bottom', but we might also call it the loss of institutions. This no doubt accounts for the fact that sociologists, while fascinated by such phenomena, have been reluctant to tackle them head on: how can one speak sociologically about situations that seem to challenge the terms of sociological discourse itself? On the other hand, it is perhaps only by exploring these extremes that we can appreciate the fact that 'making social worlds', far from being just another aspect of social life, is the most basic of human achievements.

References

Ashworth, T. (1980) *Trench Warfare 1914–1918: The Live and Let Live System*, London, Macmillan.

Bartov, O. (1992) *Hitler's Army: Soldiers, Nazis, and War in the Third Reich*, Oxford, Oxford University Press.

Bettelheim, B. (1979 [1943]) *Surviving and Other Essays*, New York, NY, Alfred A. Knopf.

Blumenberg, H. (1985) *Work on Myth*, Cambridge, MA, MIT Press.

Bohrer, K.H. (1994) *Suddenness: On the Moment of Aesthetic Appearance*, New York, NY, Columbia University Press.

Borowski, T. (1976 [1959]) *This Way for the Gas, Ladies and Gentlemen*, Harmondsworth, Penguin.

Bourke, J. (1999) *An Intimate History of Killing*, London, Granta.

Browning, C.R. (1992) *Ordinary Men: Reserve Police Battalion 101 and the Final Solution in Poland*, New York, NY, HarperCollins.

Elias, N. (2000) 'On changes in aggressiveness' in *The Civilizing Process*, Oxford, Blackwell.

Freud, S. (1984 [1920]) 'Beyond the pleasure principle', *The Penguin Freud Library*, Harmondsworth, Penguin.

Gehlen, A. (1988 [1940]) *Man, His Nature and Place in the World*, New York, NY, Columbia University Press.

Goffman, E. (1963) *Asylums*, Harmondsworth, Penguin.

Goldhagen, D.J. (1996) *Hitler's Willing Executioners: Ordinary Germans and the Holocaust*, New York, NY, Alfred A. Knopf.

Graves, R. (1999 [1929]) *Goodbye to All That*, Harmondsworth, Penguin.

Herling, G. (2005 [1951]) *A World Apart*, London, Penguin Books.

Hynes, S. (1997) *The Soldier's Tale*, London, Pimlico.

Jünger, E. (2003 [1920]) *Storm of Steel*, Harmondsworth, Penguin.

Keegan, J. (1976) *The Face of Battle*, London, Cape.

Langbein, H. (2004 [1975]) *People in Auschwitz*, Chapel Hill, NC, University of North Carolina Press.

Levi, P. (1987 [1958]) 'If this is a man' in *If This Is a Man and The Truce*, London, Abacus.

Remarque, E.M. (1994 [1929]) *All Quiet on the Western Front*, London, Vintage.

Scarry, E. (1985) *The Body in Pain: The Making and Unmaking of the World*, Oxford, Oxford University Press.

Semprun, J. (1964 [1963]) *The Long Voyage*, New York, NY, Grove Press.

Shils, E. and Janowitz, M. (1948) 'Cohesion and disintegration in the Wehrmacht in World War II', *Public Opinion Quarterly*, vol. 12, no. 2, pp. 280–315.

Todorov, T. (2000 [1986]) *Facing the Extreme: Moral Life in the Concentration Camps*, London, Phoenix.

Wiesel, E. (1960) *Night*, Harmondsworth, Penguin.

Afterword

Liz McFall, Paul du Gay and Simon Carter

nane be sufferit to beg within this toun but sic as sail have the tounis mark upon their hattis, bonettis or schulderris, and their mark is to be disponit at the discretioun of the bailies.

(Edinburgh council records, *c*.1576; quoted in Balfour Paul, 1887)

Dignitie: What badge or marcke would you that the poore should beare aboute them?'

Dutie: A square of blue cloth being a quarter every waie, wherein I would have printed vpon parchment the Arms of the Cyttie, the name of the partie, the paryshe, and the pencion which he or she weekly receaveth, being fastend to the vpper garment vpon the breast or backe, and the same daylie to weare; and whenever theye shoulde be founde without this marcke, not only to be sharply punnyshed, but allsoe to loose theire pencyons at the discrecion of the Governors.

Dignitie: What, woulde you have honest men or woemen, which have lyved in good state and now decayed, to bear this badge?

Dutie: God forbydde, I have no such meaning, but to be forced vpon suche as the churchewardeins and collectours with other honest men shall suspecte to be gadders and wanderers abroade.

Dignitie: Whie then, you will not allow them to comme to mens dores to receave the revercion of meate and porredge?

Dutie: Yes that I will, they shall have lybertie to goe to such worshipfull houses and others which ar accustomed to gyve almes of meate and drincke, at howers to be appoynted, allwaies having theire badges on their backe or breaste.

(Howes, 1587; quoted in Tawney and Power, 1924, p. 426)

The above quotations refer to practices of 'badging the poor' common across Europe in the early modern period (Hindle, 2004). A wide variety of both county-wide and parish-based badging schemes existed and while their purposes varied in many particulars they shared a general aim of identifying the 'deserving poor' and distinguishing them from those seen as 'undeserving'. The 'undeserving' were often to be found among the itinerant poor, the 'gadders and wanderers abroade' alluded to above whose nomadic lifestyles provoked unease. This may seem an unlikely way to conclude this book's exploration of the relationship between forms of human conduct and the making of social worlds but there are a number of reasons for introducing the example here.

First, badging, like other strategies of identification, offers a powerful example of how forms of individual human conduct are ordered, cultivated and governed in different social worlds using distinct material devices and distinct forms of mediation. Badging the poor was targeted fundamentally at marking entitlement of various sorts. Some badging schemes gave the poor permission to beg, some conferred the right to buy bread at reduced prices, some marked entitlement to receive pensions (the 'pencyons' referred to above), alms or other forms of relief (as in the reference above to 'meate or porredge'). Despite such variations, all badging schemes were inextricably linked to the ordering and policing of conduct by virtue of the normative conditions imposed on entitlement. To some extent these conditions were administrative, designed to identify the administrative entity responsible for providing relief; so, for instance, under the terms of the Elizabethan poor law of 1697, the poor would be relieved by and within their parish of origin. These administrative arrangements were inseparable from a wider proscription against those 'gadders and wanderers abroade' who persistently strayed from their parishes of birth. In a period in which itinerant and seasonal labour movement was widespread, however, relatively few people lived out their entire lives in their parishes of origin. In addition, badging schemes often established strict moral criteria, reserving entitlement to relief to members of the 'deserving' poor who conformed to behavioural standards including, for example, church attendance, sobriety and deference.

Figure 1
Beggar's badge made of lead

As the historian Steve Hindle argues in his (2004) discussion of badging schemes, pronounced – and not especially subtle – shifts in the associations and consequences of badging occurred in the period between 1550 and 1750. Sixteenth-century parish badges seem to have functioned, at least to some extent, as marks of distinction identifying the deserving, respectable or honourable poor, but by the end of the seventeenth century, paupers' badges were seen increasingly as symbols of shame, dependency and humiliation. The process by which these shifts in meaning occurred calls attention to broader changes in the legislative, economic, institutional and technological context in the decades leading up to the Industrial Revolution. But it also points to the myriad ways in which questions of individual conduct are indissolubly and contingently linked to the arrangements which make up the social world. To be identified as one of the 'nomber of other ydel people, as lustie roges and common beggers' (Howes, 1587; quoted in Tawney and Power, 1924, p. 438) who, it was claimed, descended upon London in the belief that poor relief was readily available there, would of course point to some failure to conform to existing standards of conduct, but such standards do not exist independently of social worlds. Forms of specification of individuals – whether as vagabonds, rogues or beggars – are inseparable from the social practices, techniques, tools and devices through which they are instituted.

Second, badging schemes are worth thinking about at this stage as a way of revisiting and reprising the arguments marshalled throughout the five main chapters of this book. Paupers' badges can, for instance, be considered from the perspective of the central question posed by Paul du Gay in Chapter 1 – precisely how are individuals equipped to act in given situations? As du Gay argues, while the ability to act, to possess agency, has often been viewed in sociological theory as a core or essential property of being a person, theorists from Marcel Mauss to Michel Callon have questioned the existence of such fixed properties. The characteristics we understand by agency are, in practice, constituted by and distributed among the particular fixtures and fittings, arrangements and devices which go into the making up of certain sorts of person. To conduct oneself as a deserving pauper after the 1697 statute, then, meant not only possessing and wearing the right 'fittings' – the cloth pauper's badge – it meant knowing and adhering to prescribed arrangements governing such things as church attendance and sobriety but also the form of entitlement, whether to pension or 'relief', the location of almshouses and the times at which they could be called upon. From this perspective, different sorts of person are the outcome – and not the foundation – of socially organised forms of training and practices.

Similarly, Liz McFall's argument in Chapter 2, that the capacity to conduct oneself as a prudent individual in financial matters is not innate but has had, historically, to be cultivated, bears on the establishment of badging schemes. Schemes for 'badging' the poor can be considered as one part of the assemblage of tools, training and practice which has helped constitute ideals of prudent financial conduct historically. Paupers' badges may not, at all times, for all people, have carried the shame and stigma with which they became associated but their impact on financial conduct was almost certainly more deterrent than aspirational. Pauper's badges may sometimes have been seen as marks of distinction but only in certain, very particular circumstances. As Hindle (2004, p. 13) notes, in the sixteenth century wearing badges marked out the neighbourhood poor 'as deserving, publicising the fact that overseers not only thought them worthy of parish relief but had also authorised them to supplement their pensions through seeking alms from door to door'. The pauper's badge in such circumstances was a mark of respect but one which indicated a willing dependence and deferential respect towards benefactors as well as conformity to standards of thrift, diligence and sobriety. Such conditions are unlikely to have excluded the badge acting as a warning to many of the risks of imprudent financial conduct at the same time as it fed the definition and regulation of standards of 'deserving' conduct. During a time in which good credit history and social standing were practically synonymous – and in sharp contrast to the impenetrability of twenty-first century credit relations – often widely and publicly known, badges were one, very visible and very public, marker of economic status.

The regulative property of paupers' badges can also be read in the context of Tony Bennett's arguments in Chapter 3 about the role of habit in the regulation and governance of conduct. As Bennett explains, habit can be used in two main ways to help bring the analysis of individual conduct into focus. First, habit draws attention to the role of repetition and routine in durably shaping, shifting and sustaining social conduct over time; but it also opens up the analysis of conduct by highlighting forms of behaviour which have been seen as requiring change, management or regulation. Badging schemes formed part of a very deliberate attempt to intervene, manage and regulate the habits and conduct of the labouring poor, especially the itinerant poor. As Howes's *Famyliar and Frendly Discourse Dialogue Wyse* has it, 'by these meanes and throughe the carefullnes of theire governours, the diligence of the Beadells and the bearing of theire badges, the citie will be well cleansed of beggers, Roges and ydell people' (Howes; 1587, quoted in Tawney and Power, 1924, p. 427). The habits and conduct of the itinerant poor, whether wounded soldiers, masterless men or profligate youths, were the problem that badging schemes proposed in the sixteenth century were meant to resolve. By the end of the seventeenth century, Hindle (2004) argues, the sense that existing schemes of outdoor poor relief fostered a 'culture of dependency' left magistrates and legislators convinced that parish relief should be made as unattractive as possible, and this drove the transformation of paupers' badges into overt symbols of humiliation. The 1697 statute 'powerfully insisted upon the notion that idleness was an inherited condition, propagated by feckless parents who lacked the moral compass to inculcate habits of industry and discipline in their offspring' (Hindle, 2004, p. 10).

Just how seriously badging schemes took the task of managing, restraining and policing the habits of the poor can be better understood in the light of Francis Dodsworth's discussion in Chapter 4 of the use of violence in the early modern period to regulate conduct. As Dodsworth explains, violence was widely used by male heads of households and communities, as well as by the state, to enforce particular modes of conduct. Under the terms of the 1697 statute, all poor persons receiving parish relief had to wear an easily visible cloth badge on the shoulder of the right sleeve. The consequences of not adhering to the terms of the statute were sharp. Parish officers who dispensed relief to anyone not wearing a badge could be fined twenty shillings for each disbursement, while any pauper who refused the badge could be whipped and committed to Bridewell for three weeks' hard labour. Bridewell was the generic name accorded to county houses of correction established in the sixteenth century and modelled on the original Bridewell in London. The regime at such institutions was harsh even by the standards of the time. As Howes's character Dignitie remarks, the practice of punishing those whose only offence was their destitution in Bridewell alongside 'roges, beggers, strompets and pilfering theves' was extremely hard considering that the very name 'Brydewell' was so odious that any hint of it in an individual's history would 'killeth the creadit for ever' (1587; quoted in Tawney and Power, 1924, p. 439).

As remarked in Chapter 2, 'creadit' here means character generally, and more specifically the chance of ever coming into any respectable occupation, position or preferment. Added to such repercussions were the consequences faced by the children of those on poor relief. Acceptance of the badge amounted to a public admission of an individual's inability to support their offspring. The badge therefore rendered the household vulnerable to the intervention of parish officers who – under the terms of Elizabethan poor law statutes – could apprentice children as young as seven off to distant and often harsh regimes (Hindle, 2004). This circumstance, as Hindle concludes, is one plausible reason why so many of the people who refused to wear the badge were women.

If the wearers of parish badges were at times, then, on the margins of society and susceptible to sharp, violent, cruel and disproportionate forms of punishment, their situations were probably still somewhat short of the extremes described by Charles Turner in Chapter 5. As Turner explains, the term 'extreme situations' was coined by Bruno Bettelheim to describe sets of conditions in which people's accustomed mechanisms and values have become so wholly inadequate, and even potentially dangerous, that a whole new set of attitudes, values, and ways of living is required by the new situations into which they are catapulted. This is arguably a reasonable description of the circumstances in which some recipients of badging schemes found themselves.

Historically, badging schemes have not just been applied to the poor but also to a range of what John Torpey has described as 'negatively privileged status groups' (2000, p. 9). Branding or tattooing convicted criminals with letters signifying their crimes is a well-documented historical practice. In France, England and in the USA, there are records of particular offences being inscribed in a brand or tattoo, including 'M' for malefactor, a generic name for convict, 'F' for fraymaker, which referred to the crime of brawling in church, 'V' for vagabond, 'SL' for Seditious Libeller, 'D' for Drunkard, and 'A' or 'AD' for Adulterer (Gustafson, 2000).

Badges have also been used to mark criminal convictions, as represented in Nathaniel Hawthorne's novel *The Scarlet Letter* (1850 [1994]) in which the heroine, Hester Prynne, is sentenced to wear the red letter 'A' for the rest of her life to mark her crime of adultery. While it has been remarked that, according to the standards of the time, Hester got off comparatively lightly; in respect of the scarlet letter at least the sentence is an accurate reflection of sentencing in the seventeenth-century Massachusetts Bay colony in which the novel is set (Korobkin, 1997).

Figure 2

Lillian Gish as Hester Prynne in the film *The Scarlet Letter* (1926)

Badges, however, have not just been used to identify the poor and those convicted of crimes, they have also been used to identify members of a number of 'negatively privileged' groups. In the extreme situations Turner is concerned with, members of a variety of 'undesirable' groups in Nazi Germany were, notoriously, required to wear distinguishing badges: red triangles for political prisoners, pink for homosexuals, brown for gypsies, and, of course, yellow star armbands for Jews. In the camps, prisoners were tattooed with a number which identified them as individuals and as members of particular groups. As Primo Levi remarks in his memoir *The Drowned and the Saved*:

> In deference to the typically German talent for classification a true and proper code soon began to take shape: men were tattooed on the outside of the arm and women on the inside; the number of the Zigeuner, the gypsies, had to be preceded by a Z. The number of a Jew, starting in May 1944 (that is, with the mass arrival of Hungarian Jews)

had to be preceded by an A, which shortly afterward was replaced
by a B.

(Levi, 1989, p. 95)

The practice of 'badging' or marking individuals in extreme – or near
extreme – situations points to the third and final reason for considering
it as an example in the context of this closing discussion: the perspective
badging systems can yield on the character and operation of social
worlds. As noted in the Introduction, the book's main line of argument
is that attention to questions of conduct offers a central means through
which sociologists can investigate how distinctive social worlds are put
together, change and break apart. The chapters in the book move
steadily from discussion and analysis of human conduct in mundane
and everyday situations towards analysis of conduct in disordered,
violent and ultimately extreme situations. In each of the chapters, the
nature of the relationship between the individual and the social world is
a central concern. Underlying this concern are questions about how this
relationship is ordered and sustained, how it shifts over time and
whether and how it can disintegrate.

The book begins its answer to these questions by suggesting that focusing
on the minutiae of conduct offers a way into understanding how the
relationship between individuals and social worlds works. Through
studying the attributes, capacities, gestures, ideals, norms, habits, etc.
which comprise conduct, a sense of the contingency and dependency of
the individual–social connection starts to emerge. This amounts to rather
more than an argument that conduct is socially shaped; what it means is
that conduct *always* simultaneously invokes the individual and the
social. So, for instance, depositing pound coins accumulated in an
oversized whisky bottle in a savings account may appear the idiosyncratic
act of one individual but it is an act that draws on specific materials, is
informed by past community practices, and utilises the institutional
infrastructures of the financial services industries. What this example
points to is an argument that has been made throughout the book – that
specific forms of conduct require an assemblage of specific materials and
forms of mediation to convey their meanings. Thus, the accumulator of
pound coins appropriates certain materials – the whisky bottle, the bank
deposit book or card – but uses them in a manner mediated by, or made
familiar through, the fundraising activities of community organisations,
pubs and other individual savers.

If individual conduct in social worlds is ordered, regulated or governed
using specific forms of mediation and arrangements of material tools,
props and devices, this also tells us something about the character of
social worlds. As Turner points out, in philosophical anthropology,

human beings are distinguished from all other creatures by having no natural environment or habitat; instead, human beings have to construct their own means of survival by making their own 'world'. This, Turner argues, offers the most fundamental rationale for mediation. Mediation, in the form of cultural, media and social institutions, stories and narratives, traditions, belief systems, rituals and so on, helps keep a potentially hostile reality at bay and turns the world into something human beings can cope with. Added to the already established significance of material tools, props and devices for sustaining given forms of conduct, this account of the role of mediation offers a crude hint at the sort of conditions which may, potentially, challenge the operation of social worlds. In other words it may seem to suggest that, to operate relatively smoothly, social worlds require a sort of subsistence level of matter and mediation.

For those badged individuals who ultimately became the inhabitants of the camps Turner describes, the material deprivation they encountered was so extreme that the rituals and routines that normally comprise human conduct became subservient to the business of survival. The extent of this deprivation was such that the conditions in the camps, in Turner's phrase, 'considerably undermined' the functioning of social worlds routinely sustained by material and ritual forms of comportment. But – and this is a key point – Turner concludes that even in such extreme circumstances it is not clear that the social world had collapsed or disintegrated. Still in existence were basic material props, rudimentary social hierarchies and recognisable codes of behaviour. Social worlds, then, are not easily defined by some sort of quantitative measure of sufficiency in relation to matter or culture – rather the capacity of social worlds, which are recognisable in at least some particulars, to persist in the most extreme of circumstances is, in certain respects, one of the most troublesome of their characteristics.

The extremes of human conduct encountered by the inhabitants of the camps and similar regimes have of course been examined for lessons about humanity and about morality. What extreme situations offer in the context of this discussion is, however, a practical and technical lesson. Regimes like those in the camps are *made to work*. Prior to being transferred to the camps, individuals had to be identified and marked as members of an undesirable group. As described in Chapter 5, people were not only herded onto trains all over Europe, but were made to pay for the journey through a complex series of administrative and financial arrangements. Technical arrangements of this sort were necessary at each stage of the process. So, using elaborate administrative regimes, individuals were first identified, recorded, filed and then marked with armbands as members of undesirable groups. To make matters more bizarre, in places like Warsaw the required yellow armbands were sold as part of a regular business, and wearers could choose between cloth and 'fancy plastic washable' armbands (see Arendt, 1994, p. 118). Through procedures like these, badged individuals were systematically marked as separate and different from the recognised, entitled or included individuals. By such means, a social world of a very particular sort was, at least for some, made to work.

What this suggests is that social worlds are both troublesome and tenacious, persisting in some form in even the most extreme of situations. Nevertheless, what is at stake in extreme situations is the strenuous and indefensible restriction of the capacity to participate in making social worlds to certain very specifically defined groups. If extreme situations offer a lesson about the character and functioning of social worlds, it may be, in Turner's words, in the concluding section of Chapter 5:

> that wherever there is a self and wherever there is a world for that self to inhabit, there is work to be done in their maintenance, and that without the requisite equipment and settings, equipment through which our relationship to reality is mediated, a common social world as well as a defensible image of self can atrophy.

References

Arendt, H. (1994) *Eichmann in Jerusalem: A Report on the Banality of Evil*, Harmondsworth, Penguin.

Balfour Paul, J. (1887) 'On beggars' badges, with notes on the licensed mendicants of Scotland', *Proceedings of the Society of Antiquaries of Scotland* (PSAS), 14 February, p. xxi.

Gustafson, M. (2000) 'The tattoo in the later Roman Empire and beyond' in Caplan, J. (ed.) *Written on the Body*, London, Reaktion Books.

Hawthorne, N. (1850 [1994]) *The Scarlet Letter*, Harmondsworth, Penguin.

Hindle, S. (2004) 'Dependency, shame and belonging: badging the deserving poor, *c.*1550–1750', *Cultural and Social History*, vol. 1, no. 1, pp. 6–35.

Howes, J. (1587) *A Famyliar and Frendly Discourse Dialogue Wyse*, reprinted in Tawney, R.H. and Power, E. (1924) *Tudor Economic Documents*, vol. 3, pp. 421–43, London, Longmans.

Korobkin, L.H. (1997) 'The Scarlet Letter of the Law: Hawthorne and criminal justice', *NOVEL: A Forum on Fiction*, vol. 30, no. 2, pp. 193–217.

Levi, P. (1989) *The Drowned and the Saved*, London, Abacus.

The Scarlet Letter, film, directed by Victor Sjöström. USA: MGM, 1926.

Torpey, J. (2000) *The Invention of the Passport: Surveillance, Citizenship and the State*, Cambridge, Cambridge University Press.

Acknowledgements

Grateful acknowledgement is made to the following sources:

Cover

Photograph: Copyright © Mike Goldwater/Reportage/Getty Images.

Text

Reading 1.1: Mauss, M. translated by Brewster, B. (1973) 'Techniques of the body', *Economy and Society*, Vol. 2, Taylor & Francis. Reprinted by permission of the publisher (Taylor & Francis Ltd, http://www. informaworld.com); *Reading 2.1*: Elias, N. (1994) *The Civilizing Process: The History of Manners and State Formation and Civilization*, translated by Edmund Jephcott, Blackwell Publishing. This edition copyright © Norbert Elias Stichting 1994. English translation copyright © Basil Blackwell Ltd 1982; *Reading 2.3*: Muldrew, C. (1993) 'Interpreting the market: the ethics of credit and community relations in early modern England', *Social History*, 1993, Taylor & Francis. Reprinted by permission of the publisher (Taylor & Francis Ltd., http://www.informaworld.com); *Reading 2.4*: Hunt, J. and Fry, B. (2007) *Spendaholics: Top Tips*, www.bbc. co.uk/bbcthree/programmes/spendaholics. Copyright © BBC MMVII; *Pages 142-8*: Elias, N. (2000) The *Civilizing Process: Sociogeneric and Psychogeneric Investigations*, Blackwell Publishing. This edition copyright © Norbert Elias Strichting 1994, 2000. English translation copyright © Basil Blackwell Ltd 1982; *Pages 159-67*: from *If This is a Man* by Primo Levi, published by Bodley Head. Reprinted by permission of The Random House Group Ltd.

Figures

Figure 1.1: www.armystudyguide.com; *Figure 1.2*: Copyright © Alexis Bertrand; *Figure 1.3 left*: Copyright © Catherine Grandclement-Chaffy; *Figure 1.3 right*: Copyright © Franck Cochoy; *Figure 1.4*: Copyright © John Lewis Partnership Archive Collection; *Figure 1.5*: The Sainsbury Archive, Museum in Docklands; *Figure 2.1*: Copyright © Lowe and Partners/photographer Richard Pullar; *Figure 2.2*: National Archives of Scotland GD254/1105/5; *Figure 3.2*: Mary Evans Picture Library; *Figures 3.3 and 3.4*: from *Distinction: A Social Critique of the Judgement of Taste*, Pierre Bourdieu, translated by Richard Nice, Copyright © 1979 by Les Editions de Minuit, this translation Copyright © 1984 by the President and Fellows of Harvard College and Routledge & Kegan Paul. Reproduced by permission of Taylor & Francis Books UK; *Figure 4.1*: Lambeth Palace Library/Bridgeman Art Library; *Figures 4.3 and 4.4*: Mary Evans Picture Library; *Figure 4.5*: Copyright © Topham/PA/TopFoto.co.uk; *Figure 2 (Afterword)*: MGM/The Kobal Collection.

Every effort has been made to locate all copyright-owners, but if any have been overlooked the publishers will make the necessary arrangements at the first opportunity.

Index

Note: Emboldened words in the index and main text indicate key words in the interactive glossary which is available for students on the DD308 *Making social worlds* course.